소프트웨어전공 기초 영어

(개정판)

이성옥 지음

성진미디어

▣ 저자 이성옥(jesuissarah@pcu.ac.kr)

- 한양대학교에서 영미언어를 수행했고 고려대학교 교육대학원에서는 영어교육으로 석사학위를 배재대학교 컴퓨터공학과와 한국기술교육대학교 HRD학과에서 각각 박사학위를 받음
- 중등기관과 대학, 직업훈련기관에서 영어와 컴퓨터 분야 취업교육을 실시했고 연구소를 대상으로 기술사업화 분야의 컨설팅을 해 왔으며 IT분야의 프로젝트형 교수법(PBT:Project-based Training)을 개발하여 분기마다 교사들에게 강의함
- 현재, 배재대학교 컴퓨터공학과 교수로 재직 중이며 주요 연구분야는 빅데이터, 머신러닝, 딥러닝, 컴퓨터 교육이다.

소프트웨어전공 기초 영어 (개정판)

저 자 | 이성옥
발행인 | 채희선
발행처 | 성진미디어
발행일 | 2023년 10월 28일
등 록 | 제311-2010-23호

전 화 | 02)374-4363(대표)
팩 스 | 02)375-4362
주 소 | 서울시 은평구 증산동 248 중앙하이츠상가 B101호

ISBN 978-89-98308-62-9

값 18,000원

Preface

컴퓨터를 전공하는 대학생이나 다른 전공, 특히나 인문계통에 있는 대학생들에게도 영어는 우리나라 사람이라면 응당 넘어야하는 관문입니다. 대학에 진학하고 성인이 되었더라도 영어 공부를 계속해야 한다는 부담은 누구에게나 동일합니다.

제가 이 책을 집필한 이유는 우선, 영어에 어려움을 겪는 친구들에게 어려운 전공 내용이 나와도 어떻게든 해낼 수 있는 자신감을 주고 싶어서 집필하였습니다. IT에 대한 부분을 자꾸 영어로 접하게 되면 눈에 익숙해지게 되고 스트레스에서 무뎌지게 됩니다. 또한 소프트웨어 분야에 대하여 알고 싶지만 기본 지식이 없어서 난감한 학생들에게 컴퓨터 개론과 같은 기초 내용에서부터 접근했으면 하는 바램으로 이 책을 구성하게 되었습니다.

소프트웨어 관련 단어나 내용의 상당수는 영어 기반입니다. 개발언어로 프로젝트를 수행하거나 과제를 하다가 어려울 때 검색을 하게 되면 영어 문서나 사이트를 찾게 됩니다. 이러한 상황이 나올 때마다 답답함을 호소하는 학생들이 많습니다.

IT 분야의 수요가 증가함에 따라 전공학생들 뿐만 아니라 비전공의 학생들도 이 업계로 진출하고 있습니다. 컴퓨터 분야로 취업하기 위하여 방학을 활용하여 스터디하는 친구들이 많아지고 있습니다. 이런 분들은 컴퓨터 관련 상식을 공부하는 동시에 영어 실력도 키워야합니다.

저는 자주 학생들에게 외국어를 배우기에 지금처럼 최적인 시기는 없다고 이야기합니다. 10여 년 전과 비교하면 현재의 외국어 관련 기술은 놀랍습니다. 스마트폰의 대중화와 더불어 각종 어플리케이션과 생성형 AI의 등장은 외국어 습득 및 활용에 있어서 큰 도움을 주고 있습니다. 지금이야말로 예전에 포기했던 영어를 배워야할 때입니다. 다소 내용이 생경하다 할지라도 여러분들의 의지만 있다면 언어의 장벽이 여러분들의 학업이나 진로를 방해하지 않을 것이라고 감히 말씀드립니다.

끝으로 이 책의 개정판을 낼 수 있도록 여러모로 도움을 주신 배재대학교 SW중점대학과 교직원 여러분들, 출판사에 깊이 감사드립니다.

저자 이성옥

Contents

Contents

Contents

Contents

Chapter 01

The Fourth Industrial Revolution and Artificial Intelligence

4차 산업혁명과 인공지능

학습순서

【 INTRO 】

'4차 산업혁명'은 IT와 관련되지 않은 사람들에게도 이제는 굉장히 익숙한 단어입니다. 미래사회라는 이미지를 우리에게 떠오르게 하지만 정작 그 용어가 의미하는 바와 분야에 대해서는 정확하게 알기 힘듭니다. 제1장에서는 4차 산업혁명이란 어떤 것을 의미하고 어떤 기술이 우리와 우리의 삶을 변화시키고 있는 지 알아보도록 하겠습니다.

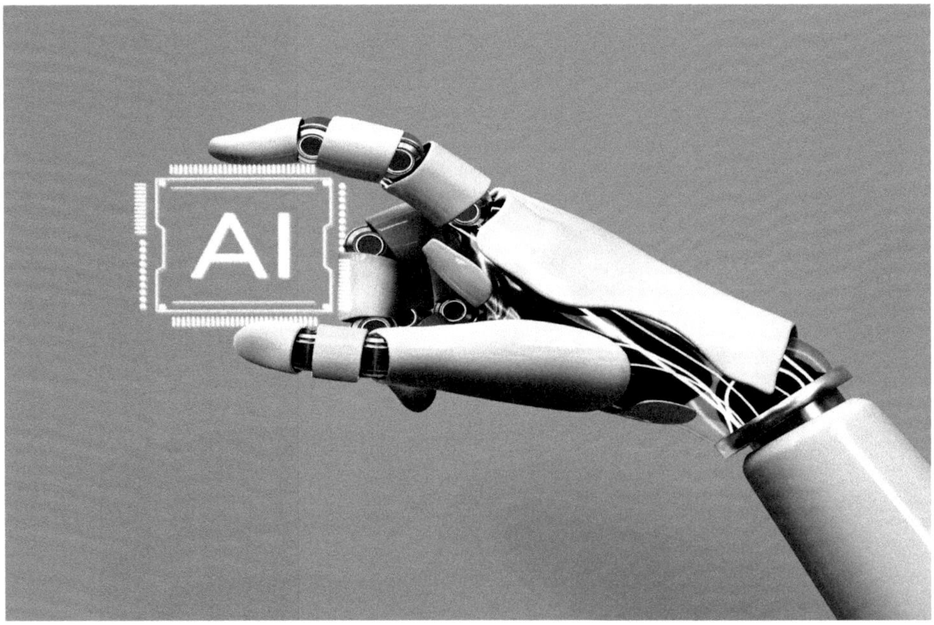

The word Fourth Industrial Revolution is now a familiar keyword for all non-IT related people. It is a naming that reminds us of the image of a future society, but it is hard to know exactly what the term means and what it is in the field. So in our first chapter, let's look at what the Fourth Industrial Revolution means and what technology is changing us and our lives.

1) The Fourth Industrial Revolution[1] 4차 산업혁명

The fourth industrial revolution (or Industry 4.0) is the ongoing automation of traditional manufacturing and industrial practices, using modern smart technology.

Large-scale machine-to-machine communication (M2M) and the internet of things (IoT) are integrated for increased automation, improved communication and self-monitoring, and production of smart machines that can analyze and diagnose issues without the need for human intervention.

4차 산업 혁명(또는 산업 4.0)은 현대적인 스마트 기술을 사용하여 기존의 제조 및 산업 관행을 지속적으로 자동화하는 것이다.

대규모 기계간 통신(M2M, Machine-to-Machine Communication)과 사물인터넷(IoT)이 통합되어 자동화, 통신 및 자가 모니터링 향상, 스마트 머신의 생산 등을 통해 사람의 개입 없이 문제를 분석 및 진단할 수 있다.

Vocabulary

the fourth industrial revolution : 4차 산업혁명
traditional : 전통의
practice : 실천, 관행
modern : 현대의, 근대의
manufacturing : 제조업의
automation : 자동화
ongoing : 계속 진행 중인
analyze and diagnose : 분석하고 진단하다
human intervention : 사람의 개입

1 https://en.wikipedia.org/wiki/Fourth_Industrial_Revolution

2) Industry 4.0 Design Principles[2] Industry 4.0 설계 원칙

As the fourth industrial revolution, industry 4.0 is a trend that is changing the way we live and work.

Technological advancements in the areas of artificial intelligence, cloud computing and smart devices have meant disruptive technologies are now part of everyday life for both individuals and businesses.

Researchers have identified six design principles that are crucial for businesses to embrace in order to realize the full benefits of industry 4.0 technology.

These design principles are – interoperability, virtualization, decentralization, real-time capability, service orientation, and modularity.

4차 산업 혁명인 industry 4.0은 우리가 생활하고 일하는 방식을 변화시키고 있는 트렌드이다.

인공지능, 클라우드 컴퓨팅과 스마트 기기 분야의 기술 발전은 파괴적 기술이 이제 개인과 기업 모두의 일상 생활의 일부가 됨을 의미한다.

연구자들은 기업이 industry 4.0 기술의 모든 장점을 실현하기 위해 수용해야 하는 6가지 설계 원칙을 찾았다.

이러한 설계 원칙은 상호운용성, 가상현실화, 분산, 실시간 기능, 서비스 지향과 모듈화이다.

---

2 https://www.rmit.edu.au/news/c4de/industry-4-0-design-principles

Vocabulary

technological advancements : 기술 발전
disruptive technologies : 파괴적인 기술
individuals and businesses : 개인과 기업
principles : 원칙
crucial : 중대한, 결정적인
identify : 찾다, 확인하다
benefits : 이점
embrace : 껴안다, 수용하다
interoperability : 상호운용성, 서비스 상호 이용
virtualization : 가상현실화
decentralization : 분산
real-time capability : 실시간 기능
service orientation : 서비스 지향
modularity : 모듈화

① Interoperability

Interoperability refers to the ability of objects, machines and people in a business to communicate, exchange data and coordinate activities.

This ability to connect everything in a company, everywhere and with everyone is essential to take advantage of the insights provided by data to increase efficiency and improve processes.

Implementing and embracing new technology has only limited capacity if the product or system cannot exchange contextual information with other products and systems. Similarly, interaction between machines and humans remains limited to simple and defined cases without interoperability.

Interoperability cannot happen without connectivity so as a first step, businesses must digitize their operations by utilizing cloud computing for software programs and data storage. The next step is to start integrating open source platforms and software into business operations.

Allowing the open exchange of information between systems helps business reduce the costs of information collection and management, reduce unnecessary duplication and leverage third party applications when needed.

① 상호운용성

상호운용성은 기업 내의 객체, 기계 및 사람들이 데이터 교환 및 활동을 통신하고 조정하는 능력을 말한다.

기업의 모든 것을 어디에서나 모든 사람들과 연결하는 이러한 능력은 데이터에서 제공하는 통찰력을 활용하여 효율성과 프로세스를 높이는 데에 필수적이다.

제품이나 시스템이 다른 제품 및 시스템과 맥락적인 정보를 교환할 수 없는 경우 새로운 기술을 구현하고 수용하는 능력은 한계가 있다. 마찬가지로 기계와 인간 간 상호작용은 상호운용성이 없는 단순한 예로 정의된다.

상호운용성은 연결 없이는 이루어질 수 없으므로 첫 번째 단계로 기업은 소프트웨어 프로그램 및 데이터 스토리지에 클라우드 컴퓨팅을 활용하여 운영을 디지털화해야 한다. 다음 단계는 오픈 소스 플랫폼과 소프트웨어를 비즈니스 운영에 통합한다.

시스템 간에 개방적인 정보 교환을 허용함으로 기업은 정보 수집 및 관리 비용을 절감하고, 불필요한 중복을 줄이며, 필요할 때 타사 애플리케이션을 활용할 수 있다.

Vocabulary

object : 물건, 물체
refer to : 언급하다, 지칭하다, 나타낸다
ability : 능력, 할 수 있음
machine : 기계
essential : 필수적인, 본질적인
take advantage of : 이용하다
insights : 통찰력
increase efficiency : 효율성을 높이다
improve processes : 프로세스를 개선하다
implement and embrace : 구현하고 수용하다
limited capacity : 제한된 능력
contextual information : 맥락적인 정보
similarly : 마찬가지로, 유사하게
interaction : 상호작용
connectivity : 연결(성)
open source platforms and software : 오픈소스 플랫폼과 소프트웨어
integrate : 통합시키다, 통합되다
digitize : 디지털화하다
utilize : 활용하다
reduce the costs of information collection and management : 정보수집과 관리비용을 절감하다
reduce unnecessary duplication : 불필요한 중복 비용을 줄이다
leverage third party applications when needed : 필요한 경우 타사 애플리케이션을 활용한다

② Virtualization

Virtualization refers to two different scenarios:
One virtual resource is created from multiple physical resources.

Many virtual resources are created from one or more physical resources.

In the first scenario, the hardware environment of a business is simulated by creating digital 'twins' of physical assets using data from sensors. In the second scenario, software is used to divide one physical server into multiple virtual servers that act like unique physical devices. Digital twins, or 3D models, are used to optimize machine performance, allowing 'what if' scenarios to be run and the impact of new equipment to be tested.

They can also act as companions for physical objects for operators to view the real-time status of the machine, analyse performance, test solutions and identify potential issues before they arise. This can help you extend the life of your business' physical assets, uncover operation inefficiencies, reduce maintenance costs and understand your equipment better.

For industries that don't rely on large equipment and machines, such as aged care and education, virtualization can be used to reduce hardware costs and the number of physical resources needed. With virtualization, applications, desktops, servers and data are no longer dependent on one physical device, improving reliability and enabling add-ons to be included when required. As with everything, start small with virtualization, moving smaller applications and equipment into a virtualized environment before transitioning critical assets.

② 가상화

가상화는 다음과 같은 두 가지 시나리오를 의미한다. 하나의 가상 리소스는 여러 물리적 리소스에서 생성된다. 많은 가상 리소스가 하나 이상의 물리적 리소스에서 생성된다.

첫 번째 시나리오에서는 센서의 데이터를 사용하여 물리적 자산의 디지털 '쌍둥이'를 생성하여 기업의 하드웨어 환경을 시뮬레이션 한다. 두 번째 시나리오에서는 소프트웨어를 사용하여 하나의 물리적 서버를 고유한 물리적 장치처럼 작동하는 여러 가상 서버로 나눈다. 디지털 트윈 또는 3D 모델은 기계 성능을 최적화하는 데 사용되며, 이를 통해 '가상' 시나리오를 실행하고 새 장비의 영향을 테스트할 수 있다.

또한 운영자가 기계의 실시간 상태를 보고, 성능을 분석하고, 해결책을 테스트하고, 문제가 발생하기 전에 잠재적 문제를 식별할 수 있도록 물리적 객체의 동반자 역할을 할 수 있다. 이를 통해 비즈니스 물리적 자산의 수명을 연장하고, 운영 비효율성을 파악하며, 유지보수 비용을 절감하고, 장비를 더 잘 이해할 수 있다.

고령 관리 및 교육 등 대규모 장비와 시스템에 의존하지 않는 업계의 경우 가상화를 사용하여 하드웨어 비용과 필요한 물리적 리소스의 수를 줄일 수 있다. 가상화로 애플리케이션, 데스크톱, 서버 및 데이터가 더 이상 하나의 물리적 장치에 의존하지 않게 되어, 안정성이 향상되고 필요할 때 추가 기능을 포함할 수 있다. 모든 것과 마찬가지로, 중요한 자산을 전환하기 전에 가상화를 통해 소규모 애플리케이션 및 장비를 가상화 환경으로 전환하면서 소규모로 시작해보아라.

Vocabulary

virtual resource : 가상 리소스
multiple physical resources : 여러 물리적 리소스
creating digital 'twins' : 디지털 트윈을 생성하며
physical assets : 물리적 자산
divide : 나누다
divide one physical server into multiple virtual servers : 하나의 물리적 서버를 여러 가상 서버로 나누다
act like : ~처럼 행동하다
unique : 유일한, 특별한
optimize machine performance : 기계의 성능을 최적화 하다
the impact of new equipment : 새로운 장비의 영향

companion : 동반자
operator : 운영자
view : 견해, 관점, 보다
extend : 더 길게 만들다, 연장하다

③ Decentralization

Decentralization is something that businesses have been embracing for years, moving systems to components rather than a central computer to enable unlimited scalability and flexibility.

Storing and transferring data in the cloud is a form of decentralization, as is the automation of manual, repetitive tasks.

Both redistribute functions or tasks away from a central location.

With industry 4.0 however, all technology is decentralized, facilitating the creation of decentralized systems across all industries on a global scale.

In advanced manufacturing, 3D printing is making it possible for businesses to have small, decentralized factories in different locations; in agriculture, decentralized ledger technology is tracing the origin of food products to reduce fraud; in aged care, motion sensors, wearable technology and voice-activated systems are moving care outside of provider settings into the home; and in education, online courses are supporting self-directed learning.

Since this is a macro trend, inevitably any business embracing new technology will start to see decentralization within their operations. However, leaders can encourage this process by spreading out decision-making to include more operators in the field and leaving day to day operations to small teams.

③ 분산

분산은 기업이 수년간 수용해 온 것으로서 시스템을 중앙 컴퓨터가 아닌 구성 요소로 이동하여 무한한 확장과 유연을 가능하게 한다.

클라우드에 데이터를 저장하고 전송하는 것은 수작업과 반복 작업을 자동화하는 것과 같이 분산의 한 형태이다. 두 기능 모두 중앙 위치에서 떨어진 곳에 기능 또는 작업을 다시 배포한다. 그러나 Industry 4.0은 모든 기술이 분산되어 전 세계적으로 모든 산업에 분산된 시스템을 쉽게 구축하도록 촉진한다.

첨단 제조 분야에서 3D 프린팅은 기업이 여러 지역에서 소규모 분산형 공장을 운영할 수 있도록 해준다. 농업 분야에서는 분산 원장 기술이 식품 제품의 원산지를 추적하여 사기를 줄이고 있다. 노인 요양에서, 모션 센서, 웨어러블 기술 및 음성 인식 시스템은 외부 제공자 설정에서 가정으로 돌봄을 이동시키고 있다. 교육 분야에서는 온라인 강좌가 자율 학습을 지원하고 있다.

이는 거시적 추세이기 때문에 어쩔 수 없어 새로운 기술을 받아들이는 모든 비즈니스는 운영 내에서 분권화를 경험하게 될 것이다. 그러나 리더들은 더 많은 운영자들을 현장에 포함하고자 의사 결정을 확장하고 일상적인 운영을 소규모 팀에 맡김으로 이러한 과정을 장려할 수 있다.

Vocabulary

decentralization : 분산
move : 움직이다
enable : (사람에게) ~을 할 수 있게 하다
central : 중심되는, 가장 중요한
component : (구성) 요소, 부품

central computer : 중앙 컴퓨터
unlimited : 무제한의, 무한정의
scalability : 확장성
flexibility : 유연성
storing and transferring data : 데이터를 저장하고 전송하는 것
a form of decentralization : 분산의 한 형태
manual : 수동의
repetitive tasks : 반복적인 작업
automation : 자동화
redistribute : 재분배하다
facilitate : 용이하게 하다
advanced manufacturing : 첨단 제조
factory : 공장
agriculture : 농업
ledger : (은행/사업체 등에서 거래 내역을 적은) 원장
trace : 추적하다
fraud : 사기
voice-activated systems : 음성 작동 시스템
self-directed learning : 자기 주도적 학습
macro trend : 거시적인 추세
inevitably : 불가피하게
encourage : 격려하다, 권장/장려하다
spreading out : 더 널리 퍼지다
decision-making : 의사결정

④ Real-time capability

Real-time capability refers to the collection and analysis of data in real-time, allowing decisions to be made immediately and at every moment.

This enables you to see what's happening in your business, what can be improved and where productivity opportunities lie.

It also allows you to analyse micro trends, immediately respond to failures in production lines or take a proactive approach to anomalies or inefficiencies.

Thanks to the proliferation of sensors and internet-connected devices, most businesses already have access to large amounts of real-time data.

The challenge lies in processing and analysing the data so that business operations can be continuously optimized.

This is where open source tools are critical, allowing small and medium sized enterprises (SMEs) to build an inexpensive and integrated reporting platform for insights across multiple data sources.

Cloud computing means this information can be managed in real-time without the need to wait for reports, with many services offering embedded analytics that can be viewed anywhere and at any time.

④ 실시간 기능

실시간 기능은 실시간으로 데이터를 수집 및 분석하여 의사결정을 즉시 수행할 수 있는 기능을 일컫는다. 이를 통해 비즈니스에서 무슨 일이 일어나고 있는지, 무엇을 개선할 수 있는지, 그리고 생산성 기회는 어디에 있는지 파악할 수 있다. 또한 마이크로 트렌드를 분석하고, 생산 라인의 장애에 즉시 대응하거나, 이상 징후나 비효율성에 대해 사전 예방적인 접근 방식을 취할 수 있다.

센서와 인터넷 연결 장치의 확산으로 대부분의 기업은 이미 대량의 실시간 데이터에 액세스할 수 있다. 문제는 비즈니스 운영을 지속적으로 최적화할 수 있도록 데이터를 처리하고 분석한다.

바로 이 때 SME(중소기업)가 여러 데이터 소스에 대한 통찰력을 얻을 수 있는 저렴하고 통합된 보고 플랫폼을 구축할 수 있는 오픈 소스 툴이 매우 중요하다. 클라우드 컴퓨팅은 보고서를 기다릴 필요 없이 이러한 정보를 실시간으로 관리할 수 있다는 것을 의미하며, 많은 서비스가 언제 어디서나 볼 수 있는 내장된 분석을 제공한다.

Vocabulary

real-time : 실시간
capability : 능력, 역량
collection and analysis : 수집, 분석
allow : 허락, 허용, 용납하다
immediately : 즉시, 즉각
productivity : 생산성
opportunities : 기회
respond : 응답하다
failures : 실패
production lines : 생산라인
proactive approach : 사전 예방적 접근 방식
anomalies or inefficiencies : 이상 징후나 비효율성
proliferation : 확산, 급증
continuously optimized : 지속적으로 최적화된
small and medium sized enterprises (SMEs) : 중소기업
embedded analytics : 내장된 분석 기능

⑤ Service orientation

The real-time capability made possible thanks to big data and the free flow of information thanks to interoperable systems enables businesses to better meet customer needs.

This allows businesses to adapt to customer's changing needs and expectations as they occur, providing a personalized service.

As a result, there is a shift in focus occurring across all industries to customers rather than products and to tailored services rather than mass production.

In agriculture, a growing number of farmers are using insights gained from data to make equipment more efficient and to optimize their supply chains and distribution models.

In aged care, cloud computing and Internet of Things (IoT) devices allow caregivers, doctors and patients to easily share information, enabling providers to streamline medication schedules, health reports, exercise regimes and more.

In advanced manufacturing, technologies like 3D printing are enabling factories to produce small-batch, customizable products quickly and cheaply.

Finally, in education, data technologies can be used to build student profiles to better understand how students learn and tailor instruction to their specific needs.

At the heart of these services is data collection and analysis, which provide businesses with predictive modelling capabilities.

In order to differentiate yourself from competition through a service orientation model, your business needs to be making use of data insights to provide unique services to your customer base.

Additionally, you should start to identify repetitive, non-core activities that can be reduced or eliminated using technology so that staff can focus on critical business functions.

⑤ 서비스 지향

빅 데이터 덕분에 실시간 기능이 가능했고 상호 운용 가능한 시스템 덕분에 자유로운 정보 흐름이 가능하여 기업은 고객 요구사항을 더 잘 충족할 수 있다. 이를 통해 기업은 변화하는 고객의 요구와 기대치에 맞춰 맞춤형 서비스를 제공할 수 있다.

그 결과, 모든 산업에서 제품이 아닌 고객, 대량 생산보다는 맞춤형 서비스로 초점이 바뀌고 있다.

농업에서 점점 더 많은 농부들이 장비를 보다 효율적으로 만들고 공급망과 유통 모델을 최적화하기 위해 데이터에서 얻은 통찰력을 이용하고 있다.

노인요양시설에서 클라우드 컴퓨팅과 사물인터넷(IoT) 장치는 간병인, 의사 및 환자가 정보를 쉽게 공유할 수 있도록 해주므로, 제공업체는 의약품 일정, 건강 보고, 운동 제도 등을 간소화할 수 있다.

고급 제조 분야에서는 3D 프린팅과 같은 기술을 통해 공장에서 맞춤 제작 가능한 소규모 제품을 빠르고 저렴하게 생산할 수 있게 되었다.

마지막으로, 교육에서 데이터 기술은 학생들이 학습하는 방법을 더 잘 이해하고 특정 요구에 맞는 교육을 제공하기 위해 학생 프로필을 구축하는 데 사용될 수 있다.

이러한 서비스의 중심에는 기업에 예측 모델링 기능을 제공하는 데이터 수집 및 분석이 있다. 서비스 지향 모델을 통해 경쟁업체와 차별화하려면 데이터 통찰력을 활용하여 고객층에 고유한 서비스를 제공해야 한다. 또한 직원이 중요한 비즈니스 기능에 집중할 수 있도록 기술사용을 줄이거나 제거할 수 있는 반복적인 비핵심 활동을 식별하기 시작해야한다.

Vocabulary

orientation : (목표하는) 방향, 지향
free flow of information : 자유로운 정보 흐름
interoperable : 상품정보 교환이 가능한
meet customer needs : 고객의 요구를 맞추다
adapt : 맞추다, 적응하다
customer's changing needs and expectations : 고객의 변화되는 니즈와 기대
tailored services : 맞춤형 서비스
farmers : 농부, 농장주
equipment : 장비, 용품
supply chains : 상품의 연쇄적인 생산 및 공급 과정
distribution : 분배
caregiver : 간병인
medication schedules : 의약품 일정
differentiate : 차별화하다
competition : 경쟁자
eliminated : 없애다, 제거하다

⑥ Modularity

Similar to service orientation, modularity refers to the ability of businesses to flexibly adapt to changing requirements and industry needs.

There are two ways to look at modularity:
A business that is split into small, well defined teams that focus on specific elements of the business operation. A business that implements modular systems, such as software platforms for accounting or HR, that allow you to purchase only what you need and add more in the future as needed. This is different to outsourcing because modular systems are designed to

interact with, and connect to, the rest of the business.

Both enable businesses to focus on what they do well. As a result, staff become specialists in core activities, offering value to customers in multiple ways. Core activities can then be expanded as the business grows, increasing business flexibility and scalability, as well as the ability of companies to respond more quickly to changing market conditions.

Identifying your business' core differentiators is the best place to start in determining how you can introduce a modular business structure. Look at where you can improve efficiencies and what tasks can be moved to software platforms to free up staff time.

⑥ 모듈화

모듈화는 서비스 지향과 마찬가지로 변화하는 요구사항과 업계 요구에 유연하게 적응할 수 있는 능력을 의미한다.

모듈화를 확인하는 방법에는 두 가지가 있다.
비즈니스 운영의 특정 요소에 초점을 맞춘 잘 정의된 소규모 팀으로 분할된 비즈니스다. 회계 또는 HR용 소프트웨어 플랫폼과 같은 모듈식 시스템을 구현하여 필요한 것만 구입하고 필요에 따라 향후 추가 작업을 수행할 수 있는 비즈니스다. 모듈식 시스템은 나머지 비즈니스와 상호 작용하고 연결되도록 설계되었기 때문에 이는 아웃소싱과 다르다. 둘 다 기업이 잘 하는 일에 집중할 수 있도록 해준다. 그 결과 직원들은 다양한 방식으로 고객에게 가치를 제공하는 핵심 활동의 전문가가 된다. 그런 다음 비즈니스 성장에 따라 핵심 활동을 확장하여 비즈니스 유연성과 확장성을 높이고 변화하는 시장 상황에 보다 신속하게 대응할 수 있다.

모듈식 비즈니스 구조를 도입하는 방법을 결정하는 데 있어 비즈니스의 핵심 차별화 요소를 파악하는 것이 가장 좋다. 효율성을 개선할 수 있는 부분과 직원 시간을 확보하기 위해 소프트웨어 플랫폼으로 이동할 수 있는 작업을 살펴보아라.

Vocabulary

modularity : 모듈 방식
similar : 비슷한, 유사한, 닮은
refer : 지시하다, 나타나다, 참고하다
split : 의견이 갈리다, 나뉘다
defined : 정의된
element : 요소
accounting : 회계
purchase : 구입하다, 사다
as a result : 그 결과
specialists : 전문가
customer : 고객
multiple ways : 다양한 방법
core activities : 핵심 활동
business flexibility and scalability : 비즈니스 유연성과 확장성
respond : 응답하다
identify : 확인하다
differentiator : 구분하는 것
determine : 결정하다

3) What Is Artificial Intelligence?[3] 인공지능이란 무엇인가?

Artificial intelligence (AI) is intelligence demonstrated by machines, unlike the natural intelligence displayed by humans and animals, which involves consciousness and emotionality. The distinction between the former and the latter categories is often revealed by the acronym chosen. 'Strong' AI is usually labelled as artificial general intelligence (AGI) while attempts

3 https://en.wikipedia.org/wiki/Artificial_intelligence

to emulate 'natural' intelligence have been called artificial biological intelligence (ABI).

Leading AI textbooks define the field as the study of "intelligent agents": any device that perceives its environment and takes actions that maximize its chance of achieving its goals. Colloquially, the term "artificial intelligence" is often used to describe machines that mimic "cognitive" functions that humans associate with the human mind, such as "learning" and "problem solving".[4]

As machines become increasingly capable, tasks considered to require "intelligence" are often removed from the definition of AI, a phenomenon known as the AI effect. For instance, optical character recognition is frequently excluded from things considered to be AI, having become a routine technology.

Modern machine capabilities generally classified as AI include successfully understanding human speech, competing at the highest level in strategic game systems (such as chess and Go), and also imperfect-information games like poker, self-driving cars, intelligent routing in content delivery networks, and military simulations.

인공지능(AI)은 인간과 동물이 보여주는 자연 지능과 달리 기계가 보여주는 지능으로 의식과 정서성을 수반한다. 전자와 후자의 범주의 구분은 종종 선택된 약어로 들어난다. '강력한' AI는 보통의 인공지능(AGI : artificial general intelligence)으로 불리는 반면, '자연적인' 지능을 모방하려는 시도는 인공 생물 지능(ABI : artificial biological intelligence)으로 불린다.

주요 AI 교재들은 이 분야를 "지능적 에이전트"의 연구로 정의한다. 즉, 환경을 인지하고 목표 달성 가능성을 최대화하기 위해 행동하는 어떤 장치를 말한다. 일상적으

4 https://sensiml.com/entity/ai/

로는 "인공 지능"이라는 용어가 종종 인간의 사고와 관련된 "학습"과 "문제 해결"과 같은 "인지" 기능을 모방하는 기계를 설명하는 데 사용된다.

기계가 점점 더 능력을 갖추게 되면서 "지능"이 필요하다고 여겨지는 작업은 종종 AI의 정의에서 제외되는 현상이 발생한다. 이를 AI 효과라고 한다. 예를 들어, 광학 문자 인식은 일상적인 기술이 되었기 때문에 AI로 간주되지 않는다.

현재 AI로 분류되는 기계의 능력에는 인간의 음성을 성공적으로 이해하는 것, 체스와 바둑과 같은 전략 게임에서 최고 수준에서 경쟁하는 것, 포커와 같은 불완전 정보 게임, 자율 주행 자동차, 콘텐츠 전달 네트워크에서의 지능적인 라우팅, 군사 시뮬레이션 등이 있다.

Artificial intelligence was founded as an academic discipline in 1955, and in the years since has experienced several waves of optimism, followed by disappointment and the loss of funding (known as an "AI winter"), followed by new approaches, success and renewed funding.

After AlphaGo defeated a professional Go player in 2015, artificial intelligence once again attracted widespread global attention. For most of its history, AI research has been divided into sub-fields that often fail to communicate with each other. These sub-fields are based on technical considerations, such as particular goals (e.g. "robotics" or "machine learning"), the use of particular tools ("logic" or artificial neural networks), or deep philosophical differences. Sub-fields have also been based on social factors (particular institutions or the work of particular researchers).

The traditional problems (or goals) of AI research include reasoning, knowledge representation, planning, learning, natural language processing, perception and the ability to move and manipulate objects. AGI is among the field's long-term goals. Approaches include statistical methods, computational intelligence, and traditional symbolic AI. Many tools are used in AI, including versions of search and mathematical optimization, artificial neural networks, and methods based on statistics, probability and economics. The AI field draws upon computer science, information engineering, mathematics, psychology, linguistics, philosophy, and many other fields.

The field was founded on the assumption that human intelligence "can be so precisely described that a machine can be made to simulate it". This raises philosophical arguments about the mind and the ethics of creating artificial beings endowed with human-like intelligence. These issues have been explored by myth, fiction and philosophy since antiquity. Some people also consider AI to be a danger to humanity if it progresses unabated. Others believe that AI, unlike previous technological revolutions, will create a risk of mass unemployment.

In the twenty-first century, AI techniques have experienced a resurgence following concurrent advances in computer power, large amounts of data, and theoretical understanding; and AI techniques have become an essential part of the technology industry, helping to solve many challenging problems in computer science, software engineering and operations research.

인공지능은 1955년에 학문적 규율로서 만들어졌고, 그 이후로 몇 년 동안 낙관의 흐름을 겪었다. 그 뒤에는 실망과 자금 손실이(AI의 겨울로 알려지는), 이 후에는 새로운 접근법, 성공 그리고 새로운 자금 지원이 뒤따랐다.

2015년 알파고가 프로 바둑기사를 꺾은 뒤 인공지능이 다시 한 번 세계적인 주목을 받았다. 지금까지 AI 연구는 대부분 의사소통에 자주 실패하는 하위 분야로 나눠져 왔다. 이러한 하위 분야는 특정 목표("로봇" 또는 "기계 학습"), 특정 도구의 사용("논리" 또는 인공 신경망) 또는 깊은 철학적 차이와 같은 기술적 고려사항에 기초한다. 하위 분야는 또한 사회적 요인(특정 기관 또는 특정 연구자의 작업)에 기초해 왔다.

AI 연구의 전통적인 문제(또는목표)는 추론, 지식 표현, 계획, 학습, 자연어 처리, 인식, 그리고 물체를 움직이고 조작하는 능력을 포함한다. AGI는 이 분야의 장기적인 목표 중 하나이다. 접근법에는 통계적 방법, 컴퓨터 지능 및 전통적 상징 AI가 포함된다. AI에는 검색과 수학적 최적화 버전, 인공신경망, 통계, 확률, 경제성을 바탕으로 한 방법 등 많은 도구가 사용된다. AI 분야는 컴퓨터 과학, 정보 공학, 수학, 심리학, 언어학, 철학, 그리고 다른 많은 분야에 기반을 두고 있다.

이 분야는 인간의 지능을 "너무 정확하게 기술하여 기계를 시뮬레이션할 수 있다"는 가정 하에 만들어졌다. 이것은 인간과 같은 지능을 타고난 인공적 존재를 창조하는 정신와 윤리에 대한 철학적 논쟁을 불러일으킨다. 이 문제들은 고대부터 신화, 소설, 철학에 의해 탐구되어 왔다. 어떤 사람들은 AI가 계속 진행되면 인류를 위협하는 것이라고 생각한다. 다른 사람들은 AI가 이전의 기술혁명과 달리 대량 실업의 위험을 초래할 것이라고 믿는다.

21세기에 AI 기술은 컴퓨터 파워, 대량의 데이터 및 이론적 이해의 동시 발전에 따라 다시 부상했다. 그리고 AI 기술은 컴퓨터 과학, 소프트웨어 공학, 운영 연구의 많은 난제들을 해결하는 데 도움을 주면서 기술 산업의 필수적인 부분이 되었다.

Vocabulary

demonstrate : **보여주다, 설명하다**
unlike : **~ 와 달리**
involve : **포함하다**
consciousness and emotionality : **의식과 정서**
distinction : **차이**
the former and the latter : **전자와 후자**
revealed : **드러나다**
acronym : **두음, 머리글자**
label : **라벨, 꼬리표를 붙이다**

attempt : 시도하다
emulate : 모방하다
biological : 생물학의
leading : 선두적인
achieve : 성취하다
colloquially : 구어체로, 회화체로
mimic : 흉내를 내다
cognitive functions : 인지적인 기능
removed : 제거된
definition : 정의
phenomenon : 현상
optical character recognition : 광학문자인식
frequently : 빈번하게
excluded : 제외되는
classified : 주제별로 분류된
compete : 경쟁하다
academic discipline : 학문적 규율
found : 설립하다, 만들다, ~의 기반을 두다
optimism : 낙관론
disappointment : 실망, 낙심
defeated : 패배한
attract : 마음을 끌다, 불러일으키다
widespread : 광범위한
subfield : 하위 분야
artificial neural network : 인공신경망
philosophical : 철학의
institution : 기관
traditional : 전통적인
reasoning : 논리, 추론
manipulate : 조종하다
approach : 접근

mathematical optimization : 수학적 최적화
statistics, probability and economics : 통계, 확률, 경제학
assumption : 가정, 추정
myth, fiction and philosophy : 신화, 소설, 철학
unabated : 조금도 수그러들지 않는
technological revolutions : 기술 혁명
mass unemployment : 대량실업
challenging : 도전적인

4) History of Artificial Intelligence[5] AI의 역사

Artificial Intelligence is not a new word and not a new technology for researchers. This technology is much older than you would imagine. Even there are the myths of Mechanical men in Ancient Greek and Egyptian Myths. Some milestones in the history of AI define the journey from the AI generation to the present day[6].

Maturation of Artificial Intelligence (1943-1952)

Year 1943: The first work which is now recognized as AI was done by Warren McCulloch and Walter pits in 1943. They proposed a model of artificial neurons.

Year 1949: Donald Hebb demonstrated an updating rule for modifying the connection strength between neurons. His rule is now called Hebbian learning.

Year 1950: The Alan Turing who was an English mathematician and pioneered Machine learning in 1950. Alan Turing publishes "Computing Machinery and Intelligence" in which he proposed a test. The test can

5 https://en.wikipedia.org/wiki/History_of_artificial_intelligence

6 https://www.javatpoint.com/history-of-artificial-intelligence

check the machine's ability to exhibit intelligent behavior equivalent to human intelligence, called a Turing test.

인공지능은 연구자들에게 새로운 단어도, 새로운 기술도 아니다. 이 기술은 당신이 상상하는 것보다 훨씬 오래되었다. 고대 그리스와 이집트 신화에는 기계인에 대한 신화도 있다. AI의 역사에서 몇 가지 이정표는 AI 세대에서 현재까지의 여정을 정의한다.

인공지능의 성숙(1943-1952)

1943년: 현재 AI로 알려진 첫 번째 연구는 1943년 워렌 맥컬록과 월터 피츠에 의해 이루어졌다. 그들은 인공 뉴런의 모델을 제안했다.
1949년: 도널드 헵은 뉴런 사이의 연결 강도를 수정하기 위한 최신 규칙을 보여주었다. 그의 규칙은 지금 헵비안 학습으로 불린다.
1950년: 1950년 영국 수학자이자 기계 학습을 개척한 앨런 튜링. 앨런 튜링은 테스트를 제안했던 "컴퓨팅 머신과 인텔리전스"를 출판한다. 이 테스트는 튜링 테스트라고 불리는 인간의 지능과 동등한 지능을 보일 수 있는 기계의 능력을 점검할 수 있다.

The birth of Artificial Intelligence (1952-1956)

Year 1955: An Allen Newell and Herbert A. Simon created the "first artificial intelligence program" which was named as "Logic Theorist". This program had proved 38 of 52 Mathematics theorems, and find new and more elegant proofs for some theorems.
Year 1956: The word "Artificial Intelligence" first adopted by American Computer scientist John McCarthy at the Dartmouth Conference. For the first time, AI coined as an academic field.
At that time high-level computer languages such as FORTRAN, LISP, or COBOL were invented. And the enthusiasm for AI was very high at that time.

인공지능의 탄생(1952-1956)

1955년: 앨런 뉴웰과 허버트 A. 사이먼은 "첫 번째 인공지능 프로그램"을 만들었다. 그 이름은 "논리 이론가"였다. 이 프로그램은 52개의 수학 이론 중 38개를 증명했고, 몇몇 이론들에 대한 새롭고 더 우아한 증거를 찾아냈다.
1956년: "인공지능"이라는 단어는 다트머스 컨퍼런스에서 미국 컴퓨터 과학자 존 매카시에 의해 처음 채택되었다. AI가 학문 분야로 처음 등장했다. 그 당시에 포트란, LISP 또는 COBOL과 같은 고급 컴퓨터 언어가 발명되었다. 당시 AI에 대한 열기도 뜨거웠다.

The golden years-Early enthusiasm (1956-1974)

Year 1966: The researchers emphasized developing algorithms which can solve mathematical problems. Joseph Weizenbaum created the first chatbot in 1966, which was named as ELIZA.
Year 1972: The first intelligent humanoid robot was built in Japan which was named as WABOT-1.

황금기-초기의 열정(1956~1974)

1966년: 연구자들은 수학 문제를 해결할 수 있는 알고리즘 개발을 강조했다. 조셉 바이젠바움은 1966년에 ELIZA라는 이름을 가진 최초의 챗봇을 만들었다.
1972년: 최초의 지능형 휴머노이드 로봇은 일본에서 만들어졌으며, 이 로봇은 WABOT-1이라고 이름 붙여졌다.

The first AI winter (1974-1980)

The duration between years 1974 to 1980 was the first AI winter duration. AI winter refers to the time period where computer scientist dealt with a severe shortage of funding from government for AI researches. During AI winters, an interest of publicity on artificial intelligence was decreased.

첫 번째 AI 겨울(1974~1980)

1974년부터 1980년까지가 최초의 AI 겨울 기간이었다. AI 겨울은 컴퓨터 과학자가 정부로부터 심각한 연구비 부족을 겪은 시기를 말한다. AI 겨울에는 인공지능에 대한 관심도가 낮아졌다.

A boom of AI (1980-1987)

Year 1980: After AI winter duration, AI came back with "Expert System". Expert systems were programmed that emulate the decision-making ability of a human expert. In the Year 1980, the first national conference of the American Association of Artificial Intelligence was held at Stanford University.

AI 붐(1980-1987)

1980년: AI 겨울기간 이후, AI는 "전문가 시스템"으로 돌아왔다. 전문가 시스템은 인간 전문가의 의사결정 능력을 모방하도록 프로그램되었다. 1980년에, 미국 인공지능 협회의 첫 번째 전국 회의가 스탠포드 대학교에서 열렸다.

The second AI winter (1987-1993)

The duration between the years 1987 to 1993 was the second AI Winter duration. Again, investors and government stopped in funding for AI research as due to high cost but not efficient result. The expert system such as XCON was very cost effective.

두 번째 AI 겨울(1987-1993)

1987년부터 1993년까지의 기간이 두 번째 AI 겨울 기간이었다.
투자자들과 정부는 높은 비용이 들지만 효율적인 결과를 얻지 못했기 때문에 AI 연구에 대한 자금 지원을 중단했다. XCON과 같은 전문가 시스템은 굉장히 비용 효율적이었다.

The emergence of intelligent agents (1993–2011)

Year 1997: In the year 1997, IBM Deep Blue beats world chess champion, Gary Kasparov, and became the first computer to beat a world chess champion.
Year 2002: for the first time, AI entered the home in the form of Roomba, a vacuum cleaner.
Year 2006: AI came in the Business world till the year 2006. Companies like Facebook, Twitter, and Netflix also started using AI.

지능형 에이전트의 출현(1993~2011)

1997년: 1997년에 IBM Deep Blue는 세계 체스 챔피언인 Gary Kasparov를 누르고 세계 체스 챔피언을 이긴 최초의 컴퓨터가 되었다.
2002년: AI가 처음으로 진공청소기인 Roomba의 형태로 가정에 들어왔다.
2006년: 2006년까지 비즈니스 세계에서 AI가 유행했다. 페이스북, 트위터, 넷플릭스 같은 회사들도 AI를 사용하기 시작했다.

Deep learning, big data and artificial general intelligence (2011–present)

Year 2011: In the year 2011, IBM's Watson won jeopardy, a quiz show, where it had to solve the complex questions as well as riddles. Watson had proved that it could understand natural language and can solve tricky questions quickly.
Year 2012: Google has launched an Android app feature "Google now", which was able to provide information to the user as a prediction.
Year 2014: In the year 2014, Chatbot "Eugene Goostman" won a competition in the infamous "Turing test“.
Year 2018: The "Project Debater" from IBM debated on complex topics with two master debaters and also performed extremely well.
Google has demonstrated an AI program "Duplex" which was a virtual assistant and which had taken hairdresser appointment on call, and lady

on other side didn't notice that she was talking with the machine. Now AI has developed to a remarkable level. The concept of Deep learning, big data, and data science are now trending like a boom. Nowadays companies like Google, Facebook, IBM, and Amazon are working with AI and creating amazing devices. The future of Artificial Intelligence is inspiring and will come with high intelligence.

딥러닝, 빅데이터 및 인공지능(2011년-현재)

2011년: 2011년 IBM의 Watson은 복잡한 문제와 수수께끼를 풀어야하는 퀴즈쇼인 jeopardy에서 우승하였다. 왓슨은 그것이 자연어를 이해할 수 있고 까다로운 질문들을 빨리 풀 수 있다는 것을 증명했다.
2012년: 구글은 사용자에게 예측 정보를 제공할 수 있는 안드로이드 앱 기능 "Google now"를 출시했다.
2014년 : 2014년, 챗봇 "유진 구스트먼"은 악명 높은 "튜링 테스트" 대회에서 우승했다.
2018년: IBM의 "프로젝트 디베이터"는 두 명의 주요 토론자와 함께 복잡한 주제에 대해 토론했고 매우 좋은 성과를 거두었다.
구글이 가상 비서로 미용사 직책을 맡았던 '듀플렉스' 프로그램을 선보였는데도 정작 옆집 여성은 자신이 기계와 대화하는 것을 눈치채지 못했다.
이제 AI는 놀라운 수준으로 발전했다. 딥러닝, 빅 데이터 및 데이터 과학 개념은 현재 붐과 같은 추세를 보이고 있다. 오늘날 구글, 페이스북, IBM, 그리고 아마존과 같은 회사들은 AI와 함께 일하며 놀라운 장치를 만들고 있다. 인공지능의 미래는 고무적이고 높은 지능과 함께 올 것이다.

Vocabulary

researcher : 연구자
Mechanical men : 기계인
Ancient Greek and Egyptian Myths : 고대 그리스와 이집트 신화
milestones : 중요한 사건들
recognize : 인정하다
propose: 제안하다
a model of artificial neurons : 인공뉴런의 모델
demonstrate an updating rule : 최신 규칙을 시연하다
mathematician : 수학자
pioneer : 개척하다
publish : 출판하다
exhibit : 보이다
equivalent to : ~와 동등한
theorist : 이론가
prove : 증명하다
theorem : (수학에서의) 정리
adopt : 채택하다
invent : 발명하다
enthusiasm : 열정
severe shortage of funding : 심각한 자금 부족
publicity : 매스컴의 관심, 홍보
emulate : 모방하다
emergence : 출현
beat : 이기다
complex : 복잡한
prediction : 예측, 예견
competition : 대회
infamous : 악명높은
remarkable level : 놀라운 수준
inspiring : 고무하는, 영감을 주는

5) Machine Learning[7] 머신러닝(기계학습)

Machine learning is a subset of artificial intelligence (AI). It is focused on teaching computers to learn from data and to improve with experience instead of being explicitly programmed to do so. In machine learning, algorithms are trained to find patterns and correlations in large data sets and to make the best decisions and predictions based on that analysis. Machine learning applications improve with use and become more accurate the more data they have access to. Applications of machine learning are all around us in our homes, our shopping carts, our entertainment media, and our healthcare.

How is machine learning related to AI?

Machine learning – and its components of deep learning and neural networks – all fit as concentric subsets of AI. AI processes data to make decisions and predictions. Machine learning algorithms allow AI to not only process that data, but to use it to learn and get smarter, without needing any additional programming. Artificial intelligence is the parent of all the machine learning subsets beneath it. Within the first subset is machine learning; within that is deep learning, and then neural networks within that.

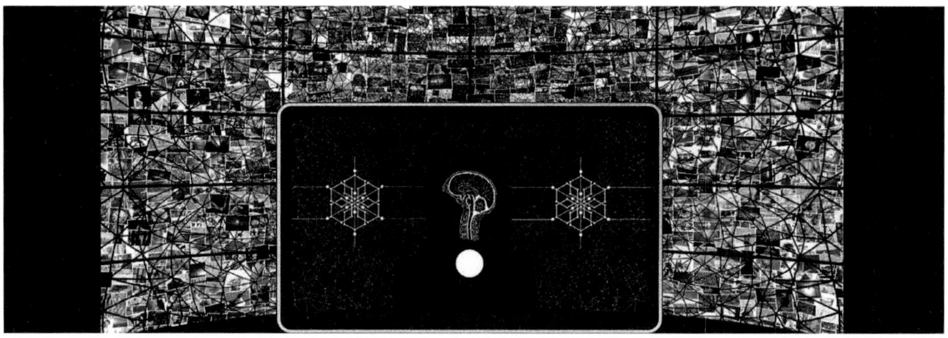

7 https://insights.sap.com/what-is-machine-learning/

How does machine learning work?

Machine learning is comprised of different types of machine learning models, using various algorithmic techniques. Depending upon the nature of the data and the desired outcome, one of four learning models can be used: supervised, unsupervised, semi-supervised, or reinforcement. Within each of those models, one or more algorithmic techniques may be applied – relative to the data sets in use and the intended results. Machine learning algorithms are basically designed to classify things, find patterns, predict outcomes, and make informed decisions. Algorithms can be used one at a time or combined to achieve the best possible accuracy when complex and more unpredictable data is involved.

머신러닝(기계학습)은 인공지능(AI)의 하위 집합이다. 머신러닝은 컴퓨터가 명시적으로 프로그래밍 되지 않고 데이터를 통해 배우고 경험을 통해 개선하도록 가르치는데 초점을 맞추고 있다. 머신러닝에서 알고리즘은 대규모 데이터 집합에서 패턴과 상관관계를 찾고 해당 분석을 기반으로 최선의 결정과 예측을 하도록 훈련된다. 머신러닝 애플리케이션은 사용과 함께 향상되고 더 많은 데이터에 액세스할수록 정확도가 높아진다. 머신러닝 애플리케이션은 가정, 쇼핑 카트, 엔터테인먼트 미디어 및 의료 등 우리 주변 어디에나 있다.

머신러닝은 AI와 어떤 관련이 있나?

머신러닝(Machine Learning)과 딥러닝(Deep Learning) 및 신경망(Neural Network) 구성 요소는 모두 AI의 중심이 같은 하위 집합으로 적합하다. AI는 데이터를 처리해 의사결정과 예측을 한다. 머신러닝 알고리즘은 별도의 프로그래밍 없이도 데이터를 처리할 수 있을 뿐 아니라 학습과 스마트화에 활용할 수 있다. 인공지능은 그 밑에 있는 모든 머신러닝 하위 집합의 모체이다. 첫 번째 부분 집합 안에는 머신러닝(기계학습)이 있고, 그 안에는 딥러닝이 있고, 그 안에 신경망이 있다.

머신러닝은 어떻게 작동하나?

머신러닝은 다양한 알고리즘 기법을 사용하여 다양한 유형의 머신러닝 모델로 구성되어 있다. 데이터의 특성 및 원하는 결과에 따라 4가지 학습 모델(지도, 비지도, 준지도 또는 강화) 중 하나를 사용할 수 있다. 이러한 각 모델 내에서 사용 중인 데이터 세트 및 의도된 결과와 관련하여 하나 이상의 알고리즘 기법을 적용할 수 있다. 머신러닝 알고리즘은 기본적으로 사물을 분류하고, 패턴을 찾고, 결과를 예측하고, 정보에 입각한 결정을 내리도록 설계되었다. 알고리즘은 한 번에 하나씩 사용하거나 조합하여 복잡하고 예측 불가능한 데이터가 포함된 경우 최상의 정확도를 달성할 수 있다.

Vocabulary

subset : 하위집합
explicitly : 명시적으로, 명쾌하게
correlation : 상관관계
prediction : 예측
component : 요소
concentric : 중심이 같은, 동심의
additional : 추가의
beneath : ~ 아래의
comprise : ~로 구성되다
desired : 바랬던
supervised, unsupervised, semi-supervised, or reinforcement : 지도학습, 비지도학습, 준지도학습 또는 강화학습
relative : ~와 관련지은
intended : 의도된
classify : 분류하다
combine : 결합하다
achieve : 달성하다, 성취하다
accuracy : 정확도
involve : 포함하다, 관련시키다

6) Deep Learning 딥러닝[8]

Deep learning is called "deep" because it includes many layers of the neural network and massive volumes of complex and disparate data. To achieve deep learning, the system engages with multiple layers in the network, extracting increasingly higher-level outputs. For example, a deep learning system that is processing nature images and looking for Gloriosa daisies will – at the first layer – recognize a plant. As it moves through the neural layers, it will then identify a flower, then a daisy, and finally a Gloriosa daisy. Examples of deep learning applications include speech recognition, image classification, and pharmaceutical analysis.

머신러닝의 하위 집합인 딥러닝은 신경 네트워크의 많은 계층과 복잡하고 이질적인 방대한 양의 데이터를 포함하기 때문에 "딥"이라고 불린다. 딥러닝을 달성하기 위해, 시스템은 네트워크의 여러 계층과 연계되어 점점 더 높은 수준의 출력을 추출한

8 https://insights.sap.com/what-is-machine-learning/

다. 예를 들어, 자연 이미지를 처리하고 글로리오사 데이지스를 찾는 딥러닝 시스템은 첫 번`째 계층에서 식물을 인식한다. 신경망을 통과하면서 꽃 한 송이, 데이지 한 송이, 그리고 마지막으로 글로리오사 데이지 한 송이를 식별할 것이다. 딥러닝 애플리케이션의 예로는 음성 인식, 영상 분류, 약물 분석이 있다.

Vocabulary

demonstrate : 보여주다, 설명하다
massive : 부피가 큰
disparate : 서로 다른, 이질적인
engage : 관계하다
multiple layers : 여러 층
extract : 추출하다
output : 출력
process : 처리하다
recognize : 인식하다
speech recognition, image classification, and pharmaceutical analysis : 음성인식, 이미지 분류, 약물 분석

☞ 잠깐 쉬어가기 ....

이세돌과 알파고의 대국 (출처 https://www.latimes.com/world/asia/la-fg-la-fg-0312-south-korea-go-player-20160311-story.html)

여러분은 혹시 2016년 3월 이세돌 9구단이 알파고와 대국을 겨뤘던 그 때를 기억하십니까?

오직 인간만이 해결할 수 있다고 여겨졌던 성역인 바둑까지도 AI가 이겼습니다. 1997년 IBM의 딥블루가 세계 체스 챔피언 가리 카스파로프를 이겼었던 적이 있죠. 구글의 인공지능 회사인 '딥마인드'가 개발한 알파고는 이 전부터 전문 바둑 기사들과 대국을 겨루며 승리를 이어가다가 드디어 2016년 세계 최상위 프로 기사인 이세돌까지 4승 1패로 승리하였습니다. 당시 드디어 인공지능의 시대가 왔다고 전 세계적으로 모든 언론사에서 대서특필 하였습니다. 그 이후로도 알파고는 세계 랭킹 1위인 커제 9단를 포함하여 전 세계 최고수들을 대상으로 모두 승리를 하였고 이 과정을 거치면서 강화학습을 통하여 점차 진화하였습니다. 알파고를 개발한 딥마인드는 알파고 이후, 머신러닝분야에 다양한 연구를 해오다가 2023년 4월 '구글 브레인'과 합병을 발표하고 사명을 '구글 딥마인드'로 바꾸었습니다. 오픈 AI로 촉발된 생성형 인공지능 경쟁에서 구글이 우위를 확보하겠다는 전략으로 해석됩니다.

연습문제

exercises

1~5. 다음 빈 칸에 들어가는 단어로 적절한 것을 넣으세요.

1. These design principles are - (①), virtualization, (②), real-time capability, service orientation, and (③).

정답 : ______________________________

2. ( ) publishes "Computing Machinery and Intelligence" in which he proposed a test. The test can check the machine's ability to exhibit intelligent behavior equivalent to human intelligence, called a Turing test.

정답 : ______________________________

3. In the year 1997, ( ) beats world chess champion, Gary Kasparov, and became the first computer to beat a world chess champion.

정답 : ______________________________

4. ( ) is called "deep" because it includes many layers of the neural network and massive volumes of complex and disparate data.

정답 : ______________________________

5. The word "Artificial Intelligence" first adopted by American Computer scientist ( ) at the Dartmouth Conference. For the first time, AI coined as an academic field.

정답 : ______________________________

6~10. 다음 It이 지칭하는 것을 영어로 쓰세요.

6. It is something that businesses have been embracing for years, moving systems to components rather than a central computer to enable unlimited scalability and flexibility.

정답 : ______________________________

7. It is intelligence demonstrated by machines, unlike the natural intelligence displayed by humans and animals, which involves consciousness and emotionality.

정답 : ______________________________

8. It is focused on teaching computers to learn from data and to improve with experience – instead of being explicitly programmed to do so.

정답 : ______________________________

9. In the year 2011, it won jeopardy, a quiz show, where it had to solve the complex questions as well as riddles.

정답 : ______________________________

10. It refers to the collection and analysis of data in real-time, allowing decisions to be made immediately and at every moment.

정답 : ______________________________

연습문제 해답

1. ① interoperability, ② decentralization, ③ modularity
2. Alan Turing 3. IBM Deep Blue 4. Deep learning 5. John McCarthy
6. Decentralization 7. Artificial intelligence 8. Machine learning
9. IBM's Watson 10. Real-time capability

Chapter

02 Generative Artificial Intelligence
생성형 AI

학습순서

1) Introduction to Generative AI
2) Applications of Generative AI
3) Limitations of Generative AI
4) The Future of Generative AI

잠깐 쉬어가기

연습문제

【 INTRO 】

여러분 중에 Chat GPT나 생성형 AI 서비스를 사용해본 적이 있나요? 2022년 하반기부터 등장하여 어느 순간 우리의 삶 가운데 친숙하게 들어와버린 생성형 AI는 과연 어디까지 영향을 미칠 수 있을까요? '4박 5일 해외 여행을 일정, 국가 등을 달리하여 50만원 예산으로 3가지 유형의 계획을 세워줘'라고 Chat GPT 프롬프트에 입력하였더니 일정과 국가까지 생각보다 세부적이고 다양하게 플랜을 짠 경험이 있습니다. 질문에 대한 답이 생성되고 나면 그와 관련되어 파생될 수 있는 여러 질문들을 물어볼 수 있게끔 잠재적인 질문 또한 제공됩니다. 이처럼 우리가 생활하면서 궁금한 것들을 AI에게 손쉽게 물어볼 수 있습니다. 과거에는 구글이나 네이버를 통하여 검색하여서 정답을 발견하기까지 시간을 할애해야했다면 이제는 검색해야하는 수고를 생성형 AI가 덜어주게 된 것입니다. 그렇다면 생성형 AI는 무얼까요? 2장에서는 생성형 AI와 적용 사례, 한계점과 앞으로의 전망 등을 알아보도록 하겠습니다.

Have any of you ever used Chat GPT or generative AI services? Since its emergence in the second half of 2022, generative AI has become familiar to us at some point in our lives. How far can generative AI influence us? When I inputted "Plan a 4-night, 5-day overseas trip with a budget of 500,000 KRW, with three different types varying the itinerary and country" into the Chat GPT prompt, I had an experience where it generated detailed and diverse plans regarding the itinerary and country. Not only did it provide answers to my questions but also potential follow-up questions related to them. This allows us to easily ask AI about things we are curious about in our daily lives. In the past, we had to spend time searching on platforms like Google or Naver to find answers, but now generative AI relieves us from that search effort. So what is generative AI? In Chapter 2, we will explore generative AI.

1) Introduction to Generative AI 생성형 AI의 개요[1]

What is Generative AI?

Generative artificial intelligence (AI) is artificial intelligence capable of generating text, images, or other media, using generative models. Generative AI models learn the patterns and structure of their input training data and then generate new data that has similar characteristics.

In the early 2020s, advances in transformer-based deep neural networks enabled a number of generative AI systems notable for accepting natural language prompts as input. These include large language model chatbots such as ChatGPT, Bing Chat, Bard, and LLaMA, and text-to-image artificial intelligence art systems such as Stable Diffusion, Midjourney, and DALL-E.

Generative AI has uses across a wide range of industries, including art, writing, software development, product design, healthcare, finance, gaming, marketing, and fashion. Investment in generative AI surged during the early 2020s, with large companies such as Microsoft, Google, and Baidu as well as numerous smaller firms developing generative AI models.

1 https://en.wikipedia.org/wiki/Generative_artificial_intelligence
https://www.gartner.com/en/topics/generative-ai

생성형 AI란?

생성형 AI는 생성 모델을 사용하여 텍스트, 이미지 또는 기타 미디어를 생성할 수 있는 인공 지능이다. 생성형 AI 모델은 입력 훈련 데이터의 패턴과 구조를 학습한 다음 유사한 특성을 가진 새로운 데이터를 생성한다.

2020년대 초반, transformer 기반 딥 뉴럴 네트워크의 발전으로 자연어 프롬프트를 입력으로 받는 몇 가지의 생성형 AI 시스템이 등장했다. 이에는 ChatGPT, Bing Chat, Bard 및 LLaMA와 같은 대형 언어 모델 챗봇과 Stable Diffusion, Midjourney 및 DALL-E와 같은 텍스트-이미지 인공 지능 아트 시스템이 포함된다.

생성형 AI는 예술, 글쓰기, 소프트웨어 개발, 제품 디자인, 의료, 금융, 게임, 마케팅 및 패션을 비롯한 다양한 산업에서 사용된다. 2020년대 초반에는 Microsoft, Google 및 Baidu와 같은 대기업과 많은 중소기업들이 Generative AI 모델을 개발하며 투자가 급증했다.

History of Generative AI

The earliest work on Generative AI can be traced back to the 1950s when computer scientists were exploring the idea of using algorithms to create new data. One of the first examples of Generative AI was the Markov Chain, which is a statistical model that can be used to generate new sequences of data based on an input sequence.[2] Since then, artists and researchers have used generative artificial intelligence to create new works. By the early 1970s, Harold Cohen was creating and exhibiting works created by AARON, the computer program Cohen created to generate paintings. Today, generative AI has uses across a wide range of industries, including art, writing, software development, product design, healthcare, finance, gaming, marketing, and fashion.

2 https://lore.com/generative-ai-history

생성형 AI의 역사

생성형 AI는 새로운 데이터를 생성하기 위해 알고리즘을 사용하는 개념으로, 1950년대에 처음 등장했다. 생성형 AI의 초기 예시 중 하나는 입력 시퀀스를 기반으로 새로운 데이터 시퀀스를 생성할 수 있는 통계 모델인 Markov Chain이다. 이후 예술가와 연구자들은 generative artificial intelligence를 사용하여 새로운 작품을 만들었다. 1970년대 초반, Harold Cohen은 AARON이라는 컴퓨터 프로그램을 만들어 그림을 생성하고 전시하기도 했다. 현재 생성형 AI는 예술, 글쓰기, 소프트웨어 개발, 제품 디자인, 의료, 금융, 게임, 마케팅 및 패션을 비롯한 다양한 산업에서 사용되고 있다.

Types of Generative AI

The main types of generative models used in practice today include autoregressive models, variational autoencoders (VAEs), and generative adversarial networks (GANs).[3] Unimodal systems take only one type of input whereas multimodal systems can take more than one type of input. For example, one version of OpenAI's GPT-4 accepts both text and image inputs. Generative AI most commonly creates content in response to natural language requests – it doesn't require knowledge of or entering code – but the enterprise use cases are numerous and include innovations in drug and chip design and material science development.

생성형 AI의 유형

생성형 AI의 주요 모델로는 autoregressive models, variational autoencoders (VAEs), 그리고 generative adversarial networks (GANs)가 있다. Unimodal systems는 하나의 유형의 입력만 받을 수 있으며, multimodal systems는 여러 유형의 입력을 받을 수 있다. 예를 들어, OpenAI의 GPT-4 중 하나는 텍스트와 이미지 입력을 모두 받을 수 있다. 생성형 AI는 대개 자연어 요청에 대한 콘텐츠를 생성한다. 즉, 코드를 알 필요가 없다. 그러나 기업에서 사용되는 경우에는 약물 및 칩 디자인 및 재료 과학 개발 등 다양한 혁신이 가능하다.

3 https://www.mlq.ai/what-is-generative-ai/

Vocabulary

generative : 발생의, 생성의
capable of : ~할 수 있는
notable for : ~ 으로 유명한
finance : 재정, 재무
surge : 밀려들다, 휩싸다
firm : 회사
statistical model : 통계적 모형
researcher : 연구원, 조사자
exhibit : 전시하다, 보이다
a wide range of : 광범위한, 다양한
autoregressive : 자기회기
variational autoencoders (VAEs) : 변분 오토인코더
generative adversarial networks (GANs) : 생성적 적대 신경망
innovation : 혁신

2) Applications of Generative AI 생성형 AI의 적용[4]

Image Generation

Generative AI can be used to create realistic images from text descriptions or other inputs. This technology has the ability to generate diverse outputs, including unique visual content such as images and videos.[5]
One example of this is OpenAI's DALL-E, which can generate images from text descriptions. Another example is the Bing Image Creator, which is powered by a more advanced version of DALL-E and produces high-quality results quickly.[6]

Generative AI has become a powerful tool in the realm of image generation. One of the most notable applications is in Generative Adversarial Networks (GANs)[7]. GANs consist of two neural networks, a generator and a discriminator, that work together to create realistic images from random noise.[8] The generator creates images and presents them to the discriminator. The discriminator then decides whether each image is real (from the original dataset) or fake (created by the generator). Over time, the generator learns to create increasingly realistic images to fool the discriminator. This process results in generated images that can be almost indistinguishable from real ones.

Applications of GANs in image generation include creating art, synthesizing photos of human faces (e.g., NVIDIA's StyleGAN), enhancing low-resolution images, and even generating medical imaging data for research purposes.

---

4 https://www.gartner.com/en/topics/generative-ai

5 https://openai.com/research/dall-e

6 https://www.zdnet.com/article/best-ai-art-generator/

7 https://towardsdatascience.com/generative-adversarial-networks-explained-34472718707a

8 https://arxiv.org/abs/1812.04948

이미지 생성

생성형 AI는 텍스트 설명 또는 기타 입력에서 현실적인 이미지를 생성하는 데 사용될 수 있다. 이 기술은 이미지 및 비디오와 같은 고유한 시각적 콘텐츠를 포함한 다양한 출력을 생성할 수 있다. OpenAI의 DALL · E는 텍스트 설명을 사용하여 이미지를 생성하는 데 사용되며, 텍스트-이미지 쌍 데이터 세트를 사용한다. 또한 Bing Image Creator는 DALL-E의 더 발전된 버전으로 구동되며, 고품질 결과물을 빠르게 생성한다.

생성형 AI는 이미지 생성 분야에서 강력한 도구가 되었다. 가장 주목할 만한 응용 분야 중 하나는 Generative Adversarial Networks (GANs)이다. GAN은 무작위 노이즈에서 사실적인 이미지를 생성하기 위해 함께 작동하는 생성자와 판별자라는 두 개의 신경망으로 구성된다. 생성자는 이미지를 생성하고 판별자에게 제시한다. 판별자는 각 이미지가 실제(원본 데이터 세트에서)인지 가짜(생성자가 생성한)인지 결정한다. 시간이 지남에 따라 생성자는 판별자를 속이기 위해 점점 더 사실적인 이미지를 생성하는 법을 배운다. 이 과정은 실제 이미지와 거의 구별할 수 없는 생성된 이미지를 생성한다.

GAN의 이미지 생성 응용 분야에는 예술 작품 만들기, 인간 얼굴 사진 합성(예: NVIDIA의 StyleGAN), 저해상도 이미지 향상, 심지어 연구 목적으로 의료 영상 데이터 생성이 포함된다.

Music Generation

Generative AI can also be used to create original music from text prompts or other inputs. This technology has the ability to generate diverse outputs, including unique audio content such as music and speech. One example of this is OpenAI's Jukebox, which generates music as raw audio in a variety of genres and artist styles[9]. Another example is Mubert, which instantly generates tracks perfectly tailored to your content on any platform.[10]

음악 생성

9 https://openai.com/research/jukebox

10 https://mubert.com/

생성형 AI는 텍스트 프롬프트 또는 다른 입력에서 원래 음악을 만들 수도 있다. 이 기술은 다양한 출력을 생성할 수 있으며, 음악 및 음성과 같은 독특한 오디오 콘텐츠를 포함한다. 이 중 하나의 예는 OpenAI의 Jukebox로, 다양한 장르와 아티스트 스타일의 음악을 원시 오디오로 생성한다. 또 다른 예는 Mubert로, 어떤 플랫폼에서든 완벽하게 맞춤화된 트랙을 즉시 생성한다.

Natural Language Generation

Generative AI can be used to generate natural language text that appears to be written by a human. This technology has the ability to generate diverse outputs, including unique written content such as articles and stories. One example of this is GPT-3, a generative pre-trained transformer developed by OpenAI that can generate human-like text. Another example is ChatGPT, a chatbot capable of very human-seeming interactions.

자연어 생성

생성형 AI는 사람이 작성한 것처럼 보이는 자연어 텍스트를 생성하는 데 사용할 수 있다. 이 기술은 다양한 출력을 생성할 수 있으며, 기사 및 이야기와 같은 독특한 작성 콘텐츠를 포함한다. 이 중 하나의 예는 OpenAI가 개발한 GPT-3로, 인간과 같은 텍스트를 생성하는 생성 전처리 변환기이다. 또 다른 예는 ChatGPT로, 매우 인간과 같은 상호작용이 가능한 챗봇이다.

Other Applications

Generative AI has many other applications across different industries and business functions, including healthcare, marketing, sales, education, and customer service. For example, in healthcare, generative AI can be used for early detection of certain diseases or for patient interactions and support.[11] In marketing and sales, generative AI can be used for writing or improving content by producing draft text in a specific style or length or for adding

11 https://www.synthesia.io/post/generative-ai-examples

subtitles or dubbing educational content in different languages.[12] These are just a few examples of the many potential applications of generative AI.

기타 응용 분야

생성형 AI는 건강 관리, 마케팅, 판매, 교육 및 고객 서비스와 같은 다양한 산업 및 비즈니스 기능에서 많은 다른 응용 분야가 있다. 예를 들어, 건강 관리에서 생성형 AI는 특정 질병의 조기 발견 또는 환자 상호 작용 및 지원에 사용될 수 있다. 마케팅 및 판매에서 생성형 AI는 특정 스타일 또는 길이의 초안 텍스트를 작성하거나 개선하여 콘텐츠를 작성하거나 다른 언어로 교육 콘텐츠에 자막 또는 더빙을 추가하는 데 사용될 수 있다. 이들은 Generative AI의 많은 잠재적인 응용 분야 중 몇 가지 예다.

Vocabulary

realistic : 현실적인
description : 서술, 묘사
diverse : 다양한
unique visual content : 독특한 시각적 내용
realm : 영역
two neural networks : 두 가지 신경망
a generator and a discriminator : 생성자와 판별자
present : 나타내다, 보여주다
fake : 가짜의
indistinguishable : 구별할 수 없는
synthesizing : 합성하는
enhancing : 강화하는
low-resolution image : 저해상도 이미지
text prompts : 텍스트 프롬프트
a variety of : 다양한
tailored : 맞춤형의

12 https://www.coursera.org/articles/what-is-generative-ai

appear : 보이다
seem : 보이다
early detection : 조기 발견
disease : 질병
interaction : 상호작용
improve : 개선하다
specific style : 특정 스타일
subtitle : 자막
potential : 잠재적인

3) Limitations of Generative AI 생성형 AI의 한계[13]

Generative AI is a type of artificial intelligence that can create new content from existing data, such as text, images, audio, video, and more. Generative AI has many potential applications across different domains and industries, such as art, entertainment, education, healthcare, design, and more. However, generative AI also has some limitations that need to be considered and addressed. Some of the main limitations of generative AI are:

Quality of generated outputs: Generative AI is limited by the quality and quantity of its training data. The more accurate and diverse the training data is, the more accurate and diverse the generated output will be. However, if the training data is noisy, incomplete, or biased, the generated output will also reflect these flaws. For example, if a generative AI model is trained on images of human faces that are mostly white and male, it will have difficulty generating realistic images of faces that are non-white or female.[14]

Control over the generated outputs: Generative AI is often unpredictable

13 https://www.harvardonline.harvard.edu/blog/benefits-limitations-generative-ai

14 https://fact.technology/learn/generative-ai-advantages-limitations-and-challenges/

and uncontrollable in its generation process. It can produce outputs that are unexpected, inappropriate, or harmful. For example, a generative AI model that generates text from prompts can produce text that is offensive, misleading, or false.[15] Therefore, it is important to have mechanisms to monitor and regulate the generation process and ensure that the generated outputs are aligned with the intended goals and values.

Computational requirements: Generative AI requires a lot of computational resources and power to train and run its models. Generative AI models are often very large and complex, requiring millions or billions of parameters and data points to learn from. For example, ChatGPT is a chatbot that uses generative AI and natural language processing to simulate human-like conversations.[16] It has 175 billion parameters and was trained on 45 terabytes of text data. Therefore, it is challenging to deploy and scale generative AI models in real-world scenarios.

생성형 AI는 기존의 데이터, 예를 들어 텍스트, 이미지, 오디오, 비디오 등으로부터 새로운 콘텐츠를 생성할 수 있는 인공지능의 한 분야이다. 생성형 AI는 예술, 엔터테인먼트, 교육, 의료, 디자인 등 다양한 분야와 산업에서 잠재적인 응용이 많다. 그러나 생성형 AI에도 고려하고 해결해야 할 한계점이 있습니다. 생성형 AI의 주요한 한계점은 다음과 같다:

생성된 콘텐츠의 품질: 생성형 AI는 학습 데이터의 품질과 양에 제한된다. 학습 데이터가 정확하고 다양할수록 생성된 콘텐츠도 정확하고 다양해진다. 그러나 학습 데이터가 잡음이 많거나 불완전하거나 편향되어 있으면 생성된 콘텐츠도 이러한 결함을 반영한다. 예를 들어, 인간의 얼굴 이미지를 주로 백인 남성으로 학습한 생성형 AI 모델은 비백인이나 여성의 얼굴 이미지를 현실적으로 생성하는 데 어려움을 겪을 수 있다.

생성된 콘텐츠의 제어: 생성형 AI는 종종 생성 과정에서 예측할 수 없고 통제할 수 없다. 기대하지 않거나 부적절하거나 해로운 콘텐츠를 생성할 수 있다. 예를 들어, 프롬프트로부터 텍스트를 생성하는 생성형 AI 모델은 모욕적이거나 오해를 불러일으키거나 거짓인

15 https://www.harvardonline.harvard.edu/blog/benefits-limitations-generative-ai

16 https://www.oneai.com/learn/generative-ai-limitations

텍스트를 생성할 수 있다. 따라서 생성 과정을 모니터링하고 규제하고 생성된 콘텐츠가 의도한 목표와 가치와 일치하는지 확인하는 메커니즘이 필요하다.

계산 요구사항: 생성형 AI는 학습과 실행에 많은 계산 자원과 파워를 요구한다. 생성형 AI 모델은 종종 매우 크고 복잡하며, 수백만 혹은 수십억 개의 파라미터와 데이터 포인트로부터 학습한다. 예를 들어, ChatGPT는 생성형 AI와 자연어 처리를 사용하여 인간과 같은 대화를 시뮬레이션하는 챗봇이다. ChatGPT는 1750억 개의 파라미터를 가지고 45 테라바이트의 텍스트 데이터로 학습되었다. 따라서 실제 상황에서 생성형 AI 모델을 배포하고 확장하는 것은 어려운 일이다.

Bias and fairness: Generative AI can inherit or amplify the bias and unfairness that exist in the training data or the generation process. Bias and unfairness can affect the quality and diversity of the generated outputs, as well as the social and ethical implications of their use. For example, a generative AI model that generates music from text can produce music that is biased towards certain genres or cultures based on the text input or the training data.[17] Therefore, it is important to ensure that generative AI models are fair and inclusive to all groups and perspectives.

Explainability and interpretability: Generative AI is often difficult to explain and interpret in terms of how it works and why it produces certain outputs. Generative AI models are often black boxes that do not reveal their internal logic or reasoning. For example, a generative AI model that generates images from text can produce images that are creative but also confusing or illogical based on the text input. Therefore, it is important to increase the transparency and accountability of generative AI models and their outputs.

Safety and security: Generative AI can pose safety and security risks to its users and society at large. Generative AI can be used for malicious purposes, such as generating fake or misleading content, impersonating or deceiving people, or attacking or compromising other systems. For example, a generative

17 https://lingarogroup.com/blog/the-limitations-of-generative-ai-according-to-generative-ai

AI model that generates voice or video from text can create deepfakes that can manipulate or harm people's reputation or privacy. Therefore, it is important to ensure that generative AI models are secure and trustworthy.

These are some of the main limitations of generative AI that need to be considered and addressed. Generative AI is a powerful technology that can create new content from existing data in various forms, such as images, music, text, and more. However, generative AI is not perfect and can produce inaccurate or biased results. Therefore, when using generative AI, human verification and supervision are required and it should be used in an ethical and responsible manner.

편향과 공정성: 생성형 AI는 학습 데이터나 생성 과정에 존재하는 편향과 불공정성을 상속하거나 확대할 수 있다. 편향과 불공정성은 생성된 콘텐츠의 품질과 다양성, 그리고 그 사용에 따른 사회적, 윤리적 영향에 영향을 줄 수 있다. 예를 들어, 텍스트로부터 음악을 생성하는 생성형 AI 모델은 텍스트 입력이나 학습 데이터에 따라 특정 장르나 문화에 대한 음악을 편향시킬 수 있다. 따라서 생성형 AI 모델이 모든 집단과 관점에 대해 공정하고 포괄적인지 확인하는 것이 중요하다.

설명력과 해석력: 생성형 AI는 작동 방식과 특정 콘텐츠를 생성하는 이유에 대해 설명하고 해석하기 어렵다. 생성형 AI 모델은 종종 내부 로직이나 추론을 드러내지 않는 블랙박스다. 예를 들어, 텍스트로부터 이미지를 생성하는 생성형 AI 모델은 창의적이지만 혼란스럽거나 비논리적인 이미지를 텍스트 입력에 기반하여 생성할 수 있다. 따라서 생성형 AI 모델과 그 콘텐츠의 투명성과 책임감을 높이는 것이 중요하다.

안전성과 보안성: 생성형 AI는 사용자와 사회 전체에 대한 안전과 보안 위협을 초래할 수 있다. 생성형 AI는 가짜나 오해를 불러일으키는 콘텐츠를 생성하거나 사람들을 사칭하거나 속이거나 다른 시스템을 공격하거나 손상시키는 등의 악의적인 목적으로 사용될 수 있다. 가령, 텍스트로부터 음성이나 비디오를 생성하는 생성형 AI 모델은 사람들의 명성이나 사생활을 조작하거나 해치는 딥페이크를 생성할 수 있다. 따라서 생성형 AI 모델이 안전하고 신뢰할 수 있는지 확인하는 것이 중요하다.

이것들은 고려하고 해결해야 할 생성형 AI의 주요한 한계점들이다. 생성형 AI는 이미지, 음악, 텍스트 등 다양한 형태로 기존의 데이터로부터 새로운 콘텐츠를 생성할 수 있는 강력한 기술이다. 그러나 생성형 AI는 완벽하지 않고 부정확하거나 편향된 결과를 생성할 수 있다. 따라서 생성형 AI를 사용할 때에는 인간의 검증과 감독이 필요하며 윤리적이고 책임감 있는 방식으로 사용해야 한다.

Vocabulary

domain : 분야
quality and quantity : 품질과 양
training data : 학습/훈련 데이터
accurate : 정확한
noisy, incomplete, or biased : 잡음이 있고 불완전하고 편향된
reflect these flaws : 이러한 결함을 반영하다
unpredictable and uncontrollable : 예측할 수 없고 통제할 수 없는
generation process : 생성 과정
offensive, misleading, or false : 모욕적이고 오해의 소지가 있거나 또는 거짓인
regulate : 규제하다
be aligned with : ~와 일치하다
intended goals and values : 의도한 목표와 가치
resource : 자원
conversation : 대화
deploy and scale : 배포하고 확장하다
bias and fairness : 편향과 공정성
inherit or amplify : 상속하거나 확대하다
quality and diversity : 품질과 다양성
ensure : 확인하다
inclusive : 포괄적인
perspective : 관점
explainability and interpretability : 설명력과 해석력
explain and interpret : 설명하고 해석하다

in terms of : ~한 관점에서
reveal : 드러내다
internal logic or reasoning : 내부 로직이나 추론
confusing : 혼란스러운
transparency and accountability : 투명성과 책임감
safety and security : 안정성과 보안성
malicious : 악의적인
impersonating or deceiving : 사칭하거나 속이는
attacking or compromising : 공격하거나 손상시키는
manipulate : 조작하다
harm : 해 끼치다
reputation : 평판, 명성
trustworthy : 신뢰할 만한
verification and supervision : 검증과 감독
ethical and responsible manner : 윤리적이고 책임감있는 방식

4) The Future of Generative AI 생성형 AI의 미래[18]

Generative AI is a type of artificial intelligence that can create new content from existing data, such as text, images, audio, video, and more. Generative AI has many potential applications across different domains and industries, such as art, entertainment, education, healthcare, design, and more. However, what does the future of generative AI look like? How will it impact our lives and society in the coming years? Here are some possible scenarios and predictions based on the current trends and developments of generative AI:

Generative AI will become more accessible and democratized. As generative

18 https://www.forbes.com/sites/bernardmarr/2023/05/31/the-future-of-generative-ai-beyond-chatgpt/

AI tools become more user-friendly and affordable, more people will be able to use them for various purposes, such as learning, creating, expressing, and communicating. For example, ChatGPT is a chatbot that uses generative AI and natural language processing to simulate human-like conversations. It is available to the public for free and can help users with a variety of tasks, such as drafting emails, essays, code, and more. Similarly, DALL · E 2 is a tool that can generate images from text prompts using a large language model.[19] Users can input any text description and get a variety of images that match the description.

Generative AI will become more specialized and domain-specific. As generative AI models become larger and more complex, they will also become more tailored and customized to specific domains and contexts. For example, Stable Diffusion is a tool that can generate high-quality images from sketches or text using a diffusion model. Users can draw a rough sketch or write a text description and get a realistic image that fills in the details. Similarly, Jukebox is a tool that can generate music from text or audio using a large neural network.[20] Users can input any text or audio prompt and get a variety of music samples that match the prompt.

생성형 AI는 기존의 데이터, 예를 들어 텍스트, 이미지, 오디오, 비디오 등으로부터 새로운 콘텐츠를 생성할 수 있는 인공지능의 한 분야이다. 생성형 AI는 예술, 엔터테인먼트, 교육, 의료, 디자인 등 다양한 분야와 산업에서 잠재적인 응용이 많다. 그러나 생성형 AI의 미래는 어떻게 될까? 앞으로 몇 년 동안 우리의 삶과 사회에 어떤 영향을 미칠까? 다음은 현재의 추세와 발전에 기반한 생성형 AI의 미래에 대한 몇 가지 가능한 시나리오와 예측이다:

생성형 AI는 접근성과 민주화가 증가할 것이다. 생성형 AI 도구가 사용자 친화적이고 저렴해지면서 더 많은 사람들이 학습, 창작, 표현, 의사소통 등 다양한 목적으로 사용할 수 있게 될 것이다. 예를 들어, ChatGPT는 생성형 AI와 자연어 처리를 사용하여 인

19 https://www.harvardonline.harvard.edu/blog/future-generative-ai

20 https://www.forbes.com/sites/bernardmarr/2023/07/25/the-future-of-manufacturing-generative-ai-and-beyond

간과 같은 대화를 시뮬레이션하는 챗봇이다. 이것은 무료로 공개되어 있으며 사용자들이 이메일, 에세이, 코드 등 다양한 작업을 수행하는 데 도움을 줄 수 있다. 마찬가지로, DALL · E 2는 큰 언어 모델을 사용하여 텍스트 프롬프트로부터 이미지를 생성하는 도구다. 사용자들은 어떤 텍스트 설명이든 입력하고 그 설명에 맞는 다양한 이미지를 얻을 수 있다.

생성형 AI는 전문화되고 도메인별로 맞춤화될 것이다. 생성형 AI 모델이 커지고 복잡해지면서 특정 분야와 상황에 맞게 조정되고 맞춤화될 것이다. 예를 들어, Stable Diffusion은 확산 모델을 사용하여 스케치나 텍스트로부터 고품질의 이미지를 생성하는 도구다. 사용자들은 대략적인 스케치나 텍스트 설명을 그리거나 쓰고 세부 사항이 채워진 현실적인 이미지를 얻을 수 있다. 마찬가지로, Jukebox는 큰 신경망을 사용하여 텍스트나 오디오로부터 음악을 생성하는 도구다. 사용자들은 어떤 텍스트나 오디오 프롬프트든 입력하고 그 프롬프트에 맞는 다양한 음악 샘플을 얻을 수 있다.

Generative AI will become more collaborative and interactive. As generative AI models become more intelligent and adaptable, they will also become more capable of collaborating and interacting with humans and other models. For example, Midjourney is a tool that can generate adaptive music for different scenarios using an algorithmic composer. Users can select any mood, activity, or genre and get personalized music that adapts to their preferences and feedback. Similarly, AI Dungeon is a tool that can generate interactive stories based on user choices using a large language model. Users can input any genre, setting, or character and get a unique story that evolves according to their actions.

Generative AI will become more ethical and responsible. As generative AI models become more powerful and influential, they will also become more subject to ethical and social scrutiny and regulation. For example,[21] generative AI models can produce fake or misleading content, such as deepfakes or fake news, that can manipulate or harm people's reputation or privacy. Therefore, it

---

21 https://www.technologyreview.com/2023/04/27/1072102/the-future-of-generative-ai-is-niche-not-generalized/

is important to ensure that generative AI models are secure and trustworthy, as well as fair and inclusive to all groups and perspectives.

These are some of the possible scenarios and predictions for the future of generative AI. Generative AI is a powerful technology that can create new content from existing data in various forms, such as images, music, text, and more. However, generative AI is not perfect and can produce inaccurate or biased results. Therefore, when using generative AI, human verification and supervision are required and it should be used in an ethical and responsible manner.

생성형 AI는 협력적이고 상호작용적이 될 것이다. 생성형 AI 모델이 더 똑똑하고 적응력 있게 되면서 인간과 다른 모델과 협력하고 상호작용하는 능력도 갖게 될 것이다. 예를 들어, Midjourney는 알고리즘 작곡가를 사용하여 다른 시나리오에 맞는 적응형 음악을 생성하는 도구다. 사용자들은 어떤 기분, 활동, 장르든 선택하고 자신의 취향과 피드백에 맞게 적응하는 개인화된 음악을 얻을 수 있다. 마찬가지로, AI Dungeon은 큰 언어 모델을 사용하여 사용자의 선택에 따라 상호작용하는 이야기를 생성하는 도구다. 사용자들은 어떤 장르, 설정, 캐릭터든 입력하고 자신의 행동에 따라 변화하는 독특한 이야기를 얻을 수 있다.

생성형 AI는 윤리적이고 책임감 있게 될 것이다. 생성형 AI 모델이 더 강력하고 영향력 있게 되면서 윤리적이고 사회적인 검토와 규제의 대상이 될 것이다. 예를 들어, 생성형 AI 모델은 가짜나 오해를 불러일으키는 콘텐츠, 예를 들어 딥페이크나 가짜 뉴스 등을 생성하여 사람들의 명예나 사생활을 조작하거나 해치는 등의 악의적인 목적으로 사용될 수 있다. 따라서 생성형 AI 모델이 안전하고 신뢰할 수 있으며 모든 집단과 관점에 대해 공정하고 포괄적인지 확인하는 것이 중요하다.

이것들은 생성형 AI의 미래에 대한 몇 가지 가능한 시나리오와 예측이다. 생성형 AI는 이미지, 음악, 텍스트 등 다양한 형태로 기존의 데이터로부터 새로운 콘텐츠를 생성할 수 있는 강력한 기술이다. 그러나 생성형 AI는 완벽하지 않고 부정확하거나 편향된 결과를 생성할 수 있다. 따라서 생성형 AI를 사용할 때에는 인간의 검증과 감독이 필요하며 윤리적이고 책임감 있는 방식으로 사용해야 한다.

Vocabulary

potential : 잠재적인
prediction : 예측
democratized : 민주화된
user-friendly and affordable : 친화적이고 저렴한
for free : 무료로
specialized : 전문적인
complex : 복잡한
diffusion model: 확산모델
draw a rough sketch : 대략적인 스케치를 그리다
fill : 채우다
collaborative and interactive : 협력적이고 상호작용적인
intelligent and adaptable : 똑똑하고 적응력있는
using an algorithmic composer : 알고리즘 작곡가를 사용하여
preference : 기호/선호
evolve : 진화하다
according to : ~에 따라
ethical and responsible : 윤리적이고 책임감있는
subject to : 영향을 받는, 종속하는
ethical and social scrutiny and regulation : 윤리적이고 사회적인 검토와 규제
deepfakes or fake news : 딥페이크나 가짜 뉴스
inclusive : 포괄적인

잠깐 쉬어가기 ....

AI에 대항하여 피켓시위를 하는 작가 (출처 https://apnews.com/article/artificial-intelligence-hollywood-strikes-explained-writers-actors-e872bd63ab52c3ea9f7d6e825240a202))

생성형 AI는 예술 분야에 밀접하게 영향을 미치고 있다. 최근에는 구글과 유니버설 뮤직이 생성형 AI분야에서 협업한다는 소식을 보도하였다. 아티스트의 목소리나 기존 음악을 사용하여 AI가 새로운 창작물을 만들어 낼 수가 있다. 저작권을 침해할 수 있기 때문에 아티스트들의 반발이 심하지만, 구글과 유니버설 뮤직의 협업은 '딥페이크(deep fake)' 에 대응하기 위함이라 알려져 있다.

또한 AI는 헐리우드 작가조합 파업의 주요 원인 중 하나로 여겨진다. 작가들은 AI가 그들의 창의성과 수입을 위협한다고 느끼며 작가조합에서는 AI로 생성된 작품을 금지하고 인간 작가를 우선시하도록 요구하고 있다. AI는 이미 다른 창의적 분야에도 영향을 미쳐 왔으며, 헐리우드에서는 AI가 앞으로 콘텐츠의 미래에 큰 역할을 할 것이라고 믿는다.

우리나라에서도 챗GPT가 드라마 대본을 쓴 사례가 있다. 부산의 한 대학에서는 한국콘텐츠진흥원의 지원을 받아 챗GPT가 생성한 대본으로 인공지능 배우가 연기한 4부작 (각 15분) 드라마 〈미스터리 에이 (A)양〉을 제작해 공개한 바 있다. 또한, 김대식 카이스트 교수는 챗GPT에게 '주인공이 출생의 비밀이 있을 것', '주인공이 죽을병에 걸릴 것', '삼각관계가 나올 것'이라는 조건을 제시하고 막장 드라마 대본을 작성하게 했다. 이 대본은 약 30장 분량으로, 주인공 지선이 입양됐다는 진실과 암 진단을 받고 친구들의 남자친구를 뺏기 시작하는 이야기이다. 챗GPT는 이러한 사례를 통해 드라마 대본을 쓰는 능력을 보여주었지만, 그것이 작가들의 창의성과 표현력을 대체할 수 있는지는 아직 논란의 여지가 있다.

연습문제

exercises

1~5. 다음 빈 칸에 들어가는 단어로 적절한 것을 넣으세요.

1. (　　　) artificial intelligence (AI) is artificial intelligence capable of generating text, images, or other media, using generative models.

정답 : ____________________

2. GANs consist of two neural networks, a generator and a (　　　), that work together to create realistic images from random noise.

정답 : ____________________

3. Generative AI is limited by the (①) and (②) of its training data.

정답 : ____________________

4. A generative AI model that generates voice or video from text can create (　　　) that can manipulate or harm people's reputation or privacy.

정답 : ____________________

5. Generative AI is a powerful technology that can create new content from (　　　) data in various forms, such as images, music, text, and more.

정답 : ____________________

6~10 다음 It이 지칭하는 것을 영어로 쓰세요.

6. It creates images and presents them to the discriminator.

정답 : ____________________

7. It most commonly creates content in response to natural language requests.
정답 : ______________________________

8. If it is noisy, incomplete, or biased, the generated output will also reflect these flaws.
정답 : ______________________________

9. It is a tool that can generate images from text prompts using a large language model.
정답 : ______________________________

10. Generative AI has become a powerful tool in the realm of it. One of the most notable applications is in Generative Adversarial Networks (GANs)
정답 : ______________________________

연습문제 해답

1. Generative
2. discriminator
3. quality, quantity
4. deepfakes
5. existing
6. The generator
7. Generative AI
8. the training data
9. DALL · E 2
10. image generation

Chapter 03

History of Computers

컴퓨터 역사

학습순서

1) What is Computers?
2) The History of Computers

잠깐 쉬어가기

연습문제

【 INTRO 】

여러분은 컴퓨터 없는 일상을 살아갈 수 있습니까?
만약 우리 삶에 컴퓨터가 없다면 우리는 지금까지 누려왔던 당연한 것들을 누릴 수 없을 것이며 엄청난 불편함을 감내해야할 것입니다. 사회, 산업 전반 모든 일들이 컴퓨터를 통하여 구동되고 있으며, 우리 또한 컴퓨터를 통하여 학업, 취업, 생활과 관련된 모든 것을 처리하고 있습니다. 우리 삶의 일부분이 되어 버린 컴퓨터와 그 역사에 대해서 알아보도록 합시다.

Could you live your daily life without a computer? If we live without computers, we would not be able to enjoy the daily life we have taken for granted, and would have to endure enormous inconvenience. Everything in our society and industry is driven by computers nowadays, and we are always dealing with everything related to school, employment, and life through them. Let's learn about computers and the history that have become part of our lives.

1) What is Computers? 컴퓨터란?[1]

A computer is a machine that can be programmed to carry out sequences of arithmetic or logical operations automatically. Modern computers can perform generic sets of operations known as programs. These programs enable computers to perform a wide range of tasks. A computer system is a "complete" computer that includes the hardware, operating system (main software), and peripheral equipment needed and used for "full" operation. This term may also refer to a group of computers that are linked and function together, such as a computer network or computer cluster.

A broad range of industrial and consumer products use computers as control systems. Simple special-purpose devices like microwave ovens and remote controls are included, as are factory devices like industrial robots and computer-aided design, as well as general-purpose devices like personal computers and mobile devices like smartphones. Computers power the Internet, which links hundreds of millions of other computers and users.

Early computers were meant to be used only for calculations. Simple manual instruments like the abacus have aided people in doing calculations since ancient times. Early in the Industrial Revolution, some mechanical devices were built to automate long tedious tasks, such as guiding patterns for looms. More sophisticated electrical machines did specialized analog calculations in the early 20th century. The first digital electronic calculating machines were developed during World War II. The first semiconductor transistors in the late 1940s were followed by the silicon-based MOSFET (MOS transistor) and monolithic integrated circuit (IC) chip technologies in the late 1950s, leading to the microprocessor and the microcomputer revolution in the 1970s. The speed, power and versatility of computers have been increasing dramatically ever since then, with

1 https://en.wikipedia.org/wiki/Computer

transistor counts increasing at a rapid pace (as predicted by Moore's law), leading to the Digital Revolution during the late 20th to early 21st centuries.

Conventionally, a modern computer consists of at least one processing element, typically a central processing unit (CPU) in the form of a microprocessor, along with some type of computer memory, typically semiconductor memory chips. The processing element carries out arithmetic and logical operations, and a sequencing and control unit can change the order of operations in response to stored information. Peripheral devices include input devices (keyboards, mice, joystick, etc.), output devices (monitor screens, printers, etc.), and input/output devices that perform both functions (e.g., the 2000s-era touchscreen). Peripheral devices allow information to be retrieved from an external source and they enable the result of operations to be saved and retrieved.

컴퓨터는 일련의 산술 연산이나 논리 연산을 자동으로 수행하도록 프로그래밍 할 수 있는 기계다. 현대의 컴퓨터는 프로그램이라고 알려진 일반 작업 세트를 수행할 수 있다. 이러한 프로그램을 통해 컴퓨터는 다양한 작업을 수행할 수 있다. 컴퓨터 시스템은 하드웨어, 운영 체제(주 소프트웨어) 및 "전체" 작동에 필요하고 사용되는 주변 장치를 포함하는 "완전한" 컴퓨터다. 이 용어는 컴퓨터 네트워크 또는 컴퓨터 클러스터와 같이 연결되고 함께 작동하는 컴퓨터 그룹을 나타낼 수도 있다.

다양한 산업용 및 소비자 제품은 컴퓨터를 제어 시스템으로 사용한다. 전자레인지와 리모컨과 같은 간단한 특수 목적 기기들과 산업용 로봇이나 컴퓨터 보조 디자인과 같은 공장 기기들 그리고 일반 목적으로 쓰는 장치인 개인용 컴퓨터나 스마트폰과 같은 모바일 기기들이 포함되어 있다. 컴퓨터는 수 억 대의 다른 컴퓨터와 사용자를 연결하는 인터넷에 전원을 공급한다.

초기 컴퓨터는 계산용으로만 사용되도록 되어 있었다. 주판과 같은 간단한 수작업 도구는 고대부터 사람들이 계산을 하는 데 도움을 주었다. 산업 혁명 초기에, 몇몇 기계 장치들은 베틀에 패턴을 안내하는 것과 같은 길고 지루한 작업을 자동화하기 위해 만들어졌다. 더 정교한 전기 기계는 20세기 초에 전문화된 아날로그 계산을 했다. 최초의 디지털 전자계산기는 2차 세계대전 중에 개발되었다. 1940년대 후반 최초의 반도체 트랜지스터는 1950년대 후반 실리콘 기반 MOSFET(MOS 트랜지스터) 및 단일 집적회로(IC) 칩 기술에 이어 1970년대 마이크로프로세서와 마이크로컴퓨터 혁명으로 이어졌다. 그 이후로 컴퓨터의 속도, 전력 및 다양한 기능성은 급격히 증가하여 트랜지스터 수가 빠른 속도로 증가하고 있으며, 20세기 후반에서 21세기 초반까지 디지털 혁명으로 이어졌다.

일반적으로 현대 컴퓨터는 최소 하나의 처리 요소(일반적으로 마이크로프로세서 형태의 중앙 처리 장치(CPU)와 특정 유형의 컴퓨터 메모리(일반적으로 반도체 메모리 칩)로 구성된다. 처리 요소는 산술 및 논리적 연산을 수행하며, 순서 및 제어 장치는 저장된 정보에 대응하여 작업 순서를 변경할 수 있다. 주변 장치에는 입력 장치(키보드, 마우스, 조이스틱 등), 출력 장치(모니터 화면, 프린터 등), 두 기능을 모두 수행하는 입/출력 장치(예: 2000년대 터치스크린)가 포함된다. 주변 장치를 사용하면 외부 소스에서 정보를 검색할 수 있으며 작업 결과를 저장하고 검색할 수 있다.

Vocabulary

machine : 기계
carry out : 수행하다
sequences : 일련의 연속적인 사건들
arithmetic or logical operations : 산술연산 또는 논리연산
modern : 현대의, 최신의
generic sets of operations : 일반 작업 세트
task : 작업
complete : 완전한
hardware, operating system : 하드웨어, 운영체제
peripheral equipment : 주변 장치
industrial and consumer products : 산업용 및 소비자 제품

special-purpose devices : 특수 목적 기기들
power : 전원을 공급하다
calculation : 계산
simple manual instrument : 간단한 수동 도구
abacus : 주판
Industrial Revolution : 산업혁명
mechanical devices : 기계 장치들
tedious tasks : 지루한 작업
automate : 자동화하다
sophisticated : 세련된, 정교한
semiconductor transistor : 반도체 트랜지스터
monolithic integrated circuit (IC) chip technologies: 단일 집적회로(IC) 칩 기술
versatility : 다재, 다예, 다능, 융통성 있음
conventionally : 진부하게
consist of : ~로 구성되다
arithmetic and logical operations : 산술 및 논리 연산
retrieve : 회수하다, 검색하다

2) The History of Computers[2] 컴퓨터의 역사

While today we use computers for both work and play, the computer was actually created for an entirely different purpose. In 1880, the population of the United States had grown so large that it took seven years to formulate the results of the U.S. Census. So, the government looked for a faster way to get the job done, which is why punch-card computers were invented that took up an entire room. While that's how the story starts, it's certainly not where it ends. Let's explore everything that happened leading up to that, in between, and after.

2 https://www.g2.com/articles/history-of-computers

Computers in the 1800s

1801: In France, weaver and merchant Joseph Marie Jacquard creates a loom that uses wooden punch cards to automate the design of woven fabrics. Early computers would use similar punch cards.
1822: Thanks to funding from the English government, mathematician Charles Babbage invents a steam-driven calculating machine that was able to compute tables of numbers.
1890: Inventor Herman Hollerith designs the punch card system to calculate the 1880 U.S. census. It took him three years to create, and it saved the government $5 million. He would eventually go on to establish a company that would become IBM.

오늘날 우리는 업무와 놀이에 모두 컴퓨터를 사용하지만, 실제로 컴퓨터는 완전히 다른 목적으로 만들어졌다. 1880년에 미국의 인구는 너무 많이 증가해서 미국 인구조사 결과를 공식화하는 데 7년이 걸렸다. 그래서 정부는 이 일을 끝낼 수 있는 더 빠른 방법을 찾았고, 그래서 방 전체를 차지하는 펀치 카드 컴퓨터가 발명되었다. 이야기는 그렇게 시작하지만 끝이 아닌 것은 확실하다. 그 중간과 이후에 일어난 모든 일을 살펴보도록 하겠다.

1800년대 컴퓨터

1801: 프랑스에서, 직조공이자 상인인 조셉 마리 자카드는 직물의 디자인을 자동화하기 위해 나무 펀치 카드를 사용하는 베틀을 만든다. 초기 컴퓨터들은 비슷한 펀치 카드를 사용했을 것이다.
1822: 영국 정부의 자금 덕에 수학자인 찰스 배비지는 숫자 표를 계산할 수 있는 증기 구동식 계산기를 발명한다.
1890: 발명가 허먼 홀러리스는 1880년 미국 인구 조사를 계산하기 위해 펀치 카드 시스템을 디자인한다. 그가 3년 걸려서 만들었고, 정부는 이로 인하여 5백만 달러를 절약한다. 후에 그는 결국 IBM이 되는 회사를 설립하게된다.

Computers from the 1900–1950s

1936: Alan Turing developed an idea for a universal machine, which he would call the Turing machine, that would be able to compute anything that is computable. The concept of modern computers was based on his idea.
1937: A professor of physics and mathematics at Iowa State University, J.V. Atanasoff, attempts to build the first computer without cams, belts, gears, or shafts.
1939: Bill Hewlett and David Packard found Hewlett-Packard in a garage in Palo Alto, California. Their first project, the HP 200A Audio Oscillator, would rapidly become a popular piece of test equipment for engineers. In fact, Walt Disney Pictures would order eight to test recording equipment and speaker systems for 12 specially equipped theaters that showed Fantasia in 1940.
Also in 1939, Bell Telephone Laboratories completes The Complex Number Calculator, designed by George Stibitz.

1900~1950년대 컴퓨터

1936년: 앨런 튜링은 그가 튜링 기계라고 부르는, 계산할 수 있는 모든 것을 계산할 수 있는 범용 기계에 대한 아이디어를 개발했다. 현대 컴퓨터의 개념은 그의 아이디어에 기초했다.
1937년: 아이오와 주립 대학의 물리학과 및 수학과 교수인 J.V. 아타나소프는 캠, 벨트,

기어 또는 축이 없는 최초의 컴퓨터를 만들려고 하였다.
1939: 빌 휴렛과 데이비드 패커드는 캘리포니아 팔로알토의 차고에서 휴렛 팩커드를 설립한다. 첫 번째 프로젝트인 HP 200A 오디오 발진기는 엔지니어들에게 인기 있는 테스트 장비로 급부상했다. 사실, 월트 디즈니 영화사는 1940년에 판타지아를 상영했던 12개의 특별 장비를 갖춘 극장의 녹음 장비와 스피커 시스템을 테스트하기 위해 8개를 주문하였다. 또한 1939년에 벨 전화연구소는 조지 스티비츠가 디자인한 복소수 계산기를 완성한다.

1941: Professor of physics and mathematics at Iowa State University J.V. Atanasoff and graduate student Clifford Berry design a computer that can solve 29 equations simultaneously. This is the first time a computer is able to house data within its own memory.
That same year, German engineer Konrad Zuse creates the Z3 computer, which used 2,300 relays, performed floating-point binary arithmetic, and had a 22-bit word length. This computer was eventually destroyed in a bombing raid in Berlin in 1943.
Additionally in 1941, Alan Turing and Harold Keen built the British Bombe, which decrypted Nazi ENIGMA-based military communications during World War II.
1943: John Mauchly and J. Presper Eckert, professors at the University of Pennsylvania, build an Electronic Numerical Integrator and Calculator (ENIAC). This is considered to be the grandfather of digital computers, as it is made up of 18,000 vacuum tubes and fills up a 20-foot by 40-foot room.

1941: 아이오와 주립 대학교 물리학과 수학과 교수 J.V.아타나소프와 대학원생 클리포드 베리는 동시에 29개의 방정식을 풀 수 있는 컴퓨터를 디자인한다. 컴퓨터가 자신의 메모리에 데이터를 저장할 수 있는 것은 이번이 처음이다.
같은 해 독일 엔지니어 콘라트 주제는 2,300개의 릴레이를 사용하고 부동 소수점 이진수 연산을 수행하며 22비트 워드 길이를 가진 Z3 컴퓨터를 만들었다. 이 컴퓨터는 1943년 베를린에서 폭격으로 파괴되었다.
1941년에 앨런 튜링과 해롤드 킨은 제2차 세계 대전 중 나치의 에니그마에 기반을 둔 군사 통신을 해독하는 영국 폭격기를 만들었다.

1943: 펜실베니아 대학의 교수인 존 모클리와 존 에커트는 에니악(ENIAC)을 만든다. 에니악은 18,000개의 진공관으로 구성되어 있고 20피트 x 40피트 크기의 방을 채우기 때문에 디지털 컴퓨터의 시초로 여겨진다.

Vocabulary

look for : 찾다
be invented : 발명되다
entire : 전체의
explore : 탐험하다
weaver : 방직공, 베짜는 사람
merchant : 상인
loom : 베틀
wooden punch card : 나무 펀치 카드
automate : 자동화하다
woven fabrics : 직물
mathematician : 수학자
steam-driven calculating machine : 증기 구동 계산기
inventor : 발명가
establish : 설립하다
census : 인구조사
universal machine : 범용 기계
computable : 계산 가능한
professor : 교수
physics and mathematics : 물리학과 수학
attempt : 시도하다
shaft : 손잡이, 화살대
garage : 차고
laboratory : 연구소
complete : 완성하다
graduate student : 대학원생

equation : 방정식
simultaneously : 동시에
perform : 수행하다
floating-point binary arithmetic : 부동 소수점 이진 산술
bombing raid : 폭격
additionally : 게다가
decrypt : 해독하다
consider : 여기다, 숙고하다
vacuum tube : 진공관
fill up : 가득 채우다

☞ 잠깐 쉬어가기 ....

이미테이션 게임 (출처 https://ko.wikipedia.org/wiki/이미테이션_게임)
앨런 튜링 (출처 https://ko.wikipedia.org/wiki/앨런_튜링)

여러분은 위에 있는 배우 많이 낯이 익죠? '닥터 스트레인지'죠. 닥터 스트레인지로 알려진 베네딕트 컴버배치가 주연한 '이미테이션 게임'은 우리나라에서 2015년에 개봉한 실화를 바탕으로 한 영화입니다. 베네딕트 컴버배치가 '앨런 튜링'의 역할을 담당하였습니다. 오른쪽 사진은 앨런 튜링(앨런 매시슨 튜링(Alan Mathison Turing): 1912. 6. 23 ~ 1954. 6. 7)입니다. 영국에서 태어난 앨런 튜링은 수학자이자 컴퓨터의 아버지로 알려져 있는 인물입니다.

튜링은 케임브리지 대학교에서 수학을 전공하고 미국으로 건너가 프린스턴 대학교에서 공부를 한 후, 다시 케임브리지로 돌아옵니다. 귀국 후에 그는 조국을 위해 일하게 됩니다. 당시에 유럽은 2차 세계대전이 일어나고 있었고 튜링은 독일의 암호화 기계인 기계인 '에니그마'를 해독하였습니다. 이는 곧 영국군이 속해있는 연합군이 승리하는 데에 영향을 주게 되었습니다. 전쟁 후에 튜링은 다시 연구자의 삶으로 돌아오게 됩니다.

튜링은 성적지향은 일반인들과 달랐는데 당시 영국은 동성애를 불법으로 간주하였습니다. 그가 동성애자임이 밝혀지자 형벌로 화학적 거세를 당하게 됩니다. 후에 튜링은 젊은 나이에 자살을 하게 됩니다.

천재 같은 튜링의 삶은 역사 속으로 사라지는 가 싶었습니다. 그러나 사람들의 튜링을 향한 청원과 컴퓨터 과학과 인공지능에 대한 그의 천재적인 업적이 인정되어, 2013년 영국 엘리자베스 2세 여왕은 튜링을 사면하게 되었습니다. 2021년부터는 영국의 50파운드에 그의 초상이 사용되고 있습니다.

연습문제

exercises

1~6. 다음 빈 칸에 들어가는 단어로 적절한 것을 넣으세요.

1. (   ) is a machine that can be programmed to carry out sequences of arithmetic or logical operations automatically.

정답 : ______________________________

2. (   ) include input devices (keyboards, mice, joystick, etc.), output devices (monitor screens, printers, etc.), and input/output devices that perform both functions (e.g., the 2000s-era touchscreen).

정답 : ______________________________

3. (   ) developed an idea for a universal machine, which he would call the Turing machine, that would be able to compute anything that is computable.

정답 : ______________________________

4. John Mauchly and J. Presper Eckert, professors at the University of Pennsylvania, build (   ).

정답 : ______________________________

5. A modern computer consists of at least one processing element, typically (   ) in the form of a microprocessor, along with some type of computer memory, typically semiconductor memory chips.

정답 : ______________________________

6. 다음 It이 지칭하는 것을 영어로 쓰세요.

It carries out arithmetic and logical operations, and a sequencing and control unit can change the order of operations in response to stored information.

정답 : ______________________________

연습문제 해답

1. A computer
2. Peripheral devices
3. Alan Turing
4. an Electronic Numerical Integrator and Calculator (ENIAC)
5. a central processing unit (CPU)
6. The processing element

Chapter

04 Computer Hardware

컴퓨터 하드웨어

학습순서

1) Computer Hardware
2) Von Neumann Architecture
3) Personal Computer(PC)

잠깐 쉬어가기

연습문제

【 INTRO 】

여러분들은 컴퓨터를 구매할 때 어떠한 것을 가장 중점에 두고 구매하나요? 어느 정도의 사양 즉, 스펙을 면밀히 조사하지 않나요? CPU를 비롯하여 각종 부품은 어떻게 되는 지 고민하다가 내가 가진 예산에 합리적인지 저울지 해본 적이 있나요? 혹은 그래픽 카드를 좋은 것으로 바꾸고 싶은데 고민해본 적이 있나요? 또는 선호하는 키보드 종류가 있을 까요? 이러한 모든 것들이 컴퓨터 하드웨어와 연관된 내용입니다. 이번 과에서는 컴퓨터 하드웨어가 무엇인지 공부해보도록 합시다.

When you buy a computer, what do you focus on the most? Do you scrutinize specifications of the computer? Have you ever thought about what would happen to the CPU and other components of the computer and tried to balance them with my budget? Or have you ever thought about changing your graphics card to a good one? Or do you have a preferred keyboard type? All of these are related to computer hardware. Let's study what computer hardware is in this chapter.

1) Computer Hardware[1] 컴퓨터 하드웨어

Computer hardware includes the physical parts of a computer, such as the case, central processing unit (CPU), monitor, mouse, keyboard, computer data storage, graphics card, sound card, speakers and motherboard.

By contrast, software is the set of instructions that can be stored and run by hardware. Hardware is so-termed because it is "hard" or rigid with respect to changes, whereas software is "soft" because it is easy to change.

Hardware is typically directed by the software to execute any command or instruction. A combination of hardware and software forms a usable computing system, although other systems exist with only hardware.

컴퓨터 하드웨어는 케이스, 중앙 처리 장치(CPU), 모니터, 마우스, 키보드, 기억 장치, 그래픽 카드, 사운드 카드, 스피커 및 마더보드와 같은 컴퓨터의 물리적 부분이 포함된다.

대조적으로, 소프트웨어는 하드웨어에 의해 저장되고 실행될 수 있는 명령어의 집합이다. 하드웨어는 변화에 대해 "단단"하거나 경직되어 있기 때문에 그렇게 불리며, 소프트웨어는 변경하기 쉽기 때문에 "부드럽다"고 한다.

하드웨어는 일반적으로 모든 명령을 실행하는 소프트웨어에 의해 지휘된다. 하드웨어와 소프트웨어의 조합은 사용 가능한 컴퓨팅 시스템을 형성하지만 다른 시스템은 하드웨어만 있다.

1 https://en.wikipedia.org/wiki/Computer_hardware

Vocabulary

By contrast : 반면
instruction : 명령
term : 용어, 칭하다, 일컫다
rigid : 엄격한, 단단한
with respect to : ~에 관하여
typically : 전형적으로, 일반적으로
execute : 실행하다
command : 커맨드/명령어
combination : 조합

2) Von Neumann Architecture[2] 폰노이만 구조

A von Neumann architecture machine, designed by physicist and mathematician John von Neumann (1903–1957) is a theoretical design for a stored program computer that serves as the basis for almost all modern computers. A von Neumann machine consists of a central processor with an arithmetic/logic unit and a control unit, a memory, mass storage, and input and output.

The von Neumann machine was created by its namesake, John von Neumann, a physicist and mathematician, in 1945, building on the work of Alan Turing. The design was published in a document called "First Draft of a Report on the EDVAC."

The report described the first stored-program computer. Earlier computers,

---

2 https://www.techopedia.com/definition/32480/von-neumann-architecture

such as the ENIAC, were hard-wired to do one task. If the computer had to perform a different task, it had to be rewired, which was a tedious process. With a stored-program computer, a general purpose computer could be built to run different programs.

물리학자 겸 수학자 존 폰 노이만 (1903-1957)에 의해 설계된 폰 노이만아키텍처 기계는 거의 모든 현대 컴퓨터의 기반이 되는 저장 프로그램 컴퓨터를 위한 이론적인 디자인이다. 폰 노이만 기계는 산술/논리 장치와 제어 장치로 되어 있는 중앙처리 장치, 메모리, 대용량 기억장치, 입출력 장치로 구성된다.

폰 노이만 기계는 물리학자이자 수학자인 존 폰 노이만이 1945년 앨런 튜링의 작품을 바탕으로 만들었다. 이 설계는 "EDVAC 보고서 초안"이라는 문서에 실려있다.

보고서는 첫 번째로 저장된 프로그램 컴퓨터에 대해 설명했다. ENIAC와 같은 초기 컴퓨터들은 한 가지 작업을 하기 위해 유선 연결되어 있었다. 컴퓨터가 다른 작업을 수행해야 한다면 다시 배선해야 했고, 이는 지루한 과정이었다. 저장된 프로그램 컴퓨터를 사용하면 범용 컴퓨터를 구축하여 다양한 프로그램을 실행할 수 있었다.

The document describes a design architecture for an electronic digital computer with these components:

- A processing unit with both an arithmetic logic unit and processor registers
- A control unit that includes an instruction register and a program counter
- Memory that stores data and instructions
- External mass storage
- Input and output mechanisms.

The von Neumann design thus forms the basis of modern computing. A similar model, the Harvard architecture, had dedicated data address and buses for both reading and writing to memory. The von Neumann architecture won out because it was simpler to implement in real hardware.

이 문서에서는 다음과 같은 구성 요소를 갖춘 전자 디지털 컴퓨터의 설계 아키텍처를 설명한다:

- 산술 논리 장치와 프로세서 레지스터가 모두 포함된 처리 장치
- 명령어 레지스터와 프로그램 카운터가 포함된 제어 장치
- 데이터와 명령어를 저장하는 메모리
- 외부 대용량 저장장치
- 입력 및 출력 메커니즘

따라서 폰 노이만 설계는 현대 컴퓨팅의 기초를 형성한다. 유사한 모델인 하버드 아키텍처는 메모리에 읽고 쓰기를 위한 전용 데이터 주소와 버스를 가지고 있었다. 폰 노이만 아키텍처(구조)는 실제 하드웨어에서 구현하기가 더 간편하기 때문에 탁월한 성능을 보였다.

Vocabulary

von Neumann architecture machine : 폰 노이만 구조 기계
theoretical : 이론적인
arithmetic/logic unit: 산술논리장치(ALU)
control unit : 제어장치
mass storage : 대용량 기억 장치
publish : 출판하다
document : 문서
hard-wired : 하드웨어에 내장된
dedicate : 전념하다, 전용으로 하다
win out : 성취하다
implement : 시행하다

3) Personal Computer(PC)[3] 개인용 컴퓨터

The personal computer is one of the most common types of computer due to its versatility and relatively low price. Desktop personal computers have a monitor, a keyboard, a mouse, and a computer case. The computer case holds the motherboard, fixed or removable disk drives for data storage, the power supply, and may contain other peripheral devices such as modems or network interfaces. Some models of desktop computers integrated the monitor and keyboard into the same case as the processor and power supply. Separating the elements allows the user to arrange the components in a pleasing, comfortable array, at the cost of managing power and data cables between them.

Laptops are designed for portability but operate similarly to desktop PCs. They may use lower-power or reduced size components, with lower performance than a similarly priced desktop computer. Laptops contain the keyboard, display, and processor in one case. The monitor in the folding upper cover of the case can be closed for transportation, to protect the screen and keyboard. Instead of a mouse, laptops may have a touchpad or pointing stick.

Tablets are portable computer that uses a touch screen as the primary input device. Tablets generally weigh less and are smaller than laptops. Some tablets include fold-out keyboards, or offer connections to separate external keyboards. Some models of laptop computers have a detachable keyboard, which allows the system to be configured as a touch-screen tablet. They are sometimes called "2-in-1 detachable laptops" or "tablet-laptop hybrids".

3 https://en.wikipedia.org/wiki/Computer_hardware

PC는 다기능성과 상대적으로 저렴한 가격 때문에 가장 일반적인 유형의 컴퓨터 중 하나이다. 데스크톱 개인용 컴퓨터에는 모니터, 키보드, 마우스 및 컴퓨터 케이스가 있다. 컴퓨터 케이스에는 데이터 저장용 마더보드, 고정식 또는 이동식 디스크 드라이브, 전원 공급 장치가 들어 있으며 모뎀이나 네트워크 인터페이스와 같은 다른 주변 장치가 들어 있을 수 있다. 일부 데스크톱 컴퓨터 모델은 모니터와 키보드를 프로세서 및 전원 공급 장치와 동일한 케이스에 통합했다. 요소를 분리하면 사용자는 전원과 데이터 케이블을 서로 연결하는 비용으로 구성요소를 만족스럽고 편안한 배열로 배열할 수 있다.

노트북은 휴대할 수 있도록 설계되었지만 데스크탑 PC와 유사하게 작동한다. 비슷한 가격의 데스크탑 컴퓨터보다 낮은 성능으로 저전력 또는 축소된 크기의 구성요소를 사용할 수 있다. 노트북에는 키보드, 디스플레이 및 프로세서가 하나의 케이스에 (모두) 포함된다. 케이스의 접이식 상부 커버에 있는 모니터는 화면과 키보드를 보호하기 위해 닫을 수 있다. 노트북은 마우스 대신 터치패드나 포인팅 스틱을 사용할 수 있다.

태블릿은 터치스크린을 기본 입력 장치로 사용하는 휴대용 컴퓨터이다. 태블릿은 일반적으로 무게가 덜 나가고 노트북보다 작다. 일부 태블릿은 접이식 키보드를 포함하거나 별도의 외부 키보드 연결을 제공한다. 일부 노트북 컴퓨터 모델에는 시스템이 터치스크린 태블릿으로 구성될 수 있도록 분리 가능한 키보드가 있다. 이러한 것들은 때때로 "2-in-1 분리형 노트북" 또는 "태블릿-노트북 하이브리드"라고 불린다.

Vocabulary

common : 흔한, 일반적인
due to : ~ 때문에
fixed : 고정된
removable disk drive : 이동식 디스크 드라이브
contain : 들어있다
element : 요소
arrange : 배열하다, 정리하다
component : 구성요소, 부품
pleasing : 만족스러운
portability : 휴대성
lower-power : 저전력
folding upper cover : 접이식 상부커버
transportation : 이동
primary : 주요한, 기본의
fold-out keyboard : 접이식 키보드
external keyboard : 외부 키보드
detachable : 분리할 수 있는

① Case

The computer case encloses most of the components of the system. It provides mechanical support and protection for internal elements such as the motherboard, disk drives, and power supplies, and controls and directs the flow of cooling air over internal components. The case is also part of the system to control electromagnetic interference radiated by the computer and protects internal parts from electrostatic discharge.

Large tower cases provide space for multiple disk drives or other peripherals and usually stand on the floor, while desktop cases provide less expansion room. All-in-one style designs include a video display built into the same case.

Portable and laptop computers require cases that provide impact protection for the unit. Hobbyists may decorate the cases with colored lights, paint, or other features, in an activity called case modding(case modification).

케이스

컴퓨터 케이스는 시스템의 대부분의 구성 요소를 포함한다. 마더보드, 디스크 드라이브 및 전원 공급 장치와 같은 내부 요소에 대한 기계적 지원과 보호를 제공하며 내부 구성 요소에 대한 냉각 공기의 흐름을 제어 및 지시한다. 또한 케이스는 컴퓨터에서 방사되는 전자기파 간섭을 제어하기 위한 시스템의 일부이며 내부 부품을 정전기 방전으로부터 보호한다.

대형 타워 케이스는 여러 개의 디스크 드라이브 또는 기타 주변 장치를 위한 공간을 제공하며 대개 바닥에 서 있는 반면, 데스크탑 케이스는 더 적은 확장 공간을 제공한다. 올인원 스타일 디자인에는 동일한 케이스에 내장된 비디오 디스플레이가 포함된다.

휴대용 및 노트북 컴퓨터에는 장치에 대한 충격 보호 기능을 제공하는 케이스가 필요하다. 취미 활동가들은 케이스 모딩(케이스 수정/변형)이라고 불리는 활동에서 케이스를 컬러 조명, 페인트칠 또는 기타 기능으로 장식할 수 있다.

② Power supply

A power supply unit (PSU) converts alternating current (AC) electric power to low-voltage direct current (DC) power for the computer. Laptops can run on built-in rechargeable battery. The PSU typically uses a switched-mode power supply (SMPS), with power MOSFETs (power metal-oxide-semiconductor field-effect transistors) used in the converters and regulator circuits of the SMPS.

전원공급장치

전원 공급 장치(PSU)는 컴퓨터의 교류(AC) 전력을 저전압 직류(DC) 전력으로 변환한다. 노트북은 내장된 충전용 배터리로 작동할 수 있다. PSU는 일반적으로 SMPS의 변환기 및 조절기 회로에 사용되는 전력 MOSFET(금속 산화막 반도체 전계효과 트랜지스터)를 사용하는 SMPS(스위치 모드 전원 공급 장치)를 사용한다.

Vocabulary

enclose : 둘러싼다

mechanical support : 기계적 지원

power supply : 전원공급장치

flow of cooling air : 냉각공기의 흐름

control and direct : 제어하고 지시하다

electromagnetic interference : 전자방해

radiate : 내뿜다

electrostatic discharge : 정전기 방전

space : 공간

stand on : 서있다

expansion room : 확장 공간
decorate : 장식하다
case modding(case modification) : 모딩(케이스 변환/수정)
convert : 변환하다
alternate : 번갈아 나오게 만들다
current (AC) electric power : 교류 전력
low-voltage direct current (DC) power : 저전압 직류(DC) 전력
built-in : 내장된
rechargeable battery : 충전식 배터리
switched-mode power supply (SMPS) : 스위치모드 전원 공급 장치
converter : 컨버터, 변환기
regulator : 레귤레이터, 조절기
circuit : 회로
MOSFET(metal-oxide-semiconductor field-effect transistor) : 금속 산화막 반도체 전계효과 트랜지스터

③ Computer motherboard

The motherboard is the main component of a computer. It is a board with integrated circuitry that connects the other parts of the computer including the CPU, the RAM, the disk drives (CD, DVD, hard disk, or any others) as well as any peripherals connected via the ports or the expansion slots. The integrated circuit (IC) chips in a computer typically contain billions of tiny metal-oxide-semiconductor field-effect transistors (MOSFETs).

Motherboard(출처 https://ko.wikipedia.org/wiki/메인보드)

Components directly attached to or to part of the motherboard include:

The CPU (central processing unit), which performs most of the calculations which enable a computer to function, and is referred to as the brain of the computer. It takes program instructions from random-access memory (RAM), interprets and processes them and then sends back results so that the relevant components can carry out the instructions. The CPU is a microprocessor, which is fabricated on a metal-oxide-semiconductor (MOS) integrated circuit (IC) chip. It is usually cooled by a heat sink and fan, or water-cooling system. Most newer CPU includes an on-die graphics processing unit (GPU). The clock speed of CPU governs how fast it executes instructions and is measured in GHz; typical values lie between 1 GHz and 5 GHz. Many modern computers have the option to overclock the CPU which enhances performance at the expense of greater thermal output and thus a need for improved cooling.

The chipset, which includes the north bridge, mediates communication between the CPU and the other components of the system, including main memory; as well as south bridge, which is connected to the north bridge, and supports auxiliary interfaces and buses; and, finally, a Super I/O chip, connected through the south bridge, which supports the slowest and most legacy components like serial ports, hardware monitoring and fan control.

컴퓨터 마더보드

마더보드는 컴퓨터의 주요 구성 요소이다. CPU, RAM, 디스크 드라이브(CD, DVD, 하드 디스크 또는 기타)와 포트 또는 확장 슬롯을 통해 연결된 주변 장치를 포함한 컴퓨터의 다른 부분을 연결하는 통합 회로가 있는 보드이다. 컴퓨터의 집적 회로(IC) 칩에는 일반적으로 수십억 개의 작은 금속 산화물 반도체 전계효과 트랜지스터(MOSFET)가 포함되어 있다.

마더보드에 직접 부착되거나 마더보드의 일부에 부착되는 구성 요소는 다음과 같다. CPU는 컴퓨터가 작동할 수 있게 하는 대부분의 계산을 수행하며 컴퓨터의 두뇌라고 불린다. RAM(Random-Access Memory)에서 프로그램 명령을 받아 해석 및 처리한 다음 결과를 보내 관련 구성 요소가 명령을 수행할 수 있도록 한다.

CPU는 MOS(Metal-Oxide-Semiconductor) 집적 회로(IC) 칩으로 제작된 마이크로프로세서이다. 보통 히트 싱크 및 팬, 또는 수냉식 시스템으로 냉각된다. 최신 CPU에는 대부분 GPU(On-Die Graphics Processing Unit)가 포함되어 있다. CPU의 클럭 속도는 명령을 실행하는 속도를 좌우하며 GHz 단위로 측정된다. 일반적인 값은 1GHz에서 5GHz 사이이다. 많은 최신 컴퓨터에는 CPU 오버클럭 옵션이 있어 열 출력을 높임으로써 냉각 성능을 개선할 필요가 있다.

노스 브릿지(North Bridge)를 포함하는 칩셋은 CPU와 메인메모리를 포함한 시스템 구성품과의 통신을 중개하고 노스 브리지와 연결된 사우스 브리지와 보조 인터페이스, 버스를 지원하며 마지막으로 느린 속도를 지원하는 슈퍼 I/O 칩을 지원한다. 직렬 포트, 하드웨어 모니터링 및 팬 제어와 같은 대부분의 레거시 구성 요소를 지원한다.

Random-access memory (RAM), which stores the code and data that are being actively accessed by the CPU. For example, when a web browser is opened on the computer it takes up memory; this is stored in the RAM until the web browser is closed. It is typically a type of dynamic RAM (DRAM), such as synchronous DRAM (SDRAM), where MOS memory chips store data on memory cells consisting of MOSFETs and MOS capacitors. RAM usually comes on dual in-line memory modules (DIMMs) in the sizes of 2GB, 4GB, and 8GB, but can be much larger.

Read-only memory (ROM), which stores the BIOS that runs when the computer is powered on or otherwise begins execution, a process known as Bootstrapping, or "booting" or "booting up". The ROM is typically a nonvolatile BIOS memory chip, which stores data on floating-gate MOSFET memory cells. The BIOS (Basic Input Output System) includes boot firmware and power management firmware. Newer motherboards use Unified Extensible Firmware Interface (UEFI) instead of BIOS.

Buses that connect the CPU to various internal components and to expand cards for graphics and sound.

The CMOS (complementary MOS) battery, which powers the CMOS memory for date and time in the BIOS chip. This battery is generally a watch battery.

The video card (also known as the graphics card), which processes computer graphics. More powerful graphics cards are better suited to handle strenuous tasks, such as playing intensive video games or running computer graphics software. A video card contains a graphics processing unit (GPU) and video memory (typically a type of SDRAM), both fabricated on MOS integrated circuit (MOS IC) chips.

Power MOSFETs make up the voltage regulator module (VRM), which controls how much voltage other hardware components receive.

RAM(Random-Access Memory)은 CPU가 능동적으로 액세스하는 코드와 데이터를 저장한다. 예를 들어 컴퓨터에서 웹 브라우저를 열면 메모리가 사용되고 웹 브라우저가 닫힐 때까지 RAM에 저장된다. MOS 메모리칩이 MOSFET와 MOS 커패시터로 구성된 메모리 셀에 데이터를 저장하는 동기식 DRAM(SDRAM)과 같은 동적램(DRAM)의 일종이다. 램은 보통 2GB, 4GB, 8GB 크기의 듀얼 인라인 메모리 모듈(DIMM)로 제공되지만 훨씬 더 클 수 있다.

ROM(Read-only Memory)은 컴퓨터의 전원이 켜지거나 실행이 시작될 때 실행되는 BIOS, 부트스트래핑 또는 "부팅" 으로 알려진 프로세스를 저장한다. ROM은 일반적으로 플로팅 게이트 MOSFET 메모리 셀에 데이터를 저장하는 비휘발성 BIOS 메모리칩이다. BIOS(Basic Input Output System)에는 부팅 펌웨어와 전원 관리 펌웨어가 포함되어 있다. 최신 마더보드는 BIOS 대신 UEFI(Unified Extensible Firmware Interface)를 사용한다.

버스는 CPU를 다양한 내부 구성요소에 연결하고 그래픽과 사운드를 위한 카드를 확장한다.

CMOS(보완적 MOS) 배터리는 BIOS 칩의 날짜 및 시간에 대해 CMOS 메모리에 전원을 공급한다. 이 배터리는 일반적으로 시계 배터리다.

비디오 카드(그래픽 카드)는 컴퓨터 그래픽을 처리한다. 보다 강력한 그래픽 카드는 집중적인 비디오 게임을 하거나 컴퓨터 그래픽 소프트웨어를 실행하는 것과 같이 어려운 작업을 처리하는 데 적합하다. 비디오 카드에는 그래픽 처리 장치(GPU)와 비디오 메모리(일반적으로 SDRAM의 일종)가 들어 있으며, 두 가지 모두 MOS 집적회로(MOSIC) 칩으로 제작된다.

전력 MOSFET는 전압 레귤레이터 모듈(VRM)을 구성하며, 이 모듈은 다른 하드웨어 구성 요소가 수신하는 전압을 제어한다.

Vocabulary

main component : 주요 구성요소
integrated circuitry : 직접회로(IC)
via : ~를 거쳐, 통하여
expansion slot : 확장슬롯
attached : 부착된
program instructions : 프로그램 지시사항
interpret and process : 해석하고 처리하다
relevant : 관련된, 연관된
fabricate : 제작하다, 날조하다
water-cooling system : 수냉식 시스템
on-die graphics processing unit (GPU) : 온다이 그래픽 처리 장치(GPU)
govern : 좌우하다, 통제하다
execute : 실행하다
typical value : 일반적인 값
enhance : 향상시키다
greater thermal output : 더 많은 열출력

mediate : 중재, 조정하다
auxiliary : 보조의
actively : 활발히
access : 접근하다
take up : 차지하다
capacitor : condenser, 축전기(주로 전자회로에서 전하를 모으는 장치)
come on : 나오다, 등장하다, 되어가다
store : 저장하다
execution : 실행
nonvolatile : 비휘발성의
floating-gate MOSFET memory cell : 부동 게이트 MOSFET 메모리 셀
boot firmware and power management firmware : 부팅 펌웨어와 전원관리 펌웨어
Unified Extensible Firmware Interface (UEFI) : 통합 확장 펌웨어 인터페이스
internal component : 내부 구성요소
suited : 적합한
strenuous : 힘이 드는, 격렬한
voltage regulator module (VRM) : 전압 레귤레이터 모듈

④ Expansion cards

An expansion card in computing is a printed circuit board that can be inserted into an expansion slot of a computer motherboard or backplane to add functionality to a computer system via the expansion bus. Expansion cards can be used to obtain or expand on features not offered by the motherboard.

확장 카드

컴퓨터 확장카드는 컴퓨터 마더보드나 백플레인의 확장 슬롯에 삽입해 확장버스를 통해 컴퓨터 시스템에 기능을 추가할 수 있는 인쇄회로기판이다. 확장 카드는 마더보드에서 제공하지 않는 기능을 얻거나 확장하는 데 사용할 수 있다.

⑤ Storage devices

A storage device is any computing hardware and digital media that is used for storing, porting and extracting data files and objects. It can hold and store information both temporarily and permanently and can be internal or external to a computer, server or any similar computing device. Data storage is a core function and fundamental component of computers.

– Fixed media

Data is stored by a computer using a variety of media. Hard disk drives (HDDs) are found in virtually all older computers, due to their high capacity and low cost, but solid-state drives (SSDs) are faster and more power efficient, although currently more expensive than hard drives in terms of dollar per gigabyte, so are often found in personal computers built post-2007. SSDs use flash memory, which stores data on MOS memory chips consisting of floating-gate MOSFET memory cells. Some systems may use a disk array controller for greater performance or reliability.

– Removable media

To transfer data between computers, an external flash memory device (such as a memory card or USB flash drive) or optical disc (such as a CD-ROM, DVD-ROM or BD-ROM) may be used. Their usefulness depends on being readable by other systems; the majority of machines have an optical disk drive (ODD), and virtually all have at least one Universal Serial Bus (USB) port.

저장 장치

저장 장치는 데이터 파일 및 객체를 저장, 포팅 및 추출하는 데 사용되는 모든 컴퓨팅 하드웨어 및 디지털 미디어다. 정보를 임시 및 영구적으로 보관하고 저장할 수 있으며 컴퓨터, 서버 또는 유사한 컴퓨팅 장치의 내부나 외부에 있을 수 있다. 데이터 저장소는 컴퓨터의 핵심 기능이자 기본 구성 요소다.

– 고정 매체

데이터는 다양한 미디어를 사용하여 컴퓨터에 저장된다. 하드 디스크 드라이브(HDD)는 대용량과 저렴한 비용으로 인해 거의 모든 구형 컴퓨터에서 찾아볼 수 있다. 솔리드 스테이트 드라이브(SSD)는 비용 면에서 하드 드라이브보다 더 비싸지만, 더 빠르고 전력 효율성이 높다. 따라서 2007년 이후에 제작된 개인용 컴퓨터에서도 자주 볼 수 있다. SSD는 부동게이트 MOSFET 메모리 셀로 구성된 MOS 메모리칩에 데이터를 저장하는 플래시 메모리를 사용한다. 일부 시스템에서는 성능 또는 신뢰성을 높이기 위해 디스크 어레이 컨트롤러를 사용할 수 있다.

– 이동식 미디어

컴퓨터 간에 데이터를 전송하려면 외장 플래시 메모리 장치(예: 메모리 카드 또는 USB 플래시 드라이브) 또는 광학 디스크(예: CD-ROM, DVD-ROM 또는 BD-ROM)를 사용할 수 있다. 이 기능의 유용성은 다른 시스템에서 읽을 수 있느냐에 따라 달라진다. 대부분의 컴퓨터에는 ODD(광학 디스크 드라이브)가 있으며, 거의 모든 컴퓨터에는 적어도 하나의 USB(범용 직렬 버스) 포트가 있다.

⑥ Input and output peripherals

Input and output devices are typically housed externally to the main computer chassis. The following are either standard or very common to many computer systems.

– Input device

Input devices allow the user to enter information into the system, or control its operation. Most personal computers have a mouse and keyboard, but laptop systems typically use a touchpad instead of a mouse. Other input devices include webcams, microphones, joysticks, and image scanners.

– Output device

Output devices are designed around the senses of human beings. For example, monitors display text that can be read, speakers produce sound that can be heard. Such devices also could include printers or a Braille embosser.

입출력 주변기기

입력 및 출력 장치는 일반적으로 메인 컴퓨터 섀시의 외부에 있다. 다음의 장치들은 표준이거나 많은 컴퓨터 시스템에 매우 일반적으로 있는 장치다.

– 입력 장치

입력 장치를 통해 사용자는 시스템에 정보를 입력하거나 시스템 작동을 제어할 수 있다. 대부분의 개인용 컴퓨터에는 마우스와 키보드가 있지만 노트북 시스템은 일반적으로 마우스 대신 터치패드를 사용한다. 다른 입력 장치로는 웹캠, 마이크, 조이스틱, 이미지 스캐너 등이 있다.

– 출력 장치

출력 장치는 인간의 감각을 중심으로 설계된다. 예를 들어 모니터는 읽을 수 있는 텍스트를 표시하고 스피커는 들을 수 있는 소리를 낸다. 그러한 장치에는 프린터나 점자 엠보서도 포함될 수 있다.

Vocabulary

expansion cards : 확장카드
insert : 삽입하다
storage devices : 저장장치
hold and store : 보관하고 저장하다
temporarily and permanently : 임시 및 영구적으로
internal or external : 내부 또는 외부
core function : 핵심 기능
fundamental : 근본적인
fixed media : 고정 매체
virtually : 거의
power efficient : 전력 효율적인
in terms of : ~의 면에서
reliability : 신뢰성
removable media : 이동식 미디어
transfer : 전송하다
external flash memory device : 외장 플래시 메모리 장치
optical disc : 광학 디스크, 레이저디스크
depend on : 의존하다, 의지하다
readable : 읽을 수 있는
majority : 다수
house : 살 곳을 주다, 보관하다
sense of human beings : 인간의 감각
Braille embosser : 점자 엠보싱기(점자를 인쇄하는 기계)

☞ 잠깐 쉬어가기 ....

에니악(출처 https://ko.wikipedia.org/wiki/에니악)

위 그림은 최초의 범용 컴퓨터라고 알려진 에니악(ENIAC : Electronic Numerical Integrator And Computer)입니다. 방 자체를 구성할 만한 사이즈인 에니악에 비해서 우리가 쓰고 있는 컴퓨터와 비교했을 때 크기 차이가 실로 놀랍지 않습니까? 그럴 만도 한 것이 에니악은 30톤짜리 컴퓨터이기 때문입니다. 초기에는 군사용으로 개발되었습니다만 완료시점이 전쟁 후라 그밖에 과학 분야에서 활용되었습니다.

30톤짜리 어마 무시한 계산기인 에니악은 17,468개의 진공관을 사용하였습니다. 에니악은 설정만 제대로 해두면 인간이 할 수 있는 계산수의 10만 배까지 연산이 가능하였다고 합니다. 에니악을 제작한 비용은 당시 미국달러로 50만 달러이며 현재 기준, 우리나라 원으로 환산하면 70억이 넘습니다. 당시 에니악을 제작하기 위하여 얼마나 공들였는지 알 수 있습니다. 현재 에니악은 미국 펜실베니아 대학과 스미소니언 박물관에서 보관되고 있습니다.

The picture above is the ENIAC (Electronic Numerical Integrator And Computer), known as the first general-purpose computer. Isn't it amazing how much smaller our computers are compared to the ENIAC, which is the size of a room itself? That's because the ENIAC is a 30-ton computer. It was originally developed for military use, but it was used in other scientific fields after the war was completed.

The ENIAC, a 30-ton calculator, used 17,468 vacuum tubes. It is said that the ENIAC could calculate up to 100,000 times the number of calculations that humans can do if it is set up properly. The cost of manufacturing the ENIAC was $500,000 in US dollars at the time, and in today's terms, it is over 7 billion won in Korean won. We can see how much effort was put into making the ENIAC at the time. The ENIAC is currently housed at the University of Pennsylvania and the Smithsonian Museum in the United States.

exercises

연습문제

1~5. 다음 빈 칸에 들어가는 단어로 적절한 것을 넣으세요.

1. (   ) is the set of instructions that can be stored and run by hardware.

정답 : ____________________

2. (   ) consists of a central processor with an arithmetic/logic unit and a control unit, a memory, mass storage, and input and output.

정답 : ____________________

3. (   ) holds the motherboard, fixed or removable disk drives for data storage, the power supply, and may contain other peripheral devices such as modems or network interfaces.

정답 : ____________________

4. (   ), which stores the code and data that are being actively accessed by the CPU.

정답 : ____________________

5. (   ), which stores the BIOS that runs when the computer is powered on or otherwise begins execution, a process known as Bootstrapping, or "booting" or "booting up".

정답 : ____________________

6~10. 다음 It이 지칭하는 것을 영어로 쓰세요.

6. It is a board with integrated circuitry that connects the other parts of the computer including the CPU, the RAM, the disk drives (CD, DVD, hard disk, or any others) as well as any peripherals connected via the ports or the expansion slots.

정답 : ______________________________

7. It is designed for portability but operate similarly to desktop PCs.

정답 : ______________________________

8. It is typically directed by the software to execute any command or instruction.

정답 : ______________________________

9. It is portable computer that uses a touch screen as the primary input device.

정답 : ______________________________

10. It can hold and store information both temporarily and permanently

정답 : ______________________________

연습문제 해답

1. Software
2. A von Neumann machine
3. The computer casee
4. Random-access memory (RAM)
5. Read-only memory (ROM)
6. The motherboard/Computer motherboard
7. A laptop
8. Hardware
9. A tablet
10. A storage device

Chapter

05 Software

소프트웨어

학습순서

1) Software
2) Types of Software
3) Operating System
4) The Purpose of an Operating System
5) The Five Most Popular Operating Systems

잠깐 쉬어가기

연습문제

【 INTRO 】

여러분들은 윈도우를 쓰고 있나요? 아니면 맥 OS를 쓰고 있나요? 여러분들의 핸드폰은 안드로이드 기반인가요, 아니면 iOS기반 인가요? 우리의 컴퓨터에는 어떤 소프트웨어가 깔려있나요? 여러분들 중에는 원하는 소프트웨어를 이용하기 위해 비용을 지불한 적이 있나요? 이러한 모든 내용이 소프트웨어라는 생태계에서 속한 것들입니다. 이번 과에서는 소프트웨어란 무엇인지 공부해보도록 합시다.

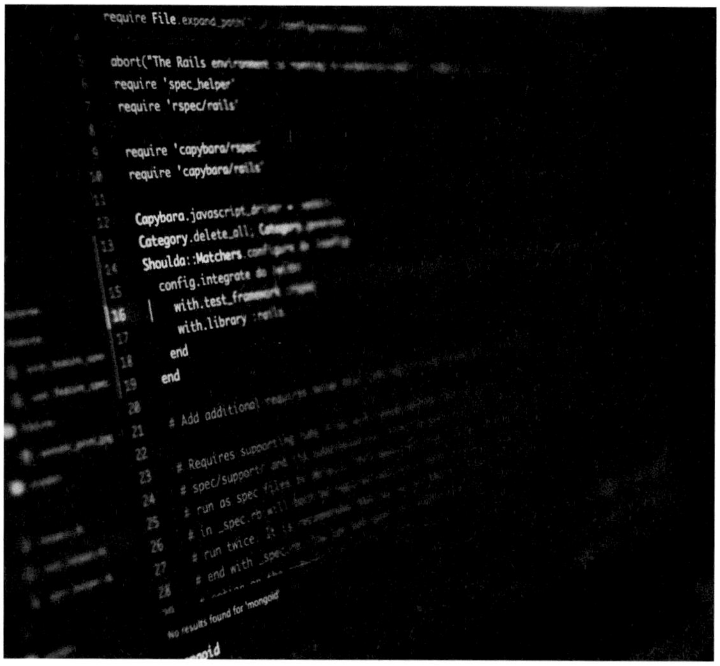

Do you use Windows? Or do you use Mac OS? Is your phone Android-based or iOS-based? What software is installed on your computers? Have any of you ever paid for the software you wanted to use? All these things belong to the ecosystem called software. In this chapter, let's study what software is.

1) Software 소프트웨어[1]

Software is a set of instructions, data, or programs used to operate a computer and execute specific tasks. In simpler terms, software tells a computer how to function. It's a generic term used to refer to applications, scripts, and programs that run on devices such as PCs, mobile phones, tablets, and other smart devices. Software contrasts with hardware, which is the physical aspects of a computer that perform the work.

Without software, most computers would be useless. For example, a web browser is a software application that allows users to access the internet. An operating system (OS) is a software program that serves as the interface between other applications and the hardware on a computer or mobile device. TCP/IP is built into all major operating systems to allow computers to communicate over long distance networks. Without the OS or the protocols built into it, it wouldn't be possible to access a web browser.

The majority of software is written in high-level programming languages due to the language being closer to natural human language as opposed to machine language. The high-level language is then translated into low-level machine code using a compiler or interpreter for the computer to understand. Software can also be written in a low-level assembly language, but it is less common.

소프트웨어는 컴퓨터를 작동시키고 특정 작업을 실행하는 데 사용되는 명령, 데이터 또는 프로그램의 집합이다. 간단히 말해서, 소프트웨어는 컴퓨터에게 작동법을 알려준다. PC, 휴대폰, 태블릿, 기타 스마트 기기와 같은 기기에서 실행되는 애플리케이션, 스크립트와 프로그램을 지칭하는 일반적 용어이다. 소프트웨어는 작업을 수행하

1 https://www.webopedia.com/definitions/software/

는 컴퓨터의 물리적 측면인 하드웨어와 대비된다.

소프트웨어가 없다면 대부분의 컴퓨터는 쓸모가 없을 것이다. 예를 들어, 웹 브라우저는 사용자가 인터넷에 액세스할 수 있는 소프트웨어 응용프로그램이다. 운영 체제(OS)는 컴퓨터나 모바일 장치의 다른 응용 프로그램과 하드웨어 간의 인터페이스 역할을 하는 소프트웨어 프로그램이다. TCP/IP는 컴퓨터가 장거리 네트워크를 통해 통신하도록 모든 주요 운영 체제에 내장되어 있다. OS나 프로토콜이 들어있지 않으면 웹 브라우저에 접근할 수 없다.

대부분의 소프트웨어는 고급 프로그래밍 언어로 작성되는데 이는 언어가 기계어와 달리 자연적인 인간 언어에 가깝기 때문이다. 그런 다음 컴퓨터가 이해할 수 있도록 컴파일러 또는 인터프리터를 사용하여 고급 언어가 낮은 수준의 시스템 코드로 변환된다. 소프트웨어도 낮은 수준의 어셈블리 언어로 작성될 수 있지만 일반적이지 않다.

Vocabulary

instructions : 명령어
operate a computer : 컴퓨터를 작동시키다
execute specific tasks : 특정 작업을 실행하다
generic term : 일반적인 용어
run : 실행되다
contrast with : ~와 대조를 이루다
physical aspects : 물리적 측면
useless : 쓸모가 없는
long distance network : 장거리 네트워크
majority : 다수
due to : ~때문에

opposed to : ~에 반대하는
translate : 변환시키다

2) Types of Software 소프트웨어의 유형[2]

① Application software

The most common type of software, application software is a computer software package that performs a specific function for a user, or in some cases, for another application. An application can be self-contained, or it can be a group of programs that run the application for the user. Examples of modern applications include office suites, graphics software, databases and database management programs, web browsers, word processors, software development tools, image editors and communication platforms.

② System software

These software programs are designed to run a computer's application programs and hardware. System software coordinates the activities and functions of the hardware and software. In addition, it controls the operations of the computer hardware and provides an environment or platform for all the other types of software to work in. The OS is the best example of system software; it manages all the other computer programs. Other examples of system software include the firmware, computer language translators and system utilities.

2 https://searchapparchitecture.techtarget.com/definition/software

③ Driver software

Also known as device drivers, this software is often considered a type of system software. Device drivers control the devices and peripherals connected to a computer, enabling them to perform their specific tasks. Every device that is connected to a computer needs at least one device driver to function. Examples include software that comes with any nonstandard hardware, including special game controllers, as well as the software that enables standard hardware, such as USB storage devices, keyboards, headphones and printers.

④ Middleware

The term middleware describes software that mediates between application and system software or between two different kinds of application software. For example, middleware enables Microsoft Windows to talk to Excel and Word. It is also used to send a remote work request from an application in a computer that has one kind of OS, to an application in a computer with a different OS. It also enables newer applications to work with legacy ones.

⑤ Programming software

Computer programmers use programming software to write code. Programming software and programming tools enable developers to develop, write, test and debug other software programs. Examples of programming software include assemblers, compilers, debuggers and interpreters.

애플리케이션 소프트웨어

가장 일반적인 유형의 소프트웨어인 응용 프로그램은 사용자 또는 경우에 따라 다른 응용 프로그램에 대해 특정 기능을 수행하는 컴퓨터 소프트웨어 패키지다. 응용 프로그램은 자체적으로 포함되거나 사용자를 위해 응용 프로그램을 실행하는 프로그램 그룹일 수 있다. 최신 애플리케이션의 예로는 오피스 제품군, 그래픽 소프트웨어, 데이터베이스 및 데이터베이스 관리 프로그램, 웹 브라우저, 워드 프로세서, 소프트웨어 개발 도구, 이미지 편집기 및 통신 플랫폼 등이 있다.

시스템 소프트웨어

이 소프트웨어 프로그램들은 컴퓨터의 응용 프로그램 및 하드웨어를 실행하도록 설계되었다. 시스템 소프트웨어는 하드웨어 및 소프트웨어의 활동과 기능을 조정한다. 또한 컴퓨터 하드웨어의 작동을 제어하고 다른 모든 유형의 소프트웨어가 작동할 수 있는 환경 또는 플랫폼을 제공한다. OS는 다른 모든 컴퓨터 프로그램을 관리하는 시스템 소프트웨어의 가장 좋은 예다. 시스템 소프트웨어의 다른 예로는 펌웨어, 컴퓨터 언어 변환기 및 시스템 유틸리티가 있다.

드라이버 소프트웨어

장치 드라이버라고도 하는 이 소프트웨어는 종종 시스템 소프트웨어의 한 유형으로 간주된다. 장치 드라이버는 컴퓨터에 연결된 장치 및 주변 장치를 제어하여 특정 작업을 수행할 수 있도록 한다. 컴퓨터에 연결된 모든 장치는 작동하려면 최소 하나의 장치 드라이버가 필요하다. 예를 들어 특수 게임 컨트롤러를 포함한 비표준 하드웨어와 함께 제공되는 소프트웨어뿐만 아니라 USB 저장 장치, 키보드, 헤드폰 및 프린터와 같은 표준 하드웨어를 사용할 수 있는 소프트웨어도 포함된다.

미들웨어

미들웨어라는 용어는 응용 프로그램과 시스템 소프트웨어 간에 또는 두 가지 다른 응용 프로그램 소프트웨어 간에 중재하는 소프트웨어를 말한다. 예를 들어, 미들웨어를 사용하면 Microsoft Windows에서 Excel 및 Word와 대화할 수 있다. OS가 한 종류인 컴퓨터의 애플리케이션에서 다른 OS가 있는 애플리케이션으로 원격 작업 요청을 보내는 데도 사용된다. 또한 새로운 애플리케이션을 기존 애플리케이션과 함께 사용할 수 있다.

프로그래밍 소프트웨어

컴퓨터 프로그래머들은 코드를 작성하기 위해 프로그래밍 소프트웨어를 사용한다. 개발자는 프로그래밍 소프트웨어 및 프로그래밍 도구를 사용하여 다른 소프트웨어 프로그램을 개발, 쓰기, 테스트 및 디버그할 수 있다. 프로그래밍 소프트웨어의 예로는 어셈블리, 컴파일러, 디버거 및 인터프리터가 있다.

Vocabulary

self-contained : 자립하는, 독립적으로 되어있는
modern application : 최신 애플리케이션
office suites : 오피스 제품군
remote work request : 원격 작업 요청
legacy : 유산(여기서는 '기존의')
enable : ~을 할 수 있게 하다, 가능하게 하다
debug : 오류를 검출하여 제거하다
assembler : 어셈블러(명령을 기계어로 전환하는 프로그램)
compiler : 컴파일러(명령어 번역 프로그램)
debugger : 디버거(다른 컴퓨터 프로그램에서 오류를 검출하여 제거하는 프로그램)
interpreter : 인터프리터(해석프로그램)

3) Operating System[3] 운영체제

An operating system (OS) is system software that manages computer hardware, software resources, and provides common services for computer programs.

Time-sharing operating systems schedule tasks for efficient use of the system and may also include accounting software for cost allocation of processor time, mass storage, printing, and other resources.

For hardware functions such as input and output and memory allocation, the operating system acts as an intermediary between programs and the computer hardware, although the application code is usually executed directly by the hardware and frequently makes system calls to an OS function or is interrupted by it. Operating systems are found on many devices that contain a computer – from cellular phones and video game consoles to web servers and supercomputers.

운영 체제(OS)는 컴퓨터 하드웨어, 소프트웨어 리소스를 관리하고 컴퓨터 프로그램에 대한 공통 서비스를 제공하는 시스템 소프트웨어다.

시간 공유 운영 체제는 시스템을 효율적으로 사용하기 위해 작업을 예약하고 프로세서 시간, 대용량 저장 장치, 인쇄 및 기타 자원의 비용 할당을 위한 회계 소프트웨어를 포함할 수도 있다.

애플리케이션 코드가 하드웨어에 의해 직접 실행되며 OS 기능에 대한 시스템 호출이 빈번하거나 시스템 기능에 의해 중단되는 경우가 많지만 입출력 및 메모리 할당과 같은 하드웨어 기능의 경우 운영 체제는 프로그램과 컴퓨터 하드웨어 사이의 중

3 https://en.wikipedia.org/wiki/Operating_system

개자 역할을 한다. 운영 체제는 휴대폰과 비디오 게임기에서부터 웹 서버, 슈퍼컴퓨터에 이르기까지 컴퓨터가 포함된 많은 장치에서 찾을 수 있다.

The dominant general-purpose desktop operating system is Microsoft Windows with a market share of around 69.51%. MacOS by Apple Inc. is in second place (20.43%), and other operating systems include Chrome OS, Linux, and various others.[4]

In the mobile sector (including smartphones and tablets), as of July 2023, Android's market share is up to 71%, while Apple's iOS is at 28.36%.[5]

Other specialized classes of operating systems (special-purpose operating systems)), such as embedded and real-time systems, exist for many applications. Security-focused operating systems also exist. Some operating systems have low system requirements (e.g. light-weight Linux distribution). Others may have higher system requirements.

Some operating systems require installation or may come pre-installed with purchased computers (OEM-installation), whereas others may run directly from media (i.e. live cd) or flash memory (i.e. USB stick).

가장 우세한 범용 데스크톱 운영체제는 시장점유율의 약 69.51%인 마이크로소프의 윈도우다. 2위(20.43%)는 애플의 mac OS다. 그 외로는 다양한 운영체제들과 크롬 OS, 리눅스 계열 등이 있다.

모바일 부문(스마트폰과 태블릿 포함)에서 2023년 7월, 안드로이드 점유율은 최대 71%에 이르고, 애플 iOS는 28.36%이다.

4 https://gs.statcounter.com/os-market-share/desktop/worldwide/

5 https://gs.statcounter.com/os-market-share/mobile/worldwide/

임베디드 및 실시간 시스템과 같은 기타 특수 운영 체제 클래스(특수 목적 운영 체제)는 많은 애플리케이션에 사용된다. 보안에 초점을 맞춘 운영 체제도 존재한다. 일부 운영 체제에서는 시스템 요구 사항이 낮습니다(예: 경량 Linux 배포). 시스템 요구 사항이 더 높은 경우도 있을 수 있다.

일부 운영 체제는 설치가 필요하거나 구입 컴퓨터(OEM 설치)와 함께 사전 설치되는 반면, 다른 운영 체제는 미디어(예: 라이브 CD) 또는 플래시 메모리(예: USB 스틱)에서 직접 실행될 수 있다.

Vocabulary

resource : 리소스
time-sharing operating systems : 시간 공유 운영 체제
efficient : 효율적인
accounting : 회계
allocation : 할당
mass storage : 대용량 기억 (장치)
intermediary : 중개자
executed : 실행된
interrupted : 중단되는
device : 장치
dominant : 우세한
general-purpose : 다목적의, 다용도의
variety : 다양성, 종류
collectively : 집합적으로, 총괄하여
growth rate : 성장률
decrease : 감소
distribution : 배포, 방식

real-time : 실시간
requirement : 요구, 필요사항
light-weight : 경량
installation : 설치

4) The Purpose of an Operating System[6] 운영체제의 목적

Operating systems contain and manage all the programs and applications that a computer or mobile device is able to run, which means managing the device's software and hardware functions.

The functions of an OS include:

Booting: Booting is the process of turning on the computer and powering up the system.

Memory management: This feature controls and coordinates the computer applications while allocating space for programs.

Loading and execution: Your OS will load, or start up, a program and then execute the program so that it opens and runs.

Data security: A good OS includes features that keep your data safe and computer programs secure. Security features are set up to keep unwanted cyberattackers at bay.

Disk management: This manages all the drives installed in a computer, including hard drives, optical disk drives, and flash drives. Disk management can also be used to divide disks, format drives, and more.

6 https://www.wgu.edu/blog/5-most-popular-operating-systems1910.html#close

운영 체제에는 컴퓨터나 모바일 장치를 실행할 수 있는 모든 프로그램과 응용 프로그램이 포함되어 관리되므로 장치의 소프트웨어와 하드웨어 기능을 관리할 수 있다.

OS의 기능은 다음과 같다.
부팅: 부팅은 컴퓨터의 전원을 켜고 시스템의 전원을 켜는 과정이다.
메모리 관리: 이 특징은 프로그램을 위한 공간을 할당하는 동안 컴퓨터 응용 프로그램을 제어하고 조정한다.
로드 및 실행: OS가 프로그램을 로드하거나 시작한 다음 프로그램을 실행하여 프로그램을 열고 실행한다.

데이터 보안: 좋은 OS에는 데이터를 안전하게 유지하고 컴퓨터 프로그램을 안전하게 유지하는 기능이 포함되어 있다. 원치 않는 사이버 공격자가 접근하지 못하도록 보안 기능이 설정되어 있다.
디스크 관리: 하드 드라이브, 광학 디스크 드라이브 및 플래시 드라이브를 포함하여 컴퓨터에 설치된 모든 드라이브를 관리한다. 디스크 관리를 사용하여 디스크를 분할하고 드라이브를 포맷할 수도 있다.

Process management: Your OS is designed to allocate resources to different computer processes, enable the processes to share information, protect them, and synchronize them.
Device controlling: Your OS will allow you to open or block access to devices like removable devices, CD/DVDs, data transfer devices, USBs, and more.

Printing controlling: As an extension of device controlling, your OS takes control of the printers that are connected to the computer, and the materials that need to be printed.
User interface: Also referred to as a UI, this is the part of the OS that allows a user to enter and receive information. This can be done with typed commands, code, and other formats.

프로세스 관리: OS는 리소스를 다른 컴퓨터 프로세스에 할당하고, 프로세스가 정보를 공유하고, 보호하고, 동기화할 수 있도록 설계되었다.

장치 제어: OS에서 이동식 장치, CD/DVD, 데이터 전송 장치, USB 등과 같은 장치에 대한 액세스를 열거나 차단할 수 있다.

인쇄 제어: 장치 제어의 확장으로서 OS는 컴퓨터에 연결된 프린터와 인쇄해야 하는 재료를 제어한다.

사용자 인터페이스: UI라고도 하며 사용자가 정보를 입력하고 받을 수 있는 OS 부분이다. 이 작업은 입력된 명령, 코드 및 기타 형식을 사용하여 수행할 수 있다.

Vocabulary

booting : 부팅
coordinate : 조정하다
execution : 실행
security : 보안
feature : 특징, 특징으로 하다
secure : 안전한
set up : 설치하다
keep : 유지하다
unwanted : 원치 않는
attacker : 공격자
at bay : 궁지에 몰린
optical : 광학의
allocate : 할당하다
synchronize : 동기화하다
extension : 확대, 확장
take control of : 제어하다
material : 재료
refer to : 언급하다, 지칭하다
typed command : 입력된 명령

5) The Five Most Popular Operating Systems[7]가장 많이 사용되는 5가지 운영 체제

There are five main types of operating systems. These five OS types are likely what run your phone, computer, or other mobile devices like a tablet. Whether you're just a normal computer and phone user or someone hoping to get involved in an IT career, knowledge of applications and systems types will help you maintain security and user access, perform routine operations, and much more.

① Microsoft Windows

The Windows OS has been around since the 1980s and has had several versions and updates (including Windows 95, Windows Vista, Windows 7/8/10, etc.) Microsoft Windows is one of the popular operating system types and is preloaded on most new PC hardware. With each new Windows update or release, Microsoft continues to work on improving their users' experience, hardware, and software, making Windows more accessible and easier to use.

Microsoft Windows contains a control panel, a desktop and desktop assistant, disk cleanup, event viewer, and more. Many users prefer Microsoft Windows because they say it's compatible with many other kinds of software. Many kinds of computer programs run best on Microsoft Windows because they're developed by Microsoft.

② Apple macOS

Head-to-head in the competition with Microsoft Windows is Apple's

7 https://www.wgu.edu/blog/5-most-popular-operating-systems1910.html#close

macOS. macOS and Windows are both examples of proprietary operating systems, meaning that the company conceptualized, designed, developed, and now sells their own OS. They're designed and sold by the companies and aren't meant to be tampered with or tweaked by users. Apple and Macintosh computers run on the proprietary macOS and OS X system, the first of which launched 20 years ago.

The macOS and Apple/Mac products are also known and beloved by their users for ease of use and continually improving user experience. Fast processing speeds, a simple desktop interface, and a wide variety of helpful resources make users excited about macOS. Many users relish the instant connection with their computers and mobile phone hardware, and enjoy the lack of bugs and hackers that Apple systems are known for.

③ Google's Android OS

The OS that companies including Google use to run its Android mobile smartphones and tablets is based on Linux distribution and other open source software. Android OS is the primary OS for Google mobile devices like smartphones and tablets. Android has gained increasing popularity since its release as an alternative to Apple's iOS for smartphone users and is continuing to increase in popularity with new updates and exciting features.

④ Apple iOS

Apple's iOS is another mobile operating system used exclusively for iPhones, some of the most popular mobile devices on the market. iOS integrations have regular updates, new expansions to software, and continually are offering new features for users even if they have older devices.

Many users appreciate the unique user interface with touch gestures, and the ease of use that iOS offers. This operating system also allows other Apple devices to connect, giving users easy connections to other devices or people.

⑤ Linux Operating System

Linux is different from Windows and Apple in that it's not a proprietary software, but rather a family of open source systems. In other words, anyone can modify and distribute it. Linux may be the least known on this list, but it's free and available in many different open source versions. Linux is popular because of its ease of customization and offers a variety of options to those who understand how to use it. If you know how to customize and work with operating systems, Linux is an ideal choice. And if this kind of coding and back-end work is interesting to you, it may be a good idea to purchase a Linux system and get started on manipulating it.

운영 체제에는 크게 다섯 가지 유형이 있다. 이러한 5가지 OS 유형은 휴대폰, 컴퓨터 또는 태블릿과 같은 기타 모바일 장치를 실행하는 OS 유형일 수 있다. 일반 컴퓨터 및 전화 사용자이든, IT 경력을 쌓고자 하는 사용자든 애플리케이션 및 시스템 유형에 대한 지식을 통해 보안 및 사용자 액세스를 유지하고 일상적인 작업을 수행하는 데 도움이 될 것이다.

마이크로소프트 윈도우즈

Windows OS는 1980년대부터 사용되었으며 여러 가지 버전 및 업데이트가 있다 (Windows 95, Windows Vista, Windows 7/8/10 등). Microsoft Windows는 널리 사용되는 운영 체제 유형 중 하나이며 대부분의 새로운 PC 하드웨어에 미리 설치되어 있다. Microsoft는 새로운 Windows 업데이트 또는 릴리스마다 사용자 경험(UX), 하드웨어 및 소프트웨어를 개선하여 Windows에 대한 접근성과 사용 편의성을 높이기 위해 계속 노력하고 있다.

마이크로소프트 윈도우즈에는 제어판, 데스크톱 및 데스크톱 어시스턴트, 디스크 정리, 이벤트 뷰어 등이 포함되어 있다. 많은 사용자들은 마이크로소프트 윈도우가 다른 많은 종류의 소프트웨어와 호환된다고 말하기 때문에 마이크로소프트 윈도우를 선호한다. 많은 종류의 컴퓨터 프로그램들이 마이크로소프트에 의해 개발되었기 때문에 마이크로소프트 윈도우에서 가장 잘 실행된다.

Apple MacOS

Microsoft Windows와의 경쟁에서 정면 승부를 하는 것은 Apple의 macOS이다. macOS와 Windows는 모두 독점 운영 체제의 예이며, 이는 Microsoft가 자체 OS를 개념화, 설계, 개발 및 판매한다는 것을 의미한다. 회사에서 설계하고 판매하며 사용자가 함부로 변경하거나 수정해서는 안 된다. 애플과 매킨토시 컴퓨터는 20년 전에 처음 출시된 독점적인 macOS와 OS X 시스템에서 실행된다.

macOS와 Apple/Mac 제품도 사용이 편리하고 사용자 경험(UX)이 지속적으로 개선되어 사용자의 사랑을 받고 있다. 빠른 처리 속도, 간단한 데스크톱 인터페이스 및 다양한 유용한 리소스를 통해 MacOS에 대한 관심이 높아진다. 많은 사용자들은 자신의 컴퓨터 및 휴대폰 하드웨어와의 즉각적인 연결을 즐기고 애플 시스템이 버그와 해커가 없다는 사실을 즐긴다.

구글의 안드로이드 OS

구글을 포함한 기업들이 안드로이드 스마트폰과 태블릿을 구동하는 OS는 리눅스 배포판과 그 외에 오픈 소스 소프트웨어를 기반으로 한다. 안드로이드 OS는 스마트폰과 태블릿과 같은 구글 모바일 기기의 기본 OS다. 안드로이드는 스마트폰 사용자를 위한 애플 iOS의 대안으로 출시 이후 인기가 높아졌으며, 새로운 업데이트와 흥미로운 기능으로 지속적인 인기를 끌고 있다.

애플 iOS

애플의 iOS는 아이폰 전용으로 사용되는 또 다른 모바일 운영 체제로, iOS 통합은 정기적인 업데이트와 소프트웨어로의 새로운 확장, 그리고 오래된 기기가 있더라도 지속적으로 새로운 기능을 제공하고 있다.
많은 사용자들이 터치 제스처가 적용된 독특한 사용자 인터페이스(UI)와 iOS가 제공하는 사용 편의성을 높이 평가하고 있다. 이 운영체제는 다른 애플 기기들도 연결할 수 있게 해 사용자가 다른 기기나 사람들과 쉽게 연결할 수 있게 해준다.

리눅스 운영 체제

리눅스는 독점 소프트웨어가 아니라 오픈 소스 시스템 제품군이라는 점에서 윈도우나 애플과 다르다. 즉, 누구나 수정하여 배포할 수 있다. Linux는 이 목록에서 가장 덜 알려져 있지만 무료이며 다양한 오픈 소스 버전에서 사용할 수 있다. 리눅스는 사용자 지정이 용이하고 사용 방법을 이해하는 사람들에게 다양한 옵션을 제공하기 때문에 인기가 있다. 운영 체제를 커스텀화하여 사용하는 방법을 알고 있다면 Linux를 선택하는 것이 좋다. 이러한 코딩 및 백엔드 작업에 관심이 있다면 Linux 시스템을 구입하여 조작하는 것이 좋다.

Vocabulary

likely : ~할 것 같은
normal : 정상적인
whether : ~인지 아닌지
get involved in : ~에 연루되다, ~에 몰두하다
routine operation : 일상적인 작업
several versions and updates : 여러 버전과 업데이트

popular : 인기있는

preloaded : 미리 설치된

release : 릴리스, 배포

improve : 향상시키다

users' experience : 사용자 경험

accessible : 접근 가능한

control panel : 제어판

desktop assistant : 데스크톱 어시스턴트

disk cleanup : 디스크 정리

prefer : 선호하다

compatible : 호환 가능한

head-to-head : 직접 대면하는, 정면 승부하는

competition : 경쟁

proprietary : 독점의

conceptualize : 개념화하다

tamper : 함부로 변경하다

tweak : 수정, 변경하다

launch : 출시하다

known : 알려진

beloved : 사랑받는

continually : 계속해서

variety : 여러 가지, 다양성

helpful resource : 유용한 리소스

relish : 좋아하다

instant connection : 즉각적인 연결

lack : 결핍

open source : 오픈소스

primary : 주된

popularity : 인기
alternative : 대안
exclusively : 독점적으로, 전용으로
integration : 통합
regular : 정기적인
appreciate : 인정하다
unique : 독특한
offer : 제공하다
in other words : 다시 말해서, 즉
modify and distribute : 수정하고 배포하다
least : 가장 덜
available : 사용가능한
customize : 고객이 원하는 대로 만들다(바꾸다), 주문 제작하다
customization : 주문에 따라 만듦, 커스텀화
ideal : 이상적인
manipulate : 조작하다

☞ 잠깐 쉬어가기 ....

여러분들이 쓰고 있는 소프트웨어를 생각해보세요. 여러분들의 노트북, 데스크탑에 깔린 프로그램이 제법 되지요? 문서 작성 소프트웨어, 디자인 및 코딩 관련된 소프트웨어, 그 때 그 때 상황에 필요한 소프트웨어를 설치하곤 합니다. 여러분은 어떤 OS를 쓰시나요? 윈도우, 맥OS, 리눅스가 대표적인 예입니다. 핸드폰에서는 안드로이드, iOS가 있죠. 간혹 원하는 프로그램을 쓰고 싶은데 여러분이 가지고 있지 않을 때, 오픈소스의 경우 구글링해서 다운받으면 되지만 오픈 소스가 아닌 것들은 저작권이 있기 때문에 구매를 해야 하죠. 가령, ms office를 개인이 구매한다고 가정하면, 연이나 월로 정액권을 끊어야하겠죠. 이렇게 소프트웨어를 사용할 때 반드시 고려해야하는 것은 저작권 문제입니다.

오픈 소스의 경우도 라이선스가 다양합니다. 만약 내가 오픈소스로 소프트웨어를 활용한다 하여도 상업적으로 이용하거나 배포할 때는 다양한 라이선스를 고려해야합니다. 크게 알아두어야 할 라이선스는 3가지 정도(GPL, LGPL, BSD)입니다.

GPL(General Public License)은 어떤 프로그램을 개발할 때, 외부에 사용하고자 한다면 프로그램 전체 소스코드를 무료로 오픈해야합니다. GPL에 비하여 완화된 라이선스는 LGPL(Lesser General Public License)로 LGPL 코드를 정적이나 동적 라이브러리로 사용하여 프로그램을 개발 및 판매, 배포할 때 개발한 소스코드를 공개하지 않아도 되는데요. 이때는 LGPL이라고 명시만 해주면 됩니다. 하지만 만약 이용하는 것에서 그치지 않고 수정하고 파생된 라이브러리를 개발하여 배포하게 되면 전체 코드를 공개해야합니다. 이것보다 더욱 완화된 라이선스는 BSD (Berkeley Software Distribution)입니다. BSD는 GPL, LGPL처럼 소스코드를 공개해야한다는 의무가 없습니다. 뿐만 아니라 상업 소프트웨어에서도 제한 없이 사용해도 됩니다. 따라서 오픈소스를 사용한다하여도 라이선스가 어떻게 되는지 알고 활용하는 것이 매우 중요하다고 할 수 있습니다.

연습문제

exercises

1~5. 다음 빈 칸에 들어가는 단어로 적절한 것을 넣으세요.

1. (   ) tells a computer how to function.

정답 : ______________________________

2. (   ) is a software program that serves as the interface between other applications and the hardware on a computer or mobile device.

정답 : ______________________________

3. The dominant general-purpose desktop operating system is (   ) with a market share of around 76.45%.

정답 : ______________________________

4.(   ) is the primary OS for Google mobile devices like smartphones and tablets.

정답 : ______________________________

5. The majority of software is written in (   ) programming languages due to the language being closer to natural human language as opposed to machine language.

정답 : ______________________________

6~10. 다음 It이 지칭하는 것을 영어로 쓰세요.

6. It is built into all major operating systems to allow computers to communicate over long distance networks.

정답 : ______________________________

7. It coordinates the activities and functions of the hardware and software.

정답 : ________________________________

8. It is the process of turning on the computer and powering up the system.

정답 : ________________________________

9. It manages all the drives installed in a computer, including hard drives, optical disk drives, and flash drives.

정답 : ________________________________

10. It is different from Windows and Apple in that it's not a proprietary software, but rather a family of open source systems.

정답 : ________________________________

연습문제 해답

1. Software
2. An operating system (OS)
3. Microsoft Windows
4. Android OS
5. high-level
6. TCP/IP
7. System software
8. Booting
9. Disk management
10. Linux

Chapter

06 Bitwise Operation

컴퓨터 구조와 연산

학습순서

【 INTRO 】

학창시절 수학 시간에 이진수, 십진수를 배웠던 기억나나요? 이진수는 0과 1만을 이용하죠. 그렇다면 우리가 일반적으로 쓰고 있는 수는 어떤 진수이죠? 바로 십진수죠. 가령, 십진수 3을 이진수로 바꾸면 11이 됩니다. 이진수 첫째자리 1은 십진수에서도 1, 이진수 둘째짜리는 1은 십진수에서는 2가 됩니다. 왜 갑자기 수학이 나왔을까요? 바로 컴퓨터가 이진수를 사용하기 때문입니다. 이진수 0, 1은 전기 신호를 의미로 전달하기에 가장 편리하기 때문입니다. 그렇다면 이번 과에서 비트에 대해서 알아보고, 비트 외에도 다른 단위에 대해서 알아보도록 하지요.

Do you remember when you were in school, you learned binary and decimal numbers in math class? Binary numbers use only 0 and 1. Then what kind of numbers are we using in general? That's a decimal number. For example, if you change decimal 3 to binary, it becomes 11. The first 1 in binary becomes 1 in decimal, and 1 in the second binary becomes 2 in decimal. Why did math suddenly come out? This is because the computer uses binary numbers. Binary numbers are very convenient for transmitting electrical signals in meaning. In this chapter, let's find out about bits and other units besides bits.

1) What's Bitwise Operation?[1] Bitwise Operation은 무엇인가?

In computer programming, a bitwise operation operates on a bit string, a bit array or a binary numeral (considered as a bit string) at the level of its individual bits. It is a fast and simple action, basic to the higher level arithmetic operations and directly supported by the processor. Most bitwise operations are presented as two-operand instructions where the result replaces one of the input operands.

On simple low-cost processors, typically, bitwise operations are substantially faster than division, several times faster than multiplication, and sometimes significantly faster than addition. While modern processors usually perform addition and multiplication just as fast as bitwise operations due to their longer instruction pipelines and other architectural design choices, bitwise operations do commonly use less power because of the reduced use of resources.

컴퓨터 프로그래밍에서 비트 연산은 개별 비트 수준에서 비트 문자열, 비트 배열 또는 이진수(비트 문자열로 간주됨)에 대해 작동한다. 빠르고 간단한 작업으로, 상위 수준의 산술 연산에 기본적이며 프로세서에서 직접 지원한다. 대부분의 비트 연산은 결과가 입력 피연산자 중 하나를 대체하는 2-연산자 명령으로 표시된다.

일반적으로 단순한 저가형 프로세서에서는 비트 단위 작업이 분할 작업보다 상당히

1 https://en.wikipedia.org/wiki/Bitwise_operation

빠르고, 곱셈 작업보다 몇 배 빠르며, 때로는 덧셈 작업보다 상당히 크게 빠르다. 최신 프로세서는 명령 파이프라인과 기타 아키텍처 설계 선택사항이 길기 때문에 대개 비트 연산만큼 빠르게 덧셈과 곱셈을 수행하지만, 비트 연산에서는 일반적으로 리소스 사용이 줄어들기 때문에 전력을 덜 사용한다.

Vocabulary

operation : 연산

operate : 작동하다

bit string : 비트 문자열

bit array : 비트배열

binary numeral : 이진수

individual : 각각의

arithmetic : 산술

bitwise operation : 비트연산

two-operand instructions : 2-연산자 명령

result : 결과

replace : 대체하다

operand : 피연산 함수

substantially : 상당히, 훨씬

division : 나누기, 분할

multiplication : 곱셈

significantly : 상당히

addition : 덧셈

modern processor : 최신 프로세서

just : 정확히, 딱

as fast as : ~만큼 빨리

due to : ~때문에

instruction pipelines : **명령 파이프라인**
architectural design choice : **아키텍처 설계 선택사항**
reduced : **줄인, 감소한**

2) Units of Information[2] 정보의 단위

In computing and telecommunications, a unit of information is the capacity of some standard data storage system or communication channel, used to measure the capacities of other systems and channels. In information theory, units of information are also used to measure the entropy of random variables and information contained in messages. he most commonly used units of data storage capacity are the bit, the capacity of a system that has only two states, and the byte (or octet), which is equivalent to eight bits.

컴퓨팅과 통신에서 정보 단위란 일부 표준 데이터 저장 시스템 또는 통신 채널의 용량으로, 다른 시스템과 채널의 용량을 측정하는 데 사용된다. 정보 이론에서 정보 단위는 랜덤 변수와 메시지에 포함된 정보의 엔트로피를 측정하는 데도 사용된다. 가장 일반적으로 사용되는 데이터 저장 용량 단위는 비트, 두 개의 상태만 있는 시스템의 용량 및 8비트에 해당하는 바이트(또는 옥텟)이다.

Bit[3]

Sometimes abbreviated as b (lowercase), bit is short for binary digit. It's a single unit of information with a value of either 0 or 1 (off or on, false or true, low or high). Eight bits make a byte, as shown in the picture. So, if you had

2 https://en.wikipedia.org/wiki/Units_of_information
3 https://www.computerhope.com/jargon/b/bit.htm

two bytes (word) it would be 16 bits (2 x 8=16), and 10 bytes would be 80 bits (10 x 8=80).

Byte[4]

A byte is a term first coined by Werner Buchholz in 1956 and later became more of a standard thanks to Bob Bemer and others. A byte is data equal to either seven or eight bits depending on whether or not it needs error correction (parity). You can think of a byte as one letter, for example, the letter 'h' is one byte or eight bits and the word 'hope' as four bytes or 32 bits (4*8).

When looking at the size of a file, a byte is the smallest measurement size listed in operating systems. However, because most files are bigger than 1,024 bytes (one kilobyte), most users see small files listed in kilobytes.

Nibble[5]

In computing, a nibble (occasionally nybble or nyble to match the spelling of byte) is a four-bit aggregation, or half an octet. It is also known as half-byte or tetrade. In a networking or telecommunication context, the nibble is often called a semi-octet, quadbit, or quartet. A nibble has sixteen (2^4) possible values. A nibble can be represented by a single hexadecimal digit (0-F) and called a hex digit.

비트

b(소문자)로 줄여 부르기도 하며, 비트는 이진수를 줄여서 부르기도 한다. 값이 0 또는 1(꺼짐 또는 켜짐, 거짓 또는 참, 낮음 또는 높음)인 단일 정보 단위다. 8비트는 1바이

4 https://www.computerhope.com/jargon/b/byte.htm

5 https://en.wikipedia.org/wiki/Nibble

트를 만든다. 따라서 2바이트(워드)가 있으면 16비트(2 x 8=16)고, 10바이트는 80비트(10 x 8=80)다.

바이트

바이트는 1956년 베르너 부흐홀츠가 처음 만든 용어로 이후에 밥 베머와 른 사람들 덕분에 표준이 됐다. 바이트는 오류 수정(패리티)이 필요한지 여부에 따라 7비트 또는 8비트에 해당하는 데이터다. 예를 들어, 'h'는 1바이트 또는 8비트이고 'hope'는 4바이트 또는 32비트(4*8)로 생각하면 된다.

파일 크기를 볼 때, 바이트는 운영 체제에 나열된 측정 크기 중 가장 작은 크기다. 그러나 대부분의 파일이 1,024바이트(1킬로바이트)보다 크기 때문에 대부분의 사용자는 작은 파일을 킬로바이트 단위로 볼 수 있다.

니블(Nibble)

컴퓨팅에서 니블(Byte의 철자와 매치하게 위해 nyble 또는 nybble이라고 함)은 4비트 집합 또는 옥텟(8비트)의 절반이다. 하프바이트 또는 테트레이드라고도 한다. 네트워킹이나 통신 맥락에서 니블은 종종 반옥텟, 쿼드비트 또는 쿼텟이라고 불린다. 니블에는 16(24)개의 가능한 값이 있다. 니블은 단일 16진수 자리(0-F)로 나타낼 수 있으며 16진수 자리라고 한다.

Vocabulary

abbreviated : 단축된
binary digit : 이진 숫자
value : 값
term : 용어
coined : 만들어진

standard : 표준, 기준
thanks to : ~때문에
depending on : ~에 따라
error correction : 오류수정
aggregation : 집합
telecommunication : 통신
context : 맥락
represent : 대표하다, 해당하다
hexadecimal : 16진법의

☞ 잠깐 쉬어가기 ....

여러분들의 컴퓨터 시스템은 32비트인가요? 64비트인가요? 위에 있는 사진이 나타내는 컴퓨터는 8비트 컴퓨터입니다. 80년대에는 아직 우리 사회에 컴퓨터가 보급되기 전이었습니다. 당시에 프로그래머였던 저희 아버지는 8비트 컴퓨터를 소장하셨고 저와 동생은 8비트 게임을 했던 추억이 돋습니다. 지금 생각해보아도 당시의 8비트 게임은 꽤 흥미로웠습니다. 최근 레트로 열풍이 불면서 8비트 컴퓨터가 중고시장에서 거래되는 경우가 왕왕 있습니다.

그리고 당시의 감성이 느껴지는 레트로 게임팩을 일반 쇼핑 사이트에서 쉽게 구매할 수 있습니다. mmorpg게임과는 다른 매력이지만 8비트 컴퓨터의 감성이 느껴집니다.

연습문제

exercises

1~5. 다음 빈 칸에 들어가는 단어로 적절한 것을 넣으세요.

1. Most bitwise operations are presented as (   ) instructions where the result replaces one of the input operands.

정답 : ____

2. Sometimes abbreviated as b (lowercase), (   ) is short for binary digit.

정답 : ____

3. If you had two bytes, it would be (   ) bits

정답 : ____

4. In computing, (   ) is a four-bit aggregation, or half an octet.

정답 : ____

5. You can think of (   ) as one letter,

정답 : ____

연습문제 해답

1. two-operand
2. bit
3. 16
4. a nibble
5. a byte

Chapter

07 Multimedia

멀티미디어

학습순서

1) Introduction
2) Major Characteristics
3) Categorization
4) Usage/Application
잠깐 쉬어가기
연습문제

【 INTRO 】

여러분 혹시 영화관에 가서 4DX로 영화 감상을 해본 적이 있나요? 요즘은 3D영화를 넘어 4D, 4DX 영화를 경험하며 수동적인 영화감상을 넘어 관객으로 하여금 실제 영화가 펼쳐지는 상황 안으로 들어가게 하게끔 느끼는 몰입감을 경험할 수 있습니다. 이처럼 멀티미디어 기술이 발달할수록 다양한 분야와 연계하여 우리 생활을 생동감 있게 바뀌고 있습니다. 학교에서는 멀티미디어 기술이 학생들의 참여도를 이끄는 데 사용되어지고 있습니다. 이번 과에서는 멀티미디어가 무엇이고 어떠한 특성을 갖으며 우리 생활 어떠한 곳에 적용될 수 있는 살펴보도록 하겠습니다.

Have you ever been to a movie theater and watched a movie in 4DX? Nowadays, you can experience 4D and 4DX movies beyond 3D movies, and you can experience immersion that makes the audience feel like they are in the actual situation of the movie, beyond passive movie viewing. As multimedia technology develops, it is changing our lives in a lively way by linking it to various fields. In schools, multimedia technology is being used to develop traditional teaching methods to engage students. In this chapter, we will explore what multimedia is, what characteristics it has, and where it can be applied in our lives.

1) Introduction[1] 개요

Multimedia is a form of communication that combines different content forms such as text, audio, images, animations, or video into a single presentation, in contrast to traditional mass media, such as printed material or audio recordings. Popular examples of multimedia include video podcasts, audio slideshows and Animated videos.

Multimedia can be recorded for playback on computers, laptops, smartphones, and other electronic devices, either on demand or in real time (streaming). In the early years of multimedia, the term "rich media" was synonymous with interactive multimedia. Over time, hypermedia extensions brought multimedia to the World Wide Web.

멀티미디어는 텍스트, 오디오, 이미지, 애니메이션 또는 비디오와 같은 다양한 콘텐츠 형식을 하나의 프리젠테이션으로 결합하는 통신 형태로서 인쇄물이나 오디오 녹음과 같은 전통적인 대중 매체와 대조된다. 널리 사용되는 멀티미디어의 예로는 비디오 팟캐스트, 오디오 슬라이드쇼 및 애니메이션 비디오가 있다.

멀티미디어를 컴퓨터, 노트북, 스마트폰 및 기타 전자 기기에 온디맨드 또는 실시간(스트리밍) 재생용으로 녹화할 수 있다. 멀티미디어 초기에는 "리치 미디어"라는 용어는 쌍방향 멀티미디어와 동의어였다. 시간이 지나면서 하이퍼미디어 확장은 멀티미디어를 월드 와이드 웹으로 가져왔다.

1 https://en.wikipedia.org/wiki/Multimedia#Multimedia

Vocabulary

combine : 결합하다
form : 종류, 유형
such as : ~와 같은
in contrast to : ~와 대조를 이루어
traditional : 전통적인
mass media : 대중매체
printed material : 인쇄물
audio recordings : 오디오 녹음
animated video : 애니메이션 비디오
be recorded : 녹음되다, 녹화되다
playback : 재생
real time : 실시간
on demand : 온디맨드, 언제든지, 초 맞춤화 서비스
synonymous : 동의어
interactive multimedia : 쌍방향 멀티미디어

2) Major Characteristics[2] 주요특성

Multimedia presentations may be viewed by person on stage, projected, transmitted, or played locally with a media player. A broadcast may be a live or recorded multimedia presentation. Broadcasts and recordings can be either analog or digital electronic media technology. Digital online multimedia may be downloaded or streamed. Streaming multimedia may be live or on-demand.

2 https://en.wikipedia.org/wiki/Multimedia#Major_characteristics

Multimedia games and simulations may be used in a physical environment with special effects, with multiple users in an online network, or locally with an offline computer, game system, or simulator.

The various formats of technological or digital multimedia may be intended to enhance the users' experience, for example to make it easier and faster to convey information. Or in entertainment or art, to transcend everyday experience.

멀티미디어 프레젠테이션은 미디어 플레이어로 무대에서 사람이 보거나, 투사하거나, 전송하거나, 로컬로 재생할 수 있다. 방송은 라이브 또는 녹화된 멀티미디어 프레젠테이션일 수 있다. 방송 및 녹화는 아날로그나 디지털 전자 미디어 기술일 수 있다. 디지털 온라인 멀티미디어는 다운로드하거나 스트리밍할 수 있다. 스트리밍 멀티미디어는 라이브 또는 온디맨드 방식일 수 있다.

멀티미디어 게임 및 시뮬레이션은 특수 효과가 있는 물리적 환경, 온라인 네트워크에 여러 사용자가 있거나 오프라인 컴퓨터, 게임 시스템 또는 시뮬레이터가 있는 로컬 환경에서 사용할 수 있다.

기술 또는 디지털 멀티미디어의 다양한 형식은 예를 들어 정보를 더 쉽고 빠르게 전달하기 위해 사용자의 경험을 향상시키기 위한 것일 수 있다. 혹은 오락이나 예술에서, 일상의 경험을 초월하기 위한 것일 수 있다.

Enhanced levels of interactivity are made possible by combining multiple forms of media content. Online multimedia is increasingly becoming object-oriented and data-driven, enabling applications with collaborative end-user innovation and personalization on multiple forms of content over time.
Examples of these range from multiple forms of content on Web sites like photo galleries with both images (pictures) and title (text) user-updated, to

simulations whose co-efficients, events, illustrations, animations or videos are modifiable, allowing the multimedia "experience" to be altered without reprogramming.

In addition to seeing and hearing, haptic technology enables virtual objects to be felt. Emerging technology involving illusions of taste and smell may also enhance the multimedia experience.

향상된 상호 작용 수준은 다양한 형태의 미디어 콘텐츠를 결합함으로써 가능하다. 온라인 멀티미디어는 점차 객체 지향적이고 데이터 중심적이 되어가고 있으며, 시간이 지남에 따라 다양한 형태의 콘텐츠에서 최종 사용자의 협업 혁신과 개인화를 맞춘 애플리케이션을 가능하게 한다.

이러한 예로는 이미지(그림)와 제목(텍스트)이 모두 업데이트된 사진 갤러리와 같은 웹사이트의 다양한 콘텐츠 형식에서부터 계수, 이벤트, 일러스트, 애니메이션 또는 비디오가 수정 가능한 시뮬레이션에 이르기까지 다양하며, 이를 통해 멀티미디어 "경험"을 재프로그래밍하지 않고도 변경할 수 있다. 촉각 기술은 보고 들을 수 있을 뿐 아니라 가상물체를 느낄 수 있게 해준다. 맛과 후각에 대한 환상을 수반하는 신기술 또한 멀티미디어 경험을 향상시킬 수 있다.

Vocabulary

multimedia presentation : 멀티미디어 연출
view : 보다
on stage : 무대에 서서, 무대 위의
project : 투사하다
transmit : 전송하다
play : 재생하다

locally : 가까이에, 국부적으로, 지방으로
broadcast : 방송
live or recorded : 라이브 또는 녹화된
electronic : 전자의
physical environment : 물리적인 환경
special effects : 특수 효과
various formats : 다양한 형식
technological : 기술의
be intended to : ~의 의도가 있다
enhance : 높이다
convey : 전달하다
transcend : 초월하다
interactivity : 상호작용
object-oriented : 객체 지향적인
data-driven : 데이터 중심적인, 데이터에 따라 처리를 하는
collaborative : 공동의, 협업적
end-user : 최종 사용자
innovation : 혁신
personalization : 개인화
range : 범위, 다양성
user-updated : 사용자로부터 업데이트된
coefficient : 계수
modifiable : 변경할 수 있는
haptic : 촉각의
in addition to : ~일 뿐만 아니라
virtual object : 가상의 물체
emerging : 최근에 만들어진
involve : 포함하다

3) Categorization[3] 분류

Multimedia may be broadly divided into linear and non-linear categories: linear active content progresses often without any navigational control for the viewers such as a cinema presentation; non-linear uses interactivity to control progress as with a video game or self-paced computer-based training. Hypermedia is an example of non-linear content.

Multimedia presentations can be live or recorded: a recorded presentation may allow interactivity via a navigation system; a live multimedia presentation may allow interactivity via an interaction with the presenter or performer.

멀티미디어는 선형 및 비선형 범주로 크게 나눌 수 있다. 선형 활성 콘텐츠는 종종 영화관 프레젠테이션과 같은 시청자를 위한 탐색 제어 없이 진행된다. 비선형 콘텐츠는 비디오 게임이나 자기 페이스에 맞는 컴퓨터 기반 훈련과 같이 상호 작용을 사용하여 진행 상황을 제어한다. 하이퍼미디어는 비선형 콘텐츠의 한 예이다.

멀티미디어 프리젠테이션은 실시간 또는 녹화할 수 있다. 기록된 프리젠테이션은 내비게이션 시스템을 통해 대화할 수 있다. 라이브 멀티미디어 프리젠테이션은 발표자 또는 퍼포머(수행자)와의 상호 작용을 통해 쌍방향 참가를 할 수 있다.

Vocabulary

broadly : 크게, 넓게

be divided into : ~로 나누어지다

linear and non-linear categories : 선형과 비선형 범주

---

3 https://en.wikipedia.org/wiki/Multimedia#Characteristics

linear active content : 선형 활성 콘텐츠
progress : 진행하다, 나아가다
navigational : 항해의
self-paced : 자기 진도에 맞춰 학습할 수 있는
via : ~를 통해서

4) Usage/Application[4] 사용/적용

Multimedia finds its application in various areas including, but not limited to, advertisements, art, education, entertainment, engineering, medicine, mathematics, business, scientific research and spatial temporal applications. Several examples are as follows:

① Entertainment and fine arts

Multimedia is heavily used in the entertainment industry, especially to develop special effects in movies and animations (VFX, 3D animation, etc.). Multimedia games are a popular pastime and are software programs available either as CD-ROMs or online. Video games class as multimedia, as such games meld animation, audio, and, most importantly, interactivity, to allow the player an immersive experience. While video games can vary in terms of animation style or audio type or even lack thereof, the element of interactivity makes them a striking example of interactive multimedia. Interactive multimedia defines multimedia applications that allow users to actively participate instead of just sitting by as passive recipients of information.

4 https://en.wikipedia.org/wiki/Multimedia#Usage/application

In the arts there are multimedia artists, whose minds are able to blend techniques using different media that in some way incorporates interaction with the viewer. Another approach entails the creation of multimedia that can be displayed in a traditional fine arts arena, such as an art gallery. Although multimedia display material may be volatile, the survivability of the content is as strong as any traditional media. Digital recording material may be just as durable and infinitely reproducible with perfect copies every time.

멀티미디어는 광고, 예술, 교육, 엔터테인먼트, 엔지니어링, 의학, 수학, 비즈니스, 과학 연구, 공간 시간 응용 등 다양한 분야에서 응용되고 있다. 몇 가지 예는 다음과 같다.

엔터테인먼트 및 미술

멀티미디어는 엔터테인먼트 산업, 특히 영화 및 애니메이션(VFX, 3D 애니메이션 등)의 특수 효과를 개발하는 데 많이 사용되고 있다. 멀티미디어 게임은 인기 있는 오락이며 CD-ROM이나 온라인으로 사용할 수 있는 소프트웨어 프로그램이다. 비디오 게임 클래스는 애니메이션, 오디오, 그리고 가장 중요한 상호작용을 융합하여 플레이어가 몰입할 수 있도록 한다. 비디오 게임은 애니메이션 스타일이나 오디오 유형에 따라 다양하거나 심지어 그 유형도 다양하지만, 상호작용의 요소는 비디오 게임을 대화형 멀티미디어의 두드러진 예로 만든다. 인터랙티브 멀티미디어는 사용자가 단순히 방관하지 않고 능동적으로 참여할 수 있는 멀티미디어 애플리케이션을 정보의 수동 수신자로 정의한다.

예술에는 멀티미디어 아티스트들이 있는데 그들의 마음은 어떤 식으로든 시청자들과의 상호작용을 포함하여 다른 매체를 사용하여 기술을 혼합할 수 있다. 미술관과 같은 전통 미술무대에서 전시할 수 있는 멀티미디어를 만드는 것도 방법이다. 멀티미디어 디스플레이 소재는 휘발성이 강할 수 있지만 콘텐츠의 생존성은 기존 미디어

못지않다. 디지털 레코딩 재료는 내구성이 뛰어나고 매회 완벽한 복사본으로 무한정 재현할 수 있다.

Vocabulary

application : 응용
various areas : 다양한 분야
limited : 제한된
spatial temporal application : 공간 시간 응용
fine arts : 미술, 순수 미술
heavily : 아주 많이
special effects : 특수 효과
popular pastime : 인기있는 취미
meld : 혼합하다
most importantly : 가장 중요하게
immersive : 몰입하는
vary : 서로 다르다
in terms of : ~의 면에서
thereof : (앞에 언급된) 그것의
striking : 두드러진
define : 정의하다
passive recipient : 수동 수신자
arts : 예술
blend : 혼합하다
incorporate : 포함하다, 통합하다
approach : 접근
entail : 수반하다
arena : 무대

volatile : 휘발성의
survivability : 생존성
durable : 내구성이 있는
infinitely : 무한히, 대단히
reproducible : 재현할 수 있는

② Engineering

Software engineers may use multimedia in computer simulations for anything from entertainment to training such as military or industrial training. Multimedia for software interfaces are often done as a collaboration between creative professionals and software engineers. Multimedia helps expand the teaching practices that can be found in engineering to allow for more innovated methods to not only educated future engineers, but to help evolve the scope of understanding of where multimedia can be used in specialized engineer careers like software engineers.

Multimedia is also allowing major car manufactures, such as Ford, and General Motors, to expand the design, and safety standards of their cars. By using a game engine and VR glasses, these companies are able to test the safety features, and the design of the car, before a prototype is even made. Building a car virtually reduces the time it takes to produce new vehicles, cutting down on the time needed to test designs, and allowing the designers to make changes in real time. It also reduces expenses, since with a virtual car making real world prototypes is no longer needed.

엔지니어링

소프트웨어 엔지니어는 엔터테인먼트에서부터 군사 또는 산업 훈련과 같은 훈련에 이르기까지 컴퓨터 시뮬레이션에 멀티미디어를 사용할 수 있다. 소프트웨어 인터페이스용 멀티미디어는 종종 크리에이티브 전문가와 소프트웨어 엔지니어 간의 협업으로 이루어진다. 멀티미디어는 엔지니어링에서 찾을 수 있는 교육 관행을 확장하여 더욱 혁신적인 방법을 교육받은 미래 엔지니어뿐만 아니라 소프트웨어 엔지니어처럼 전문화된 엔지니어 경력에서 멀티미디어가 사용될 수 있는 이해 범위를 넓히는 데 도움이 된다.

멀티미디어는 또한 포드나 제너럴 모터스와 같은 주요 자동차 제조업체들이 자동차의 디자인과 안전 기준을 확장할 수 있도록 하고 있다. 이 회사들은 게임 엔진과 VR 안경을 사용하여 시제품이 만들어지기 전에 자동차의 안전 기능과 디자인을 테스트할 수 있다. 자동차를 만들면 신차 생산에 걸리는 시간이 사실상 단축되고 디자인 테스트에 필요한 시간도 단축되며 설계자가 실시간으로 변경할 수 있다. 가상 자동차가 더 이상 실제 프로토타입을 만들 필요가 없기 때문에 비용도 절감된다.

Vocabulary

military : 군사
collaboration : 공동작업, 협력
professional : 전문직 종사자
practice : 관행
evolve : 진화하다, 발달하다
scope of understanding : 이해의 범위
specialized engineer career : 전문 엔지니어 커리어
major car manufacture : 주요 자동차 제조사
safety feature : 안전 특성

virtually : 사실상
reduce : 줄이다
vehicle : 차량, 자동차
expense : 비용

③ Virtual reality

Virtual reality (VR) is a simulated experience that can be similar to or completely different from the real world. Applications of virtual reality include entertainment (e.g. video games), education (e.g. medical or military training) and business (e.g. virtual meetings). Other distinct types of VR-style technology include augmented reality and mixed reality, sometimes referred to as extended reality or XR.

One may distinguish between two types of VR; immersive VR and text-based networked VR (also known as "Cyberspace"). The immersive VR changes your view, when you move your head. While both VRs are appropriate for training, Cyberspace is preferred for distance learning. In some cases these two types are even complementary to each other. This page mainly focuses on the immersive VR.

Currently, standard virtual reality systems use either virtual reality headsets or multi-projected environments to generate realistic images, sounds and other sensations that simulate a user's physical presence in a virtual environment. A person using virtual reality equipment is able to look around the artificial world, move around in it, and interact with virtual features or items.

The effect is commonly created by VR headsets consisting of a head-mounted display with a small screen in front of the eyes, but can also be created through specially designed rooms with multiple large screens. Virtual reality typically incorporates auditory and video feedback, but may also allow other types of sensory and force feedback through haptic technology.

VR(가상현실)은 실제 환경과 비슷하거나 완전히 다를 수 있는 시뮬레이션된 경험이다. 가상현실의 적용 분야에는 엔터테인먼트(예: 비디오 게임), 교육(예: 의료 또는 군사 훈련) 및 비즈니스(예: 가상 회의)가 포함된다. VR 스타일의 다른 뚜렷한 기술로는 증강 현실과 혼합 현실(확장 현실 또는 XR이라고도 함)이 있다.

몰입형 VR과 텍스트 기반 네트워크 VR("Cyberspace"라고도 함)의 두 가지 VR 유형을 구별할 수 있다. 몰입형 VR은 머리를 움직이면 시야가 바뀐다. 두 VR 모두 훈련에는 적합하지만 원격 학습에는 사이버 공간이 선호된다. 경우에 따라서는 이러한 두 유형이 서로 보완되기도 한다. 이 페이지는 주로 몰입형 VR을 중점적으로 다룬다.

현재 표준 가상현실 시스템은 가상현실 헤드셋 또는 다중 투영 환경을 사용하여 가상 환경에서 사용자의 물리적 존재를 시뮬레이션 하는 사실적인 이미지, 소리 및 기타 감각을 생성한다. 가상현실 장비를 사용하는 사람은 인공세계를 둘러보고, 그 안에서 움직이고, 가상 기능이나 아이템과 상호작용할 수 있다.

헤드마운트 디스플레이와 눈앞의 작은 화면으로 구성된 VR 헤드셋이 공통적으로 나타나지만 대형 스크린이 여러 개 있는 특수실을 통해서도 효과를 낼 수 있다. 가상현실은 일반적으로 청각 및 비디오 피드백을 포함하지만 촉각 기술을 통해 다른 유형의 감각 및 힘 피드백을 허용할 수도 있다.

Vocabulary

similar : 비슷한
completely different : 완전 다른
augmented reality : 증강 현실
mixed reality : 혼합 현실
extended reality : 확장 현실
immersive VR and text-based networked VR : 몰입형 VR과 텍스트 기반 네트워크형 VR
appropriate for training : 훈련에 적합한
distance learning : 원격 학습
complementary : 상호 보완적인
currently : 현재
multi-projected environments : 다중 투영 환경
realistic : 사실적인
sensation : 감각
physical presence : 물리적 존재
equipment : 장비

④ Augmented reality

Augmented reality (AR) is an interactive experience of a real-world environment where the objects that reside in the real world are enhanced by computer-generated perceptual information, sometimes across multiple sensory modalities, including visual, auditory, haptic, somatosensory and olfactory. AR can be defined as a system that incorporates three basic features: a combination of real and virtual worlds, real-time interaction, and accurate 3D registration of virtual and real objects.

The overlaid sensory information can be constructive (i.e. additive to the natural environment), or destructive (i.e. masking of the natural environment). This experience is seamlessly interwoven with the physical world such that it is perceived as an immersive aspect of the real environment. In this way, augmented reality alters one's ongoing perception of a real-world environment, whereas virtual reality completely replaces the user's real-world environment with a simulated one.

Augmented reality is related to two largely synonymous terms: mixed reality and computer-mediated reality. The primary value of augmented reality is the manner in which components of the digital world blend into a person's perception of the real world, not as a simple display of data, but through the integration of immersive sensations, which are perceived as natural parts of an environment.

증강현실

증강현실(AR)은 컴퓨터가 만들어낸 지각 정보에 의해 현실 세계에 존재하는 물체가 때로는 시각, 청각, 촉각, 체감각, 후각을 포함한 여러 감각 양식에 걸쳐 향상되는 실제 환경의 대화형 경험이다. AR은 실제와 가상의 조합, 실시간 상호 작용, 가상과 실제 개체의 정확한 3D 등록 등 세 가지 기본 기능을 통합하는 시스템으로 정의할 수 있다.

중첩된 감각 정보는 건설적(즉, 자연 환경에 부가적)이거나 파괴적(즉, 자연 환경의 변장)일 수 있다. 이러한 경험은 실제 환경의 몰입감 있는 측면으로 인식될 수 있도록 물리적 환경과 완벽하게 연계되어 있다. 이러한 방식으로 증강 현실은 실제 환경에 대한 지속적인 인식을 바꾸는 반면, 가상현실은 사용자의 실제 환경을 시뮬레이션 환경으로 완전히 대체한다.

증강 현실은 크게 동의어로 쓰이는 두 가지 용어, 즉 혼합 현실과 컴퓨터 매개 현실과 관련이 있다. 증강현실의 1차적 가치는 디지털 세계의 구성요소가 단순히 데이터를 표시하는 것이 아니라 환경의 자연스러운 부분으로 인식되는 몰입감(immorgive sensions)의 통합을 통해 사람의 실제 세계 인식에 혼합되는 방식이다.

The earliest functional AR systems that provided immersive mixed reality experiences for users were invented in the early 1990s, starting with the Virtual Fixtures system developed at the U.S. Air Force's Armstrong Laboratory in 1992. Commercial augmented reality experiences were first introduced in entertainment and gaming businesses. Subsequently, augmented reality applications have spanned commercial industries such as education, communications, medicine, and entertainment. In education, content may be accessed by scanning or viewing an image with a mobile device or by using markerless AR techniques.

Augmented reality is used to enhance natural environments or situations and offer perceptually enriched experiences. With the help of advanced AR technologies (e.g. adding computer vision, incorporating AR cameras into smartphone applications and object recognition) the information about the surrounding real world of the user becomes interactive and digitally manipulated. Information about the environment and its objects is overlaid on the real world. This information can be virtual.

Augmented Reality is any experience which is artificial and which adds to the already existing reality. or real, e.g. seeing other real sensed or measured information such as electromagnetic radio waves overlaid in exact alignment with where they actually are in space. Augmented reality also has a lot of potential in the gathering and sharing of tacit knowledge.

Augmentation techniques are typically performed in real time and in semantic contexts with environmental elements. Immersive perceptual information is sometimes combined with supplemental information like scores over a live video feed of a sporting event. This combines the benefits of both augmented reality technology and heads up display technology (HUD).

사용자에게 몰입감 넘치는 혼합현실 경험을 제공하는 최초의 기능적 AR 시스템은 1992년 미 공군 암스트롱 연구소에서 개발한 버츄얼 픽스쳐 시스템을 시작으로 1990년대 초에 발명됐다. 상업적인 증강현실 경험은 엔터테인먼트 및 게임 사업에 처음 도입되었다. 그 후, 증강현실 애플리케이션은 교육, 통신, 의학, 엔터테인먼트 등 상업 산업에 광범위하게 적용되었다. 교육에서는 모바일 기기로 영상을 스캔하거나 보거나 마커 없는 AR 기법을 사용하여 콘텐츠에 액세스할 수 있다.

증강현실은 자연환경이나 상황을 개선하고 지각적으로 풍부한 경험을 제공하기 위해 사용된다. 첨단 AR 기술(예: 컴퓨터 비전 추가, AR 카메라 스마트폰 애플리케이션 및 객체 인식에 통합)의 도움으로 사용자의 주변 실제 환경에 대한 정보가 대화형 및 디지털 방식으로 조작된다. 환경과 환경에 대한 정보가 실제 환경에 중첩되어 있다. 이 정보는 가상일 수 있다.

증강 현실은 인위적이고 이미 존재하는 현실을 더하는 모든 경험이다. 또는 실제, 예를 들어 전자기파와 같이 실제 감지되거나 측정된 다른 정보(예: 실제 공간과 정확히 일치)가 중첩되는 것을 볼 수 있다. 증강현실은 또한 암묵적 지식을 모으고 공유하는 데 많은 잠재력을 가지고 있다.

증강 기법은 일반적으로 환경 요소와 함께 실시간 및 의미적 맥락에서 수행된다. 몰입식 지각 정보는 스포츠 이벤트의 실시간 비디오 피드에서 점수와 같은 보충 정보와 결합되기도 한다. 이는 증강현실 기술과 헤드업 디스플레이 기술(HUD)의 장점을 결합한 것이다.

Vocabulary

reside : 살다, 거주하다

enhance : 향상시키다

generate : 발생시키다

perceptual : 지각의

sensory : 감각의

modality : 양식

visual, auditory, haptic, somatosensory and olfactory : 시각, 청각, 촉각, 체감각, 후각의

3D registration : 3D 정합(서로 다른 영상을 변형하여 하나의 좌표계에 나타내는 처리기법)

overlaid sensory information : 중첩된 감각 정보

constructive : 건설적

additive: 부가된, 덧셈의, 첨가물

destructive : 파괴적인

masking : 덮어 가리기, 변장, 마스킹(사진의 색체/농담 등을 수정)

seamlessly : 균일하게

interweave : 섞어 짜다, 혼합하다, 뒤섞이다

perceive : 인지하다

immersive aspect : 몰입감있는 측면

alter : 바꾸다

ongoing perception : 지속적인 인식

whereas : ~하는 반면

completely : 완전히

replace : 대체하다

synonymous term : 동의어

mixed reality and computer-mediated reality : 혼합 현실과 컴퓨터 매개 현실

primary value : 주요 가치

manner : 방식

immersive sensations : 몰입감

functional : 기능적인

invent : 발명하다

commercial : 상업적인

subsequently : 그 뒤에

span : 걸쳐 이어지다. 가로지르다

markerless : 마커 없는

enriched : 풍성한

advanced : 첨단의

surrounding : 주위의

overlay : 덮어씌우다(overlaid 과거분사)

existing reality : 존재하는 현실

electromagnetic : 전자기의

radio wave : 전파

potential : 잠재력

gathering : 수집

tacit : 암묵적인

semantic context : 의미적 맥락

immersive perceptual information : 몰입식 지각 정보

supplemental : 보충의

benefit : 이득

☞ 잠깐 쉬어가기 ....

2020년 상반기에 시작되어 21세기 이후 전 지구촌을 집어삼킨 최악의 전염병 중 하나로 기록되는 코로나바이러스 감염증 19(COVID-19)는 2023년 5월 5일 국제적 공중 보건 비상사태가 해제되었습니다. 비상 사태가 선언된지 3년 4개월 동안 공식적으로 6억 8700만명 이상의 확진자와 약 690만 명의 사망자가 발생했고, 약 133억 회의 백신이 접종되었다 합니다.

코로나 팬데믹에 의해서 우리의 삶은 그 이전과의 삶과 달라지게 되었습니다. 많은 분야에서 비대면 플랫폼이 정착되면서 새로운 라이프 스타일을 채택하게 되었습니다. 집 안에서 외부 활동을 즐기는 방법도 다양해졌고, 산업적으로는 배달앱과 라이브 커머스의 성장, 온라인 교육 플랫폼의 정착, IT업계의 성장이 도드라졌습니다.

헬스센터에 가서 다른 사람들과 부대끼며 운동하는 대신 VR콘텐츠를 통하여 자신에게 맞는 운동 루틴을 설정하여 실제처럼 운동할 수 있습니다. 집콕 여행을 통하여 세계 모든 나라의 명소 및 익스트림 스포츠를 경험할 수도 있습니다. 늦은 시간에도 언제든지 집 문 앞까지 아메리카노 한자에서부터 맛있는 식당 요리, 고급 레스토랑의 정통 코스요리까지 손 쉽게 시켜먹을 수 있게 되었습니다. 늦은 밤 슈퍼에 가서 장을 보는 대신 신선 식품을 새벽 배송을 통하여 구매하여 시원한 우유 한잔을 들이킬 수도 있습니다. 팬데믹 이후, 우리는 그 어떤 때도 경험하지 못한 새로운 세상에서 살아가고 있습니다.

연습문제

exercises

1~5. 다음 빈 칸에 들어가는 단어로 적절한 것을 넣으세요.

1. Popular examples of ( ) include video podcasts, audio slideshows and Animated videos.

정답 : ______________________________

2. The various formats of technological or digital multimedia may be intended to enhance ( ), for example to make it easier and faster to convey information.

정답 : ______________________________

3. Multimedia is heavily used in ( ), especially to develop special effects in movies and animations (VFX, 3D animation, etc.).

정답 : ______________________________

4. Augmented reality is related to two largely synonymous terms: (①) and (②).

정답 : ______________________________

5. ( ) may use multimedia in computer simulations for anything from entertainment to training such as military or industrial training.

정답 : ______________________________

6~10. 다음 It이 지칭하는 것을 영어로 쓰세요.

6. It may be a live or recorded multimedia presentation.

정답 : ______________________________

7. It is a simulated experience that can be similar to or completely different from the real world.

정답 : ______________________________

8. It can be defined as a system that incorporates three basic features: a combination of real and virtual worlds, real-time interaction, and accurate 3D registration of virtual and real objects.

정답 : ______________________________

9. It may allow interactivity via an interaction with the presenter or performer.

정답 : ______________________________

10. It enables virtual objects to be felt.

정답 : ______________________________

연습문제 해답

1. multimedia
2. the users' experience
3. the entertainment industry
4. ① mixed reality, ② computer-mediated reality
5. Software engineers
6. A broadcast
7. Virtual reality (VR)
8. AR
9. A live multimedia presentation
10. Haptic technology

Chapter 08

Database
데이터베이스

학습순서

1) Introduction
2) Terminology
3) Use Cases
4) Types of Databases
5) What is Structured Query Language (SQL)?
6) Evolution of the Database

잠깐 쉬어가기

연습문제

【 INTRO 】

모든 회사에서는 고객의 데이터 관리에 대하여 왜 이렇게 신경을 쓸까요? 바로 잘된 데이터 관리는 그 회사의 자원을 효율적으로 관리하여 매출 증대로 이어지기 때문입니다. 가령, 저는 주말마다 어떠한 특정 사이트에 들어가서 컴퓨터 관련 기기를 사곤 합니다. 회사 입장에서 이러한 고객의 구매패턴이 인지된다면 주말에 포인트 적립 2배 이벤트나 관련 기기 할인행사를 할 수 있을 것이고 이는 고객의 구매율을 높이는 방법이 될 수 있습니다. 잘된 데이터관리는 회사의 상태를 정확하게 파악하고 고객들을 하여금 충성심을 갖도록 만들게 하는 전략 중에 하나입니다. 이번 과에서는 데이터베이스가 무엇이고 어떤 유형이 있는지 살펴보도록 하겠습니다.

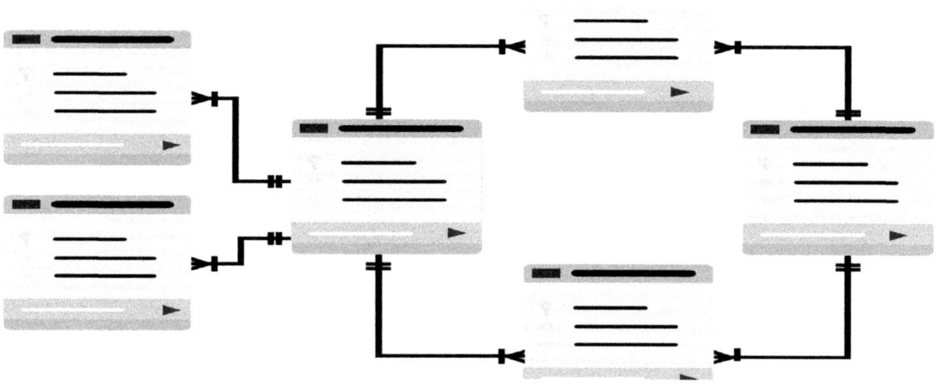

Why are all companies so concerned about managing customer data? This is because good data management efficiently manages the company's resources, leading to increased sales. For example, suppose I visited a purchase site every weekend and boought a computer-related device. If my purchase pattern was recognized on the site, the company would double the points over the weekend and it would be a way to increase the customer's purchase rate. Good data management is one of the strategies that accurately identifies the company and increases customer loyalty. In this chapter, we will learn what databases are and what types of databases they are.

1) Introduction[1] 개요

In computing, a database is an organized collection of data stored and accessed electronically from a computer system. Where databases are more complex they are often developed using formal design and modeling techniques.

The database management system (DBMS) is the software that interacts with end users, applications, and the database itself to capture and analyze the data. The DBMS software additionally encompasses the core facilities provided to administer the database. The sum total of the database, the DBMS and the associated applications can be referred to as a "database system". Often the term "database" is also used to loosely refer to any of the DBMS, the database system or an application associated with the database.

Computer scientists may classify database-management systems according to the database models that they support. Relational databases became dominant in the 1980s. These model data as rows and columns in a series of tables, and the vast majority use SQL for writing and querying data. In the 2000s, non-relational databases became popular, referred to as NoSQL because they use different query languages.

컴퓨팅에서 데이터베이스는 컴퓨터 시스템에서 전자적으로 저장되고 액세스되는 데이터의 조직화된 집합이다. 데이터베이스가 더 복잡한 경우 공식 설계 및 모델링 기법을 사용하여 개발하는 경우가 많다.

데이터베이스 관리 시스템(DBMS)은 최종 사용자, 응용프로그램 및 데이터베이스

1 https://en.wikipedia.org/wiki/Database

자체와 상호 작용하여 데이터를 캡처하고 분석하는 소프트웨어이다. DBMS 소프트웨어는 데이터베이스 관리를 위해 제공되는 핵심 기능을 추가로 포함한다. 데이터베이스, DBMS 및 관련 응용프로그램의 합계를 "데이터베이스 시스템"이라고 할 수 있다. 또한 "데이터베이스"라는 용어는 자주 DBMS, 데이터베이스 시스템 또는 데이터베이스와 관련된 응용프로그램을 지칭하는 데 대략 사용된다.

컴퓨터 과학자들은 그들이 지원하는 데이터베이스 모델에 따라 데이터베이스 관리 시스템을 분류할 수 있다. 관계형 데이터베이스는 1980년대에 주로 쓰였다. 이러한 모델 데이터는 일련의 테이블에서 행과 열로 사용되며 대다수가 SQL을 사용하여 데이터를 쓰고 쿼리를 한다. 2000년대에 서로 다른 쿼리 언어를 사용하기 때문에 NoSQL로 불리는 비관계형 데이터베이스는 인기 있게 되었다.

Vocabulary

organized collection : 조직화된 집합
electronically : 전자적으로
more complex : 더 복잡한
formal : 공식적인, 정식의
end user : 최종사용자
capture and analyze : 캡처하고 분석하다
additionally : 추가로
encompass : 포함하다, 아우르다
core facility : 핵심 기능
administer : 관리하다
associated application : 관련된 응용프로그램/애플리케이션
term : 용어
loosely : 느슨하게
classify : 분류하다

relational databases : 관계형 데이터베이스
dominant : 우세의, 주된
row : 행(가로줄)
column : 열(세로줄)
a series of : 일련의
vast majority : 대다수

2) Terminology[2] 용어

Formally, a "database" refers to a set of related data and the way it is organized. Access to this data is usually provided by a "database management system" (DBMS) consisting of an integrated set of computer software that allows users to interact with one or more databases and provides access to all of the data contained in the database (although restrictions may exist that limit access to particular data). The DBMS provides various functions that allow entry, storage and retrieval of large quantities of information and provides ways to manage how that information is organized.

Because of the close relationship between them, the term "database" is often used casually to refer to both a database and the DBMS used to manipulate it.

형식적으로 "데이터베이스"는 관련 데이터 집합과 데이터 구성 방식을 나타낸다. 이 데이터에 대한 액세스는 일반적으로 사용자가 하나 이상의 데이터베이스와 상호 작용하고 데이터베이스에 포함된 모든 데이터에 대한 액세스를 제공하는 통합 컴퓨터 소프트웨어 집합으로 구성된 "데이터베이스 관리 시스템"(DBMS)에 의해 제공된다(특정 데이터에 대한 액세스를 제한하는 제한 사항이 있을 수 있음). DBMS는 대량의 정보를 입력, 저장

2 https://en.wikipedia.org/wiki/Database#Terminology_and_overview

및 검색할 수 있는 다양한 기능을 제공하며, 정보의 구성 방식을 관리할 수 있는 방법을 제공한다.

두 데이터베이스 간의 가까운 관계 때문에 "데이터베이스"라는 용어는 데이터베이스와 데이터베이스를 조작하는 데 사용되는 DBMS를 모두 지칭하는 데 종종 사용된다.

Existing DBMSs provide various functions that allow management of a database and its data which can be classified into four main functional groups:
Data definition – Creation, modification and removal of definitions that define the organization of the data.
Update – Insertion, modification, and deletion of the actual data.
Retrieval – Providing information in a form directly usable or for further processing by other applications. The retrieved data may be made available in a form basically the same as it is stored in the database or in a new form obtained by altering or combining existing data from the database.
Administration – Registering and monitoring users, enforcing data security, monitoring performance, maintaining data integrity, dealing with concurrency control, and recovering information that has been corrupted by some event such as an unexpected system failure.

Both a database and its DBMS conform to the principles of a particular database model. "Database system" refers collectively to the database model, database management system, and database.

기존 DBMS는 데이터베이스와 데이터베이스 데이터를 관리할 수 있는 다양한 기능을 제공하며, 이 기능은 다음과 같은 4가지 주요 기능 그룹으로 분류할 수 있다.
데이터 정의 – 데이터 구성을 정의하는 정의를 생성, 수정 및 제거한다.
업데이트 – 실제 데이터를 삽입, 수정 및 삭제한다.
검색 – 직접 사용할 수 있는 형태 또는 다른 애플리케이션에서 추가로 처리할 수 있는 형태로 정보를 제공한다. 검색된 데이터는 기본적으로 데이터베이스에 저장된 것과 동일한 형태로 제공되거나 데이터베이스에서 기존 데이터를 변경하거나 결합하여 얻은 새로운 형태로 제공될 수 있다.

관리 – 사용자 등록 및 모니터링, 데이터 보안 강화, 성능 모니터링, 데이터 무결성 유지, 동시성 제어 처리, 예상치 못한 시스템 장애와 같은 일부 이벤트로 인해 손상된 정보 복구를 한다.

데이터베이스와 DBMS는 모두 특정 데이터베이스 모델의 원칙을 준수한다. "데이터베이스 시스템"은 데이터베이스 모델, 데이터베이스 관리 시스템 및 데이터베이스를 일컫는다.

Vocabulary

formally : 형식적으로
related data : 관련 데이터
integrated : 통합된
contained : 포함된
entry : 입력
retrieval : 검색
large quantities of information : 대량의 정보
casually : 약식으로
existing : 기존의
definition : 데이터 정의
insertion : 삽입
available : 사용가능한
administration : 관리
register : 등록하다

enforce : 강화하다
security : 보안
data integrity : 데이터 무결성
deal with : 처리하다, 다루다
concurrency control : 동시성 제어
recover : 되찾다, 회복하다
corrupted : 오염된, 부패된
unexpected system failure : 예상치 못한 시스템 장애
conform : 준수하다, 따르다
collectively : 집합적으로, 총괄하여

3) Use Cases[3] 사용 사례

Databases are used to support internal operations of organizations and to underpin online interactions with customers and suppliers. Databases are used to hold administrative information and more specialized data, such as engineering data or economic models. Examples include computerized library systems, flight reservation systems, computerized parts inventory systems, and many content management systems that store websites as collections of webpages in a database.

데이터베이스는 조직의 내부 운영을 지원하고 고객 및 공급업체와의 온라인 상호 작용을 뒷받침하는 데 사용된다. 데이터베이스는 관리 정보와 엔지니어링 데이터 또는 경제 모델과 같은 보다 전문화된 데이터를 보관하는 데 사용된다. 예를 들어, 전산화된 도서관 시스템, 항공편 예약 시스템, 전산화된 부품 재고 시스템, 데이터베이

3 https://en.wikipedia.org/wiki/Database#Database_management_system

스에 웹페이지 모음으로 웹사이트를 저장하는 많은 콘텐츠 관리 시스템이 있다.

Vocabulary

internal : 내부의
operation : 운영
organization : 조직
underpin : 뒷받침하다
customer : 고객
supplier : 공급자, 공급회사
administrative information : 관리 정보
more specialized data : 보다 전문화된 데이터
economic model : 경제모델
computerized : 컴퓨터화된, 전산화된
computerized library system : 전산화된 라이브러리 시스템
flight reservation system : 항공편 예약 시스템
computerized parts inventory system : 전산화된 부품 재고 시스템
collection : 수집품, 모음

4) Types of Databases[4] 데이터베이스의 유형

There are many different types of databases. The best database for a specific organization depends on how the organization intends to use the data.

4 www.oracle.com/database/what-is-database/#Types_of_databases

Relational databases

Relational databases became dominant in the 1980s. Items in a relational database are organized as a set of tables with columns and rows. Relational database technology provides the most efficient and flexible way to access structured information.

Object-oriented databases

Information in an object-oriented database is represented in the form of objects, as in object-oriented programming.

Distributed databases

A distributed database consists of two or more files located in different sites. The database may be stored on multiple computers, located in the same physical location, or scattered over different networks.

데이터베이스 유형은 매우 다양하다. 특정 조직에 가장 적합한 데이터베이스는 조직의 데이터 사용 방법에 따라 달라진다.

관계형 데이터베이스

1980년대에는 관계형 데이터베이스가 우세하였다. 관계형 데이터베이스의 항목은 열과 행이 있는 테이블 집합으로 구성된다. 관계형 데이터베이스 기술은 구조화된 정보에 액세스하는 가장 효율적이고 유연한 방법을 제공한다.

객체 지향 데이터베이스

객체 지향 데이터베이스의 정보는 객체 지향 프로그래밍에서와 같이 객체의 형태로 표현된다.

분산 데이터베이스

분산 데이터베이스는 서로 다른 사이트에 있는 둘 이상의 파일로 구성된다. 데이터베이스는 동일한 물리적 위치에 있는 여러 컴퓨터에 저장되거나 다른 네트워크에 분산될 수 있다.

Data warehouses

A central repository for data, a data warehouse is a type of database specifically designed for fast query and analysis.

NoSQL databases

A NoSQL, or nonrelational database, allows unstructured and semistructured data to be stored and manipulated (in contrast to a relational database, which defines how all data inserted into the database must be composed). NoSQL databases grew popular as web applications became more common and more complex.

Graph databases

A graph database stores data in terms of entities and the relationships between entities.

OLTP databases[5]

An OLTP database stores and manages data related to everyday operations within a system or a company. However, OLTP is focused on transaction-oriented tasks. OLTP typically deals with query processing (inserting, updating, deleting data in a database), and maintaining data integrity and effectiveness when dealing with numerous transactions simultaneously.

---

5 https://phoenixnap.com/kb/oltp-database

These are only a few of the several dozen types of databases in use today. Other, less common databases are tailored to very specific scientific, financial, or other functions.

데이터 웨어하우스

데이터의 중앙 저장소인 데이터 웨어하우스는 빠른 쿼리 및 분석을 위해 특별히 설계된 데이터베이스 유형이다.

NoSQL 데이터베이스

NoSQL, 또는 비관계형 데이터베이스는 구조화되지 않은 데이터와 반구조화된 데이터를 저장하고 조작할 수 있다(데이터베이스에 삽입된 모든 데이터가 어떻게 구성되어야 하는지를 정의하는 관계형 데이터베이스와는 대조적으로). NoSQL 데이터베이스는 웹 애플리케이션이 더 일반적이고 더 복잡해짐에 따라 인기를 얻었다.

그래프 데이터베이스

그래프 데이터베이스는 개체 및 개체 간의 관계 측면에서 데이터를 저장한다.

OLTP 데이터베이스

OLTP 데이터베이스는 시스템이나 회사 내의 일상적인 운영과 관련된 데이터를 저장하고 관리한다. 그러나 OLTP는 트랜잭션 지향 작업에 중점을 둔다. OLTP는 일반적으로 쿼리 처리(데이터베이스에 데이터 삽입, 업데이트, 삭제), 그리고 동시에 여러 트랜잭션을 처리할 때 데이터 무결성과 효율성을 유지하는 작업을 처리한다.

이들은 오늘날 사용되는 수십 가지 유형의 데이터베이스 중 일부에 불과하다. 일반적이지 않은 다른 데이터베이스는 매우 구체적인 과학, 재무 또는 기타 기능에 맞게 조정된다.

Vocabulary

depend on : 달려있다
intend to : 의도하다
relational : 관계의
object-oriented : 객체 지향의
distributed : 분산의, 배포의
scattered : 산재한, 산발적인
warehouse : 창고
central repository : 중앙의 저장소
unstructured : 체계가 없는
complex : 복잡한
entity : 개체
integrity : 무결성
effectiveness : 효과
deal with : 처리하다, 다루다
numerous transactions : 수많은 트랜잭션
simultaneously : 동시에
dozen : 십여 개
tailored : 맞춤의

5) What is Structured Query Language (SQL)?[6] SQL이란?

SQL is a programming language used by nearly all relational databases to query, manipulate, and define data, and to provide access control. SQL was first developed at IBM in the 1970s with Oracle as a major contributor, which led to implementation of the SQL ANSI standard, SQL has spurred many extensions from companies such as IBM, Oracle, and Microsoft. Although SQL is still widely used today, new programming languages are beginning to appear.

SQL은 거의 모든 관계형 데이터베이스에서 데이터를 쿼리, 조작 및 정의하고 액세스 제어를 제공하는 데 사용하는 프로그래밍 언어다. SQL은 1970년대에 IBM에서 Oracle을 주요 기여자로 처음 개발하여 SQL ANSI 표준을 구현하게 되었으며, SQL은 IBM, Oracle 및 Microsoft와 같은 회사의 많은 확장에 박차를 가했다. 오늘날에도 SQL이 널리 사용되고 있지만 새로운 프로그래밍 언어가 등장하기 시작했다.

Vocabulary

manipulate : 조작하다
define : 정의하다
major : 주요한
contributor : 기부자, 기여자
implementation : 실행, 성취
standard : 표준
spur : 박차를 가하다
extension : 확대
appear : 생기다, 발생하다

6 https://www.oracle.com/database/what-is-database/#relational

6) Evolution of the Database[7] 데이터베이스의 진화

Databases have evolved dramatically since their inception in the early 1960s. Navigational databases such as the hierarchical database (which relied on a tree-like model and allowed only a one-to-many relationship), and the network database (a more flexible model that allowed multiple relationships), were the original systems used to store and manipulate data. Although simple, these early systems were inflexible.

In the 1980s, relational databases became popular, followed by object-oriented databases in the 1990s. More recently, NoSQL databases came about as a response to the growth of the internet and the need for faster speed and processing of unstructured data. Today, cloud databases and self-driving databases are breaking new ground when it comes to how data is collected, stored, managed, and utilized.

데이터베이스는 1960년대 초에 시작된 이후 급격하게 발전해 왔다. 계층형 데이터베이스(트리 유사 모델에 의존하고 일대다 관계만 허용)와 네트워크 데이터베이스(다중 관계를 허용하는 보다 유연한 모델)와 같은 탐색 데이터베이스는 데이터를 저장하고 조작하는 데 사용되는 원래 시스템이다. 단순하지만 이러한 초기 시스템은 유연성이 없었다.

1980년대에는 관계형 데이터베이스가 대중화되었고 1990년대에는 객체 지향 데이터베이스가 그 뒤를 이었다. 보다 최근 NoSQL 데이터베이스는 인터넷의 성장과 비정형 데이터의 빠른 속도와 처리에 대한 필요성에 대한 대응으로 등장했다. 오늘날 클라우드 데이터베이스와 자율주행 데이터베이스는 데이터의 수집, 저장, 관리 및 활용 방식에 있어 새로운 지평을 열고 있다.

7 www.oracle.com/database/what-is-database/#Types_of_databases

Vocabulary

evolve : 진화하다, 발달하다

dramatically : 극적으로

inception : 시작

navigational database : 탐색 데이터베이스

hierarchical database : 계층적 데이터베이스

rely on : 의지하다

one-to-many : 일대다

flexible : 유연한

inflexible : 유연성 없는

object-oriented : 객체 지향의

recently : 최근에

response : 대응

unstructured : 체계가 없는

self-driving : 자율주행의

break new ground : 신기원을 이루다

when it comes to : ~라면, ~에 대해서라면

utilize : 활용하다

☞ 잠깐 쉬어가기 ....

쿠팡 로켓배송 차량 (출처: https://news.coupang.com/wp-content/uploads/2021/01/image-10.jpeg)

"로켓배송을 안 써본 사람은 있어도 한 번만 쓴 사람은 없다"는 말을 들어본 적이 있나요?

매일 자정되기 전에 폭풍 검색해서 다음 날 원하는 물건을 받아볼 수 있는 로켓배송 서비스, 이미 너무나 익숙하죠? 오늘 주문하면 내일 받아볼 수 있는 로켓배송을 가능하게 하는 것은 고객들의 구입 패턴과 데이터를 분석하여 미리 물류창고에 준비해두어 고객이 구매했을 때 쿠팡만의 빠른 배송 시스템으로 다음날 받아 볼 수 있도록 시스템화 해둔 것입니다. 로켓배송은 식품도 적용됩니다. '로켓프레시'를 통하여 자정 전에 주문한 우유가 다음 날 7시가 되기 전에 문 앞에 신선하게 새벽배송되어 있습니다. 이렇게 길들여진 고객들의 소비패턴에 쿠팡이 중요한 위치를 자리잡게 됩니다.

쿠팡의 물리적 인프라는 최첨단 시스템 및 소프트웨어와 접목돼 있습니다. AI와 머신러닝을 이용해 급격한 수요 증가를 예측합니다. 상품이 필요하기도 전에 물류와 배송 네트워크에 선제적으로 배치합니다. 또한 기술을 이용해 수억 건의 주문에 대한 동선을 효율적이고 역동적으로 설계합니다. 쿠팡은 고객들의 DB관리와 더불어 머신러닝을 통하여 재고율도 낮추었습니다.

2018년 10월, 매달 2900원을 내면 로켓배송 무료 이용, 30일 이내 무료 반품할 수 있는 '로켓와우 멤버십 서비스'는 출시 1주일 만에 가입자 수는 15만 명을 기록했습니다. 두 달 뒤에는 100만 명을 돌파했다. 쿠팡은 2022년 6월 와우 멤버십 가격을 2900원에서 4990원으로 올렸습니다. 그럼에도, 쿠팡 안에서 소비패턴이 익숙해진 고객들은 "그래도 싸다"는 반응을 보이며 멤버십을 유지하였습니다.

연습문제

exercises

1~5. 다음 빈 칸에 들어가는 단어로 적절한 것을 넣으세요.

1. Items in (   ) are organized as a set of tables with columns and rows.

정답 : ____

2. In computing, (   ) is an organized collection of data stored and accessed electronically from a computer system.

정답 : ____

3. More recently, (   ) came about as a response to the growth of the internet and the need for faster speed and processing of unstructured data.

정답 : ____

4. These model data as rows and columns in a series of (   ), and the vast majority use SQL for writing and querying data.

정답 : ____

5. A NoSQL, or nonrelational database, allows (   ) and semistructured data to be stored and manipulated

정답 : ____

6~10. 다음 It이 지칭하는 것을 영어로 쓰세요.

6. It is the software that interacts with end users, applications, and the database itself to capture and analyze the data.

정답 : ____

7. It is a programming language used by nearly all relational databases to query, manipulate, and define data, and to provide access control.

정답 : ______________________________

8. It consists of two or more files located in different sites. The database may be stored on multiple computers, located in the same physical location, or scattered over different networks.

정답 : ______________________________

9. It stores data in terms of entities and the relationships between entities.

정답 : ______________________________

10. It stores and manages data related to everyday operations within a system or a company, but it is focused on transaction-oriented tasks.

정답 : ______________________________

연습문제 해답

1. a relational database
2. a database
3. NoSQL databases
4. tables
5. unstructured
6. The database management system (DBMS)
7. SQL
8. A distributed database
9. A graph database
10. An OLTP database

Chapter

09 Computer Network
컴퓨터 네트워크

학습순서

1) What's a Computer Network?
2) Usage
3) Network Topology
4) Types of Network Topology
5) Types of Area Networks
6) Communication Protocols
7) OSI Model

잠깐 쉬어가기

연습문제

【 INTRO 】

한국은 전 세계적으로 가장 빠른 수준의 초고속 인터넷의 나라입니다. 그리고 우리나라는 미국 다음으로 인터넷을 연결한 앞서가는 나라입니다.1982년 한국전자통신연구원(ETRI)과 서울대학교가 세계 2번째로 통신망을 연결하였습니다. 90년대, 전화선을 활용하는 PC통신을 경험한 이후, 초고속 인터넷 서비스 시대가 열렸습니다. 그리고 현재, 우리나라 각 가정의 인터넷 보급률은 거의 100%라고 할 수 있습니다. 그렇다면 이번 과에서는 통신망이 무엇이고 어떠한 유형이 있는 지 알아보도록 합시다.

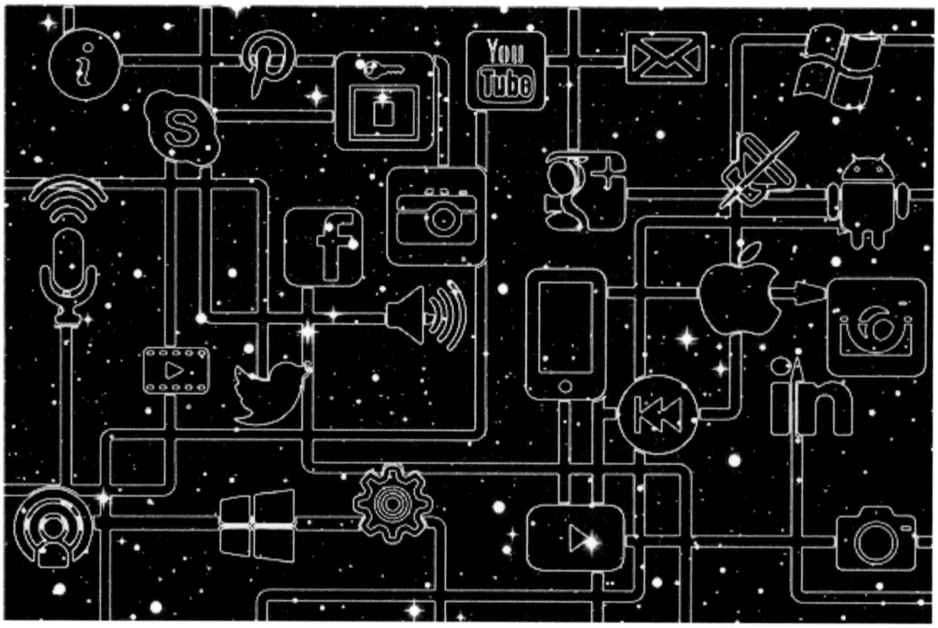

KKorea is the country with the fastest level of broadband internet in the world. And Korea is the leading country in the world after the United States to connect to the Internet. In 1982, the Electronics and Telecommunications Institute (ETRI) and Seoul National University connected the second largest communication network in the world. In the 1990s, after experiencing PC communication using telephone lines, the era of broadband Internet service opened. And now, the Internet penetration rate in each household in Korea is almost 100%. So, in this chapter, let's learn what a communication network is and what types there are.

1) What's a Computer Network?[1] 컴퓨터 네트워크란 무엇인가?

A computer network is a set of computers sharing resources located on or provided by network nodes. The computers use common communication protocols over digital interconnections to communicate with each other. These interconnections are made up of telecommunication network technologies, based on physically wired, optical, and wireless radio-frequency methods that may be arranged in a variety of network topologies.

The nodes of a computer network may include personal computers, servers, networking hardware, or other specialized or general-purpose hosts. They are identified by hostnames and network addresses. Hostnames serve as memorable labels for the nodes, rarely changed after initial assignment. Network addresses serve for locating and identifying the nodes by communication protocols such as the Internet Protocol.

Computer networks may be classified by many criteria, including the transmission medium used to carry signals, bandwidth, communications protocols to organize network traffic, the network size, the topology, traffic control mechanism, and organizational intent.

Computer networks support many applications and services, such as

---

1 https://en.wikipedia.org/wiki/Computer_network

access to the World Wide Web, digital video, digital audio, shared use of application and storage servers, printers, and fax machines, and use of email and instant messaging applications.

컴퓨터 네트워크(통신망)는 네트워크 노드에 있거나 네트워크 노드에 의해 제공되는 리소스를 공유하는 컴퓨터 집합이다. 컴퓨터는 디지털 상호 연결을 통한 공통 통신 프로토콜을 사용하여 서로 통신한다. 이러한 상호 연결은 다양한 네트워크 토폴로지에 배치될 수 있는 물리적 유선, 광학, 무선 주파수 방법을 기반으로 하는 통신 네트워크 기술로 구성된다.

컴퓨터 네트워크의 노드에는 개인용 컴퓨터, 서버, 네트워킹 하드웨어 또는 기타 특수 또는 범용 호스트가 포함될 수 있다. 호스트 이름과 네트워크 주소로 식별된다. 호스트 이름은 노드에 대해 기억 가능한 레이블 역할을 하며 초기 할당 후에는 거의 변경되지 않는다. 네트워크 주소는 인터넷 프로토콜과 같은 통신 프로토콜로 노드를 찾고 식별하는 데 사용된다.

컴퓨터 네트워크는 신호 전달에 사용되는 전송 매체, 대역폭, 네트워크 트래픽을 구성하는 통신 프로토콜, 네트워크 크기, 토폴로지, 트래픽 제어 메커니즘 및 기관의 의도를 포함한 많은 기준에 의해 분류될 수 있다.

컴퓨터 네트워크는 월드 와이드 웹, 디지털 비디오, 디지털 오디오, 애플리케이션 및 스토리지 서버 공유 사용, 프린터 및 팩스, 이메일 및 인스턴트 메시징 애플리케이션 사용과 같은 많은 애플리케이션과 서비스를 지원한다.

Vocabulary

share : 공유하다

interconnection : 상호접속

telecommunication : 전자통신

wired : 컴퓨터 시스템에 연결된

optical : 광학의

wireless : 무선의

radio-frequency : 무선 주파수

specialized : 전문화된, 전문적인

general-purpose : 다목적의, 다용도의

identified : 식별된

memorable label : 기억 가능한 레이블

rarely : 좀처럼 ~하지 않는

initial : 초기의, 처음의

assignment : 할당, 배정

criteria : 기준(criterion 단수)

transmission medium : 전송매체

bandwidth : 대역폭

traffic control mechanism : 트래픽 제어 메커니즘

intent : 의도

2) Usage[2] 사용

A computer network extends interpersonal communications by electronic means with various technologies, such as email, instant messaging, online chat, voice and video telephone calls, and video conferencing. A network allows sharing of network and computing resources.

Users may access and use resources provided by devices on the network, such as printing a document on a shared network printer or use of a shared storage device.

A network allows sharing of files, data, and other types of information giving authorized users the ability to access information stored on other computers on the network. Distributed computing uses computing resources across a network to accomplish tasks.

컴퓨터 네트워크(통신망)는 이메일, 인스턴트 메시징, 온라인 채팅, 음성 및 영상 전화 통화, 화상 회의와 같은 다양한 기술을 사용하여 전자적 수단으로 대인 통신을 확장한다. 네트워크를 통해 네트워크 및 컴퓨팅 리소스를 공유 할 수 있다.

사용자는 공유 네트워크 프린터에서 문서 인쇄 또는 공유 저장 장치 사용과 같이 네트워크의 장치에서 제공하는 리소스에 액세스하여 사용할 수 있다.

네트워크를 통해 파일, 데이터 및 기타 유형의 정보를 공유 할 수 있으므로 권한이 부여된 사용자는 네트워크의 다른 컴퓨터에 저장된 정보에 액세스 할 수 있다. 분산 컴퓨팅은 네트워크를 통해 컴퓨팅 리소스를 사용하여 작업을 수행한다.

---

2 https://en.wikipedia.org/wiki/Computer_network#Use

Vocabulary

interpersonal : 대인관계와 관련된
communication : 통신
electronic means : 전자적 수단
instant messaging : 인스턴트 메신저
video conferencing : 화상회의 시스템
authorized users : 인증된 사용자
distributed computing : 분산컴퓨팅
accomplish : 성취하다, 해내다

3) Network Topology[3] 네트워크 토폴로지

Basically, network topology is made from two words, Network and Topology. So let's understand first these two basic terms before jumping to the definition of Network Topology.

Network – Network is an arrangement where two or more computers (also referred to as nodes) communicate with each other. These computers or participants nodes actively contribute to the process of communication.

Topology – Topology is simply an arrangement of how these nodes will interact. It is a topology which governs data flow between respective nodes.

Hence, it is an arrangement of two or more nodes communicating with each other, typically over the internet through a particular medium. It

3 https://www.educba.com/what-is-network-topology/

helps to communicate between these nodes.

Network Topology is the structure and arrangement of components of a computer communication system. Internet is the key technology in the present time, and it depends upon the network topology.

There are several types of topology available such as bus topology, ring topology, star topology, tree topology, point-to-multipoint topology, point-to-point topology, world-wide-web topology. Local area network (LAN) and Wide area network (WAN) are the commonly used network topology that is installed and configured in the enterprise.

Some of the advantages of implementing network topology are proper functioning of a network, upgrading network performance, Reduces operational, implementation and maintenance cost, error or fault detection, effective utilization of resources.

기본적으로 네트워크 토폴로지는 네트워크와 토폴로지의 두 단어로 구성된다. 네트워크 토폴로지의 정의로 넘어가기 전에 먼저 이 두 가지 기본 용어를 이해하자.

네트워크 - 네트워크(통신망)는 둘 이상의 컴퓨터(노드라고도 함)가 서로 통신하는 배열이다. 이러한 컴퓨터 또는 참가자 노드는 커뮤니케이션 과정에 적극적으로 기여한다.

토폴로지 - 토폴로지란 단순히 노드가 상호 작용하는 방식을 정리한 것이다. 각 노드 간의 데이터 흐름을 제어하는 것은 토폴로지이다.

따라서 토폴로지는 일반적으로 특정 매체를 통해 인터넷을 통해 서로 통신하는 두 개 이상의 노드의 배열이다. 이러한 노드 간의 통신에 도움을 준다.

네트워크 토폴로지는 컴퓨터 통신 시스템의 구성 요소 구조 및 배열이다. 인터넷은 현재의 핵심 기술이며 네트워크 토폴로지에 따라 다르다.

버스 토폴로지, 링 토폴로지, 별 토폴로지, 트리 토폴로지, 점 대 다점 토폴로지, 점 대 점 토폴로지, 월드 와이드 웹 토폴로지 등 몇 가지 유형의 토폴로지를 사용할 수 있다. LAN(Local Area Network) 및 WAN(Wide Area Network)은 기업에서 설치 및 구성하여 일반적으로 사용되는 네트워크 토폴로지이다.

네트워크 토폴로지 구현의 장점 중 하나는 네트워크의 적절한 작동, 네트워크 성능 업그레이드, 운영, 구현 및 유지보수 비용 절감, 오류 또는 결함 감지, 리소스의 효과적인 활용이다.

Vocabulary

topology : 토폴로지(컴퓨터 네트워크의 요소들을 물리적으로 연결해 놓은 것)
definition : 정의
arrangement : 방식, 배열
contribute : 기여하는
govern : 다스리다
data flow : 데이터 흐름
particular medium : 특정 매체
present time : 현재
install : 설치하다
configure : 환경을 설정하다
enterprise : 기업, 회사
advantage : 이점, 장점
implement : 시행하다
maintenance : 유지

fault : 결함
detection : 탐지, 발견
utilization : 활용

4) Types of Network Topology[4] 토폴로지 네트워크의 유형

It could be broadly classified into the following different types. These different types are as follows:

- Bus Topology
- Mesh Topology
- Ring Topology
- Star Topology
- Tree Topology
- Point-to-Multipoint Topology
- Point-to-Point Topology
- World-Wide-Web Topology

Let's discuss each type of topology along with its advantage and disadvantage.

네트워크 토폴로지 유형

그것은 크게 다음과 같은 다른 유형으로 분류될 수 있다. 이러한 다양한 유형은 다음과 같다.

- 버스 토폴로지
- 메시 토폴로지
- 링 토폴로지

4 https://www.educba.com/what-is-network-topology/

- 별 토폴로지
- 트리 토폴로지
- 점 대 다중점 토폴로지
- 포인트 투 포인트 토폴로지
- 월드 와이드 웹 토폴로지

각 유형의 토폴로지와 장점과 단점에 대해 살펴보자.

Vocabulary

broadly : 넓게
classify : 분류하다
along with : ~에 덧붙여
advantage and disadvantage : 장점과 단점

① Bus Topology

A bus topology is a type of network in which each node present for communication is connected to a wire. This wire is responsible for transmitting a message from one participant node to another receiver node. Generally, this wire is termed or known as "Backbone." The connecting wire is rightly termed as Backbone since the network's completely smooth working depends upon the backbone wire. It is sometimes also referred to as Line Topology.

Now let us look at a few of its uses, advantages, and disadvantages.

– Uses

It is generally used over a small network such as LAN.
Here messages need to be transmitted over the limited number of participant nodes.

– Advantages

Easy to use and understand
Cost-effective
Easy to extend the network by simply adding a repeater (a repeater generally boosts the signal and helps for transmission to longer distances)

– Disadvantages

A single cable break will bring down the bus topology.
Too many participants nodes make the network slow.

① 버스 토폴로지

버스 토폴로지는 통신을 위해 존재하는 각 노드가 회선(와이어)에 연결된 네트워크 유형이다. 이 회선은 한 참가자 노드에서 다른 수신기 노드로 메시지를 전송하는 역할을 한다. 일반적으로 이 와이어를 "백본"이라 한다.
네트워크가 완전히 원활하게 작동하는 것은 백본 와이어에 따라 달라지므로 연결 와이어를 백본이라고 한다. 라인(선) 토폴로지라고도 한다.

이제 몇 가지 용도, 장점 및 단점을 살펴보도록 하자.

– 용도

일반적으로 LAN과 같은 소규모 네트워크를 통해 사용된다.
여기서 메시지는 제한된 수의 참가자 노드를 통해 전송되어야 한다.

– 장점

사용하기 쉽고 이해하기

비용 효율적

중계기를 추가하기만 하면 네트워크 확장이 용이함(중계기는 일반적으로 신호를 증폭하고 더 먼 거리로 전송하는 데 도움이 됨)

– 단점

단일 케이블 중단으로 버스 토폴로지가 중단된다.

참가자 노드가 너무 많으면 네트워크가 느려진다.

Vocabulary

wire : 전선

responsible : 책임을 지는, 원인이 되는

transmit a message : 메세지를 전송하다

receiver : 수신기

generally : 일반적으로

term : 용어, 칭하다

rightly : 마땅히, 제대로

completely : 완전히, 완벽히

smooth : 원활한

advantage and disadvantage : 장점과 단점

cost-effective : 비용 효율적인

repeater : 중계기

② Mesh Topology

As the name suggests, Mesh Topology generally forms a mesh of all the interconnected nodes. Here each node is connected to every other node through a single one-to-one communicating wire.

There is a one-to-one mapping between each node. Now let us look at a few of its uses, advantages, and disadvantages.

– Uses

A mesh topology is generally used over a large network where a single node's breakdown shall not affect the complete network. It is generally used as if a single fault in routes, wires, etc., shall not hamper complete topology.

– Advantages

Better fault-tolerance capacity

Failure of one participant nodes or other devices such as routers will not affect the complete network.

If there is a breakdown in one path between two nodes, then an alternate path is always available.

– Disadvantages

The network becomes too complex as there are large participants nodes. It becomes costly due to the set-up of multiple paths.

② 메쉬 토폴로지

이름에서 알 수 있듯이 메쉬 토폴로지는 일반적으로 상호 연결된 모든 노드의 망을 형성한다. 여기에서 각 노드는 단일 일대일 통신 와이어를 통해 다른 모든 노드에 연결된다. 각 노드 사이에는 일대일 매핑이 있다. 이제 몇 가지 용도, 장점 및 단점을 살펴보자.

– 용도

메쉬 토폴로지는 일반적으로 단일 노드의 고장이 전체 네트워크에 영향을 미치지 않는 대규모 네트워크에서 사용된다. 일반적으로 경로, 와이어 등의 단일 오류가 완전한 토폴로지를 방해하지 않는 것처럼 사용된다.

– 장점

내결함성 용량 향상
한 참가자 노드 또는 라우터와 같은 다른 장치의 오류는 전체 네트워크에 영향을 미치지 않는다.
두 노드 사이의 한 경로에 장애가 있으면 항상 대체 경로를 사용할 수 있다.

– 단점

대규모 참여 노드가 있기 때문에 네트워크가 너무 복잡해진다. 다중 경로 설정으로 인해 비용이 많이 든다.

Vocabulary

mesh : 망
interconnected : 연결된
breakdown : 고장
fault : 결함
hamper : 방해하다

tolerance : 내성, 저항력
capacity : 용량
affect : 영향을 미치다
complete : 가능한 최대한, 완벽한, 완전한
breakdown : 고장
path : 길
alternate path : 대체 경로
available : 사용가능한
complex : 복잡한

③ Ring Topology

As the name suggests, ring topology forms a ring by connecting participants nodes. Nodes are connected in such a way that a single wire forms the path whose ends are joined to form a circle. Ring topology uses the token concept where the token is transmitted along with the message for the correct delivery of the message. Now let us look at a few of its uses, advantages, and disadvantages.

– Uses

A ring topology is generally designed in such a way that it forms a ring-type network either physically or logically. These rings are made around campus or building to form a high speed flexible, reliable network.

– Advantages

No master-slave concept

Each node has its own share of responsibility.
Could work in a high capacity network

– Disadvantages

A single node failure affects the complete network.
Sometimes it becomes difficult to troubleshoot if the network is too large.
Adding or manipulating the network affects other participants nodes.

③ 링 토폴로지

이름에서 알 수 있듯이 링 토폴로지는 참가자 노드를 연결하여 링을 형성한다. 노드는 단일 와이어가 끝이 결합되어 원을 형성하는 경로를 형성하는 방식으로 연결된다. 링 토폴로지는 메시지의 올바른 전달을 위해 메시지와 함께 토큰이 전송되는 토큰 개념을 사용한다. 이제 몇 가지 용도, 장점 및 단점을 살펴보자.

– 용도

링 토폴로지는 일반적으로 물리적 또는 논리적으로 링형 네트워크를 형성하는 방식으로 설계된다. 이 링은 캠퍼스 또는 건물 주변에 만들어지며 유연하고 안정적인 고속 네트워크를 형성한다.

– 장점

마스터-슬레이브 개념 없음
각 노드에는 고유한 책임 분담이 있음.
고용량 네트워크에서 작동 가능

– 단점

단일 노드 오류는 전체 네트워크에 영향을 준다.
네트워크가 너무 큰 경우 문제를 해결하기 어려울 때가 있다.
네트워크를 추가하거나 조작하면 다른 참가자 노드에 영향을 미친다.

Vocabulary

join : 연결하다

transmit : 전송하다

correct delivery : 올바른 전달

physically or logically : 물리적 또는 논리적으로

reliable : 신뢰할만한, 안정적인

responsibility : 책임

high capacity : 대용량

failure : 실패

troubleshoot : 해결하다

④ Star Topology

A star topology generally consists of a central hub. Every participant node is directly connected to this hub. Hub acts as a central point to receive the message from the sender node and then transmits it to other participant nodes. There is no direct connection between nodes. Now let us look at a few of its uses, advantages, and disadvantages.

– Uses

A general implementation of the star topology is an Ethernet 10BaseT network.

– Advantages

A single node failure does not affect the complete network.
The network can run smoothly as far as the centralized hub is running smoothly.
It is more cost-effective since the centralized network reduces network administration cost highly.

– Disadvantages

Failure of the central hub will disrupt the whole topology.
It is slightly costly when compared to the bus topology.

④ 스타 토폴로지

스타 토폴로지는 일반적으로 중앙 허브로 구성된다. 모든 참가자 노드는 이 허브에 직접 연결된다. 허브는 발신자 노드에서 메시지를 수신한 다음 다른 참가자 노드에 전송하는 중심점 역할을 한다. 노드 사이에는 직접적인 연결이 없다. 이제 몇 가지 용도, 장점 및 단점을 살펴보자.

– 용도

스타 토폴로지의 일반적인 구현은 이더넷 10BaseT 네트워크이다.

– 장점

단일 노드 오류는 전체 네트워크에 영향을 미치지 않는다.
중앙 집중식 허브가 원활하게 실행되는 한 네트워크는 원활하게 실행될 수 있다.
중앙 집중식 네트워크는 네트워크 관리 비용을 크게 줄여주기 때문에 더욱 비용 효율적이다.

– 단점

중앙 허브에 장애가 발생하면 전체 토폴로지가 중단된다.
버스 토폴로지와 비교할 때 약간 비싸다.

Vocabulary

consist of : 구성되다
implementation : 이행
centralized hub : 중앙집중식 허브
smoothly : 순조롭게
administration : 관리
disrupt : 방해하다
slightly : 약간

⑤ Tree Topology

A tree topology is a special type of network where many participants nodes are connected to form a tree type of architecture. Generally, there is a central initiator node that could be compared to the root of a tree. This root node on extending further has different nodes connected to it, which could be compared as branches of a tree. A tree topology is a combination of bus topology and star topology. Now let us look at a few of its uses, advantages, and disadvantages.

– Uses

It is generally used where there is a requirement of communication between two networks.

– Advantages

Easily scalable since adding a new node a leaf node is easily possible

Leaf nodes could accommodate new nodes, thus forming the hierarchical chain.

Other hierarchical nodes do not get affected if particular nodes fail.

Easy to debug

– Disadvantages

A huge length of wires is required to form the hierarchical chain.

A lot of maintenance is required.

⑤ 트리 토폴로지

트리 토폴로지는 많은 참여자 노드가 연결되어 트리 유형의 아키텍처를 형성하는 특수한 유형의 네트워크이다.

일반적으로 트리의 루트와 비교할 수 있는 중앙 초기자 노드가 있다.

추가로 확장되는 이 루트 노드에는 연결된 다른 노드가 있으며, 이는 트리의 분기로 비교할 수 있다.

트리 토폴로지는 버스 토폴로지와 스타 토폴로지의 조합이다.

이제 몇 가지 용도, 장점 및 단점을 살펴보자.

– 용도

일반적으로 두 네트워크 간의 통신이 필요한 경우에 사용된다.

– 장점

새로운 노드를 리프 노드 추가가 용이하여 쉽게 확장 가능

리프 노드는 새 노드를 수용하여 계층적 체인을 형성할 수 있다.
특정 노드가 실패하더라도 다른 계층적 노드는 영향을 받지 않는다.
디버그하기 쉬움

– 단점

계층적 체인을 형성하려면 엄청난 길이의 와이어가 필요하다.
많은 유지 보수가 필요하다.

Vocabulary

initiator : 개시자
compare : 비교하다
combination : 조합
requirement : 필요조건, 요구
scalable : 확장 가능한
accommodate : 수용하다
hierarchical chain : 계층적 체인
particular : 특정한

⑥ Point–to–Multipoint Topology

A Point–to–Multipoint Topology consists of one node which acts as a sender, and on the other side are multiple nodes that act as a receiver. This communication is opposite to Point–to–Point communication. Now let us look at a few of its uses, advantages, and disadvantages.

– Uses

A radio channel broadcast or television is a typical example of it.

– Advantages

Fast
Easy to widespread a message when it needs to broadcast to a large number of nodes.

– Disadvantages

Expensive
The initial set-up is quite high.

⑥ 점대 다중점 토폴로지

점대 다중점 토폴로지는 송신자 역할을 하는 노드 하나와 수신자 역할을 하는 여러 개의 노드로 구성된다. 이 통신은 점대점 통신과는 반대이다. 이제 몇 가지 용도, 장점 및 단점을 살펴보자.

– 용도

라디오 채널 방송이나 텔레비전이 대표적인 예이다.

– 장점

빠름
많은 노드로 방송해야 할 때 메시지를 쉽게 전파할 수 있다.

– 단점

비쌈
초기 설정이 상당히 높다.

Vocabulary

sender : 송신자
receiver : 수신자
opposite : 반대의
broadcast : 방송하다
widespread : 광범위한, 널리 퍼진
initial : 처음의, 초기의
set-up : 구성

⑦ Point-to-Point Topology

A Point-to-Point Topology consists of two nodes that are communicating directly. A typical example is a telephonic call where two nodes are connected for communication. This communication is opposite to Point-to-many communication, where there are a single sender and multiple receivers. Now let us look at a few of its uses, advantages, and disadvantages.

- Uses

A telephonic call two-way radio communicating is a typical example of it.

- Advantages

Fast and secure
Single node failure does not affect others.

– Disadvantages

Expensive
High maintenance cost

⑦ 점대점 토폴로지

점대점 토폴로지는 직접 통신하는 두 개의 노드로 구성된다. 전형적인 예는 통신을 위해 두 개의 노드가 연결된 전화 통화를 들 수 있다.
이 통신은 단일 송신기와 다중 수신기가 있는 점 대 다수 통신과는 반대이다. 이제 몇 가지 용도, 장점 및 단점을 살펴보자.

– 용도

전화 통화 양방향 무선 통신이 대표적인 예이다.

– 장점

빠르고 안전함
단일 노드 장애는 다른 노드에는 영향을 미치지 않는다.

– 단점

값이 비쌈
높은 유지보수 비용

Vocabulary

telephonic call : 전화 통화
two-way : 양방향의
failure : 실패, 장애
maintenance cost : 유지보수 비용

⑧ World-Wide-Web Topology

This is one of the most popular and widely implemented types of topology. It is a wide network of interconnected web pages which are connected to each other. These pages are generally connected through hyperlinks.

⑧ 월드와이드웹 토폴로지

토폴로지 유형 중 하나이다. 이것은 서로 연결된 웹페이지의 넓은 네트워크이다. 이러한 페이지는 일반적으로 하이퍼링크를 통해 연결된다.

Vocabulary

popular : 인기 있는, 많은 사람들이 공유하는
implemented : 시행되는
interconnected : 서로 연결된
generally : 일반적으로
through : ~를 통해

5) Types of Area Networks[5] 영역 네트워크의 유형

Common types of area networks are:

- LAN: Local Area Network
- WAN: Wide Area Network
- WLAN: Wireless Local Area Network
- MAN: Metropolitan Area Network

5 https://www.lifewire.com/lans-wans-and-other-area-networks-817376

- SAN: Storage Area Network, System Area Network, Server Area Network, or sometimes Small Area Network
- CAN: Campus Area Network, Controller Area Network, or sometimes Cluster Area Network
- PAN: Personal Area Network

LAN and WAN are the two primary and best-known categories of area networks, while the others have emerged with technology advances.

영역 네트워크(통신망)의 일반적인 유형은 다음과 같다.

- LAN: 근거리 통신망
- WAN: 원거리 통신망/ 광역 통신망
- WLAN: 무선 근거리 통신망
- MAN: 대도시 지역 통신망/도시권 통신망
- SAN: 저장 지역 통신망, 시스템 영역 통신망, 서버 영역 통신망 또는 때로는 소규모 영역 통신망
- CAN: 캠퍼스 통신망, 컨트롤러 영역 네트워크 또는 때로는 클러스터 영역 네트워크
- PAN: 개인 통신망

LAN과 WAN은 영역 네트워크의 가장 잘 알려진 두 가지 주요 범주이며 나머지는 기술 발전으로 등장했다.

– LAN: Local Area Network

A LAN connects network devices over a relatively short distance. A networked office building, school, or home usually contains a single LAN, though sometimes one building contains a few small LANs (perhaps one per room), and occasionally a LAN spans a group of nearby buildings. In TCP/IP networking, a LAN is often, but not always, implemented as a single IP subnet. In addition to operating in a limited space, LANs are also typically owned, controlled, and managed by a single person or organization. These networks also tend to use certain connectivity technologies, primarily Ethernet and Token Ring.

– LAN: 근거리 통신망

LAN은 비교적 짧은 거리에 있는 네트워크 장치를 연결한다. 네트워크로 연결된 사무실 건물, 학교 또는 가정에는 일반적으로 단일 LAN이 포함되어 있지만 때로는 한 건물에 몇 개의 작은 LAN(방당 한개)이 포함되어 있고 때로는 LAN이 근처 건물 그룹에 걸쳐있다. TCP/IP 네트워킹에서 LAN은 종종 단일 IP 서브넷으로 구현되지만 항상 구현되지는 않는다. 제한된 공간에서 작동하는 것 외에도 LAN은 일반적으로 한 사람이나 조직에서 소유, 제어 및 관리를 한다. 또한 이러한 네트워크는 주로 이더넷 및 토큰링과 같은 특정 연결 기술을 사용하는 경향이 있다.

– WAN: Wide Area Network

A WAN spans a large physical distance. The internet is the largest WAN, spanning the Earth. A WAN is a geographically-dispersed collection of LANs. A network device called a router connects LANs to a WAN. In IP networking, the router maintains both a LAN address and a WAN address. A WAN differs from a LAN in several important ways. Most WANs (like the internet) aren't owned by a single organization. Instead, WANs exist under collective or distributed ownership and management. WANs tend to use technology like ATM, Frame Relay, and X.25 for connectivity over the longer distances.

– WAN: 원거리 통신망/광역 통신망

WAN은 물리적 거리가 멀다. 인터넷은 지구에 걸쳐 있는 가장 큰 WAN이다. WAN은 지리적으로 분산된 LAN 모음이다. 라우터라고 하는 네트워크 장치는 LAN을 WAN에 연결하다. IP 네트워킹에서 라우터는 LAN 주소와 WAN 주소를 모두 유지한다. WAN은 몇 가지 중요한 면에서 LAN과 다르다. 인터넷과 같은 대부분의 WAN은 단일 조직에서 소유하지 않는다. 대신 WAN은 집합적이거나 분산된 소유권 및 관리 하에 존재한다. WAN은 장거리 연결을 위해 ATM, 프레임 릴레이 및 X.25와 같은 기술을 사용하는 경향이 있다.

– LAN, WAN, and Home Networking

Residences typically employ one LAN and connect to the internet WAN through an internet service provider (ISP) using a broadband modem. The ISP provides a WAN IP address to the modem, and all the computers on the home network use LAN IP addresses (also called private IP addresses). All computers on a home LAN can communicate directly with each other but must go through a central network gateway, typically a broadband router, to reach the ISP and beyond.

– LAN, WAN 및 홈 네트워킹

주거지는 일반적으로 하나의 LAN을 사용하고 광대역 모뎀을 사용하여 인터넷 서비스 공급자(ISP)를 통해 인터넷 WAN에 연결한다. ISP는 모뎀에 WAN IP 주소를 제공하고 홈 네트워크의 모든 컴퓨터는 LAN IP 주소(사설 IP 주소라고도 함)를 사용한다. 가정용 LAN의 모든 컴퓨터는 서로 직접 통신할 수 있지만 ISP 이상에 도달하려면 중앙 네트워크 게이트웨이(일반적으로 광대역 라우터)를 거쳐야 한다.

– Other Types of Area Networks

While LAN and WAN are the most popular network types, you may also see references to these others:

Wireless Local Area Network: A LAN based on Wi-Fi wireless network technology.

Metropolitan Area Network: A network spanning a physical area larger than a LAN but smaller than a WAN, such as a city. A MAN is typically owned and operated by a single entity such as a government body or large corporation.

Campus Area Network: A network spanning multiple LANs but smaller than a MAN, such as on a university or local business campus.

Personal Area Network: A network that surrounds an individual. A wireless PAN (WPAN) might be created between Bluetooth devices.

Storage Area Network: Connects servers to data storage devices through technology like Fibre Channel.

System Area Network (also called Cluster Area Network, or CAN): Links high-performance computers with high-speed connections in a cluster configuration.

Passive Optical Local Area Network: A POLAN serves fiber by using fiber optic splitters to allow a single optical fiber to serve multiple devices.

A couple of other network types that focus on private networks include virtual private networks (VPNs) and enterprise private networks (EPNs).

– 기타 유형의 영역 네트워크

LAN 및 WAN이 가장 인기 있는 네트워크 유형이지만 다음 네트워크 유형에 대한 참조도 볼 수 있다.

Wireless Local Area Network(무선 근거리 통신망): Wi-Fi 무선 네트워크 기술을 기반으로 하는 LAN이다.

Metropolitan Area Network(광역 통신망): LAN보다 크지만 WAN(도시)보다 작은 물리적 영역에 걸쳐 있는 네트워크이다. MAN은 일반적으로 정부기관이나 대기업과 같은 단일 기업이 소유하고 운영한다.

Campus Area Network(캠퍼스 통신망): 여러 LAN에 걸쳐 있지만 대학교 또는 로컬 비즈니스 캠퍼스와 같이 MAN보다 작은 네트워크이다.

Personal Area Network(개인 통신망): 개인을 둘러싸고 있는 네트워크다. Bluetooth 장치 사이에 WPAN(무선 PAN)이 생성될 수 있다.

Storage Area Network(저장 지역 통신망): 파이버 채널과 같은 기술을 통해 서버를 데이터 스토리지 장치에 연결한다.

System Area Network(시스템 영역 통신망, 클러스트 영역 통신망 또는 CAN이라고도 함): 클러스터 구성에서 고성능 컴퓨터를 고속으로 연결한다.

Passive Optical Local Area Network(수동 광 근거리 통신망): POLAN은 광섬유 스플리터를 사용하여 하나의 광섬유가 여러 장치를 처리할 수 있도록 함으로써 광섬유를 제공한다.

사설 네트워크에 초점을 맞추는 몇 가지 다른 네트워크 유형으로는 VPN(가상 사설망)과 EPN(엔터프라이즈 사설망)이 있다.

Vocabulary

local : 지역의
metropolitan : 대도시의
primary : 주된
relatively : 비교적
distance : 거리
occasionally : 때때로
span : 걸치다
in addition to : ~일뿐 아니라
collective : 집합적인
distributed : 분산의
ownership : 소유권
residence : 거주기
employ : 쓰다
internet service provider : 인터넷 서비스 공급자
optical : 광학의
fiber : 섬유
serve : 제공하다
focus : 집중하다
virtual : 가상의
private : 사설의
enterprise : 회사

6) Communication Protocols [6] 통신 프로토콜

A communication protocol is a set of rules for exchanging information over a network. Communication protocols have various characteristics. They may be connection-oriented or connectionless, they may use circuit mode or packet switching, and they may use hierarchical addressing or flat addressing.

In a protocol stack, often constructed per the OSI model, communications functions are divided up into protocol layers, where each layer leverages the services of the layer below it until the lowest layer controls the hardware that sends information across the media. The use of protocol layering is ubiquitous across the field of computer networking.

An important example of a protocol stack is HTTP (the World Wide Web protocol) running over TCP over IP (the Internet protocols) over IEEE 802.11 (the Wi-Fi protocol). This stack is used between the wireless router and the home user's personal computer when the user is surfing the web.

통신 프로토콜은 네트워크를 통해 정보를 교환하기 위한 규칙 집합이다. 통신 프로토콜에는 다양한 특성이 있다. 연결 지향 또는 비연결일 수 있으며 회로 모드 또는 패킷 스위칭을 사용할 수 있으며 계층적 주소 지정 또는 평면 주소 지정을 사용할 수 있다.

종종 OSI 모델에 따라 구성되는 프로토콜 스택에서 통신 기능은 프로토콜 계층으로 나뉘며, 각 계층은 가장 낮은 계층이 미디어를 통해 정보를 전송하는 하드웨어를 제어할 때까지 그 아래 계층의 서비스를 활용한다. 프로토콜 계층화의 사용은 컴퓨터 네트워킹 분야 전반에 걸쳐 널리 퍼져 있다.

---

6 https://en.wikipedia.org/wiki/Computer_network#Communication_protocols

프로토콜 스택의 중요한 예는 IEEE 802.11(Wi-Fi 프로토콜)을 통해 TCP/IP(인터넷 프로토콜)를 통해 실행되는 HTTP(월드 와이드 웹 프로토콜)이다. 이 스택은 사용자가 웹 서핑을 할 때 무선 라우터와 가정용 사용자의 개인용 컴퓨터 사이에 사용된다.

Vocabulary

exchange : 교환하다

characteristic : 특징

connection-oriented : 송신할 때마다 접속을 확립하는, 연결 지향적인

circuit : 회로

hierarchical : 계층의

flat : 납작한, 평평한

constructed : 구성되는

function : 기능

divide : 나누다

layer : 계층

leverage : …에 영향력을 미치다

inherently : 본질적으로

unreliable : 신뢰할 수 없는

traverse : 가로지르다

transmission : 전송

core : 핵심

suite : 세트

addressing : 주소지정

identification : 식별

specification : 사양, 규격(스펙)

enlarged : 커진

capability : 능력, 역량

7) OSI Model [7] OSI 모델

The Open Systems Interconnection (OSI) model describes seven layers that computer systems use to communicate over a network. It was the first standard model for network communications, adopted by all major computer and telecommunication companies in the early 1980s.

The modern Internet is not based on OSI, but on the simpler TCP/IP model. However, the OSI 7-layer model is still widely used, as it helps visualize and communicate how networks operate, and helps isolate and troubleshoot networking problems.

OSI was introduced in 1983 by representatives of the major computer and telecom companies, and was adopted by ISO as an international standard in 1984.

OSI(Open Systems Interconnection) 모델은 컴퓨터 시스템이 네트워크를 통해 통신하는 데 사용하는 7개의 계층을 말한다. 1980년대 초 모든 주요 컴퓨터 및 통신 회사에서 채택한 네트워크 통신의 첫 번째 표준 모델이다.

현대 인터넷은 OSI를 기반으로 하지 않고 보다 단순한 TCP/IP 모델을 기반으로 한다. 그러나 OSI 7계층 모델은 네트워크 작동 방식을 시각화 및 전달하고 네트워킹 문제를 분리 및 해결하는 데 도움이 되므로 여전히 널리 쓰인다.

OSI는 1983년 주요 컴퓨터 및 통신 회사 대표들에 의해 도입되었으며 1984년 ISO에 의해 국제 표준으로 채택되었다.

---

7 https://www.imperva.com/learn/application-security/osi-model

Vocabulary

describe : 서술하다, 묘사하다
standard model : 표준 모델
adopted : 채택된
modern : 현대의, 근대의, 최신의
visualize : 시각화하다
operate : 작동하다
isolate : 분리하다
troubleshoot : 해결하다
representative : 대표
top down : 탑다운, 하향식
serve : 제공하다
end user : 최종 사용자

① OSI Model Explained: The OSI 7 Layers

We'll describe OSI layers "top down" from the application layer that directly serves the end user, down to the physical layer.

– Layer 7 : Application Layer

The application layer is used by end-user software such as web browsers and email clients. It provides protocols that allow software to send and receive information and present meaningful data to users. A few examples of application layer protocols are the Hypertext Transfer Protocol (HTTP), File Transfer Protocol (FTP), Post Office Protocol (POP), Simple Mail Transfer Protocol (SMTP), and Domain Name System (DNS).

① OSI 모델 설명: OSI 7 계층

최종 사용자에게 직접 서비스를 제공하는 애플리케이션 계층에서 물리적 계층까지 OSI 계층을 "하향식(탑다운)"으로 설명하겠다.

- 계층 7: 응용 계층

응용 계층은 웹 브라우저 및 전자 메일 클라이언트와 같은 최종 사용자 소프트웨어에서 사용된다. 소프트웨어가 정보를 주고받고 의미 있는 데이터를 사용자에게 제공할 수 있는 프로토콜을 제공한다. 응용 계층 프로토콜의 몇 가지 예로는 HTTP(Hypertext Transfer Protocol), FTP(파일 전송 프로토콜), POP(Post Office Protocol), SMTP(Simple Mail Transfer Protocol) 및 DNS(Domain Name System)가 있다.

- Layer 6 : Presentation Layer

The presentation layer prepares data for the application layer. It defines how two devices should encode, encrypt, and compress data so it is received correctly on the other end. The presentation layer takes any data transmitted by the application layer and prepares it for transmission over the session layer.

- 계층 6 : 표현 계층

표현 계층은 응용 계층에 대한 데이터를 준비한다. 두 장치가 데이터를 인코딩, 암호화 및 압축하여 다른 쪽 끝에서 올바르게 수신하는 방법을 정의한다. 표현 계층은 응용 계층이 전송하는 모든 데이터를 가져와 세션 계층을 통해 전송할 수 있도록 준비한다.

- Layer 5 : Session Layer

The session layer creates communication channels, called sessions, between devices. It is responsible for opening sessions, ensuring they remain open and functional while data is being transferred, and closing them when communication ends. The session layer can also set checkpoints during a data transfer–if the session is interrupted, devices can resume data transfer from the last checkpoint.

– 계층 5: 세션 계층

세션 계층은 장치 간에 세션이라고 하는 통신 채널을 만든다. 세션을 열고 데이터가 전송되는 동안 열려 있고 기능적으로 유지되도록 하고 통신이 종료되면 세션을 닫는 역할을 한다. 세션 계층은 데이터 전송 중에 체크포인트를 설정할 수도 있다. 세션이 중단된 경우 장치는 마지막 체크포인트에서 데이터 전송을 재개할 수 있다.

– Layer 4 : Transport Layer

The transport layer takes data transferred in the session layer and breaks it into "segments" on the transmitting end. It is responsible for reassembling the segments on the receiving end, turning it back into data that can be used by the session layer. The transport layer carries out flow control, sending data at a rate that matches the connection speed of the receiving device, and error control, checking if data was received incorrectly and if not, requesting it again.

– 계층 4 : 전송 계층

전송 계층은 세션 계층에서 전송된 데이터를 가져와서 전송 끝의 "세그먼트"로 나눈다. 수신 끝의 세그먼트를 재조립하여 세션 계층에서 사용할 수 있는 데이터로 다시 변환하는 역할을 담당한다. 전송 계층은 수신 장치의 연결 속도와 일치하는 속도로 데이터를 보내는 흐름 제어와 데이터가 잘못 수신되었는지 확인하고 그렇지 않은 경우 다시 요청하는 오류 제어를 수행한다.

- Layer 3 : Network Layer

The network layer has two main functions. One is breaking up segments into network packets, and reassembling the packets on the receiving end. The other is routing packets by discovering the best path across a physical network. The network layer uses network addresses (typically Internet Protocol addresses) to route packets to a destination node.

- 계층 3: 네트워크 계층

네트워크 계층에는 두 가지 주요 기능이 있다. 하나는 세그먼트를 네트워크 패킷으로 분할하고 수신 끝에서 패킷을 재조립하는 것이다. 다른 하나는 물리적 네트워크에서 최적의 경로를 검색하여 패킷을 라우팅 하는 것이다. 네트워크 계층은 네트워크 주소(일반적으로 인터넷 프로토콜 주소)를 사용하여 패킷을 대상 노드로 라우팅한다.

- Layer 2 : Data Link Layer

The data link layer establishes and terminates a connection between two physically-connected nodes on a network. It breaks up packets into frames and sends them from source to destination. This layer is composed of two parts-Logical Link Control (LLC), which identifies network protocols, performs error checking and synchronizes frames, and Media Access Control (MAC) which uses MAC addresses to connect devices and define permissions to transmit and receive data.

- 계층 2: 데이터 링크 계층

데이터 링크 계층은 네트워크에서 물리적으로 연결된 두 노드 간의 연결을 설정하고 종료한다. 패킷을 프레임으로 나누고 원본에서 목적지로 보낸다. 이 계층은 네트워크 프로토콜을 식별하고 오류 검사를 수행하고 프레임을 동기화하는 LLC(논리 링크 제어)와 MAC 주소를 사용하여 장치를 연결하고 데이터를 송수신할 수 있는 권한을 정의하는 MAC(미디어 액세스 제어)의 두 부분으로 구성된다.

– Layer 1 : Physical Layer

The physical layer is responsible for the physical cable or wireless connection between network nodes. It defines the connector, the electrical cable or wireless technology connecting the devices, and is responsible for transmission of the raw data, which is simply a series of 0s and 1s, while taking care of bit rate control.

– 계층 1: 물리 계층

물리 계층은 네트워크 노드 간의 물리적 케이블 또는 무선 연결을 담당한다. 기기를 연결하는 커넥터, 전기 케이블 또는 무선 기술을 정의하며 비트 전송률 제어와 함께 단순히 0과 1의 연속인 원시 데이터 전송을 담당한다.

Vocabulary

provide : 제공하다
meaningful : 의미 있는
presentation : 표현, 발표
encode : 인코드, 부호화하다, 암호로 바꾸다
encrypt : 암호화하다
compress : 압축하다
responsible : 책임이 있는
resume : 재개하다
reassemble : 재조립하다
carry out : 수행, 이행하다
incorrectly : 부정확하게

request : 요청하다
discover : 발견하다
destination : 목적지, 도착지
establish : 설정하다
terminate : 끝나다, 종료하다
identify : 확인하다
synchronize : 동기화하다
permission : 허락, 허가
raw data : 원래 데이터
take care of : 책임을 지다, 처리하다

② Advantages of OSI Model

The OSI model helps users and operators of computer networks:

Determine the required hardware and software to build their network.
Understand and communicate the process followed by components communicating across a network.
Perform troubleshooting, by identifying which network layer is causing an issue and focusing efforts on that layer.

The OSI model helps network device manufacturers and networking software vendors:

Create devices and software that can communicate with products from any other vendor, allowing open interoperability
Define which parts of the network their products should work with.

Communicate to users at which network layers their product operates – for example, only at the application layer, or across the stack.

② OSI 모델의 장점

OSI 모델은 컴퓨터 네트워크의 사용자와 운영자에게 다음과 같은 도움을 준다.

네트워크를 구축하는 데 필요한 하드웨어 및 소프트웨어를 결정한다.
구성 요소가 네트워크를 통해 통신하는 과정을 이해하고 전달한다.
문제를 일으키는 네트워크 계층을 식별하고 해당 계층에 집중하여 문제 해결을 수행한다.

OSI 모델은 네트워크 장치 제조업체 및 네트워킹 소프트웨어 공급업체에 다음과 같은 도움을 준다.

다른 공급업체의 제품과 통신할 수 있는 장치 및 소프트웨어를 생성하여 개방형 상호운용성을 제공한다.
제품이 작동해야 하는 네트워크 부분을 정의한다.
제품이 작동하는 네트워크 계층(예: 애플리케이션 계층 또는 스택 전체에서)을 사용자와 통신한다.

Vocabulary

users and operators : 사용자와 운영자
troubleshooting : 고장의 수리, 분쟁 조정
cause : 야기하다
component : 구성요소
issue : 문제, 쟁점
manufacturer : 제조업체
vendor : 공급업체
interoperability : 상호운용성

③ OSI vs. TCP/IP Model

The Transfer Control Protocol/Internet Protocol (TCP/IP) is older than the OSI model and was created by the US Department of Defense (DoD). A key difference between the models is that TCP/IP is simpler, collapsing several OSI layers into one:

OSI layers 5, 6, 7 are combined into one Application Layer in TCP/IP.
OSI layers 1, 2 are combined into one Network Access Layer in TCP/IP – however TCP/IP does not take responsibility for sequencing and acknowledgement functions, leaving these to the underlying transport layer.

OSI 대 TCP / IP 모델

TCP / IP (전송 제어 프로토콜 / 인터넷 프로토콜)는 OSI 모델보다 오래되었으며 미국 국방부(DoD)에서 만들었다. 모델 간의 주요 차이점은 TCP / IP가 더 간단하여 여러 OSI 계층을 하나로 축소한다는 것이다.

OSI 레이어 5, 6, 7은 TCP / IP에서 하나의 애플리케이션 계층으로 결합된다.
OSI 계층 1, 2는 TCP/IP에서 하나의 네트워크 액세스 계층으로 결합되지만 TCP/IP는 시퀀싱 및 승인 기능을 담당하지 않으므로 기본 전송 계층에 이 기능을 맡긴다.

Vocabulary

collapse : 무너지다, 붕괴되다
combine : 결합하다
take responsibility for : 책임지다
acknowledgement : 승인, 인정

☞ 잠깐 쉬어가기 ....

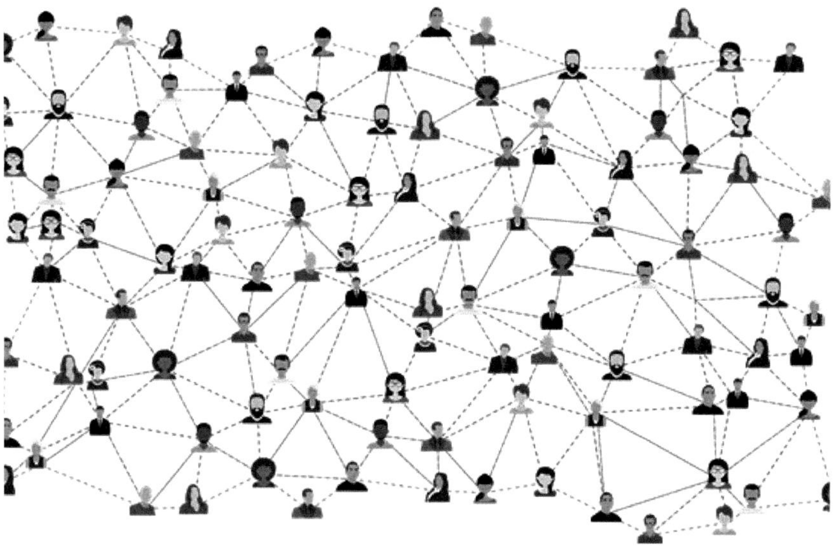

과기정통부에서 발표한 '2022 인터넷 이용 실태조사'[8]에 따르면, 우리나라의 가구 인터넷 접속률은 99.96%라고 합니다. 2,136만 가구 중 2,136만 가구가 인터넷 접속이 가능하다는 뜻은 모든 가구가 인터넷 접속이 가능하다는 이야기겠죠? 그리고 우리 나라 국민 5,081만명 중 인터넷 이용자 수는 47,253,345명, 전체 인구의 93%가 인터넷을 이용하고 있습니다. 흥미로운 점은 지난 5년간 60대 이상 고령층에서 인터넷 이용률이 증가한 것인데요, 5년 전에 60대가 88.8% 인터넷을 이용했다면 2022년에는 94% 인터넷을 이용했습니다. 또한 주 평균 인터넷 이용시간은 2018년 대비 5.6시간 증가하여 22.1시간을 사용하는 것으로 나타났습니다. 팬데믹을 거치면서 인터넷 쇼핑 이용률도 62%에서 73.7%로 월 평균 6.3회, 192,759원정도를 인터넷 쇼핑에 사용하는 것으로 집계되었습니다.

동영상 서비스 이용률은 96.1%이고, 하루 1회 이상 이용하는 사람들의 비율은 76.2%

8 https://www.nia.or.kr/site/nia_kor/ex/bbs/View.do?cbIdx=99870&bcIdx=25604&parentSeq=25604

입니다. 1인 가구 증가 및 고령사회 진입에 따라 70세 이상 인구의 동영상 서비스 이용률이 높아졌는데요, 2022년 82.4%로 2019년 47.1%에서 4년간 35.3%나 상승하였습니다. 그 중 두드러지는 증가 폭을 보이는 동영상 서비스는 유튜브(77.2%)입니다. 팬데믹과 인터넷의 발달이 맞물려서 고령층의 생활 양상까지 바꾸었다는 것은 참으로 놀랍습니다.

연습문제

exercises

1~5. 다음 빈 칸에 들어가는 단어로 적절한 것을 넣으세요.

1. (   ) of a computer network may include personal computers, servers, networking hardware, or other specialized or general-purpose hosts.

정답 : ________________________________

2. (   ) is a special type of network where many participants nodes are connected to form a tree type of architecture.

정답 : ________________________________

3. Residences typically employ one LAN and connect to the internet WAN through (   ) using a broadband modem.

정답 : ________________________________

4. The modern Internet is not based on OSI, but on the simpler (   ).

정답 : ________________________________

5. (   ) is responsible for the physical cable or wireless connection between network nodes.

정답 : ________________________________

6~10. 다음 It이 지칭하는 것을 영어로 쓰세요.

6. It extends interpersonal communications by electronic means with various technologies, such as email, instant messaging, online chat, voice and video telephone calls, and video conferencing.

정답 : ______________________________

7. It uses computing resources across a network to accomplish tasks.

정답 : ______________________________

8. It is the structure and arrangement of components of a computer communication system.

정답 : ______________________________

9. It connects network devices over a relatively short distance.

정답 : ______________________________

10. It describes seven layers that computer systems use to communicate over a network.

정답 : ______________________________

연습문제 해답

1. The nodes
2. A tree topology
3. an internet service provider (ISP)
4. TCP/IP model
5. The physical layer
6. A computer network
7. Distributed computing
8. Network Topology
9. A LAN
10. The Open Systems Interconnection (OSI) model

Chapter

10 Wireless Communication

무선 통신

학습순서

1) Introduction
2) Wireless Communication
3) Modes of Wireless Communications
4) Advantages of Wireless Communication
5) Disadvantages of Wireless Communication
6) Applications

잠깐 쉬어가기

연습문제

【 INTRO 】

여러분이 지금 있는 장소에서 와이파이 신호를 확인하면 몇 개 정도의 신호가 발견됩니까? 여러분의 물건 중에 와이파이 기능을 가지고 있는 물건은 몇 개입니까? 핸드폰을 비롯하여 태블릿, 이어폰, 스피커, 키보드, 마우스, 시계와 같은 일상의 물건에도 와이파이 기능이 탑재되어 있습니다. 또한 자동차를 비롯한 냉장고, 세탁기, 건조기를 비롯한 전자 기기 등에도 와이파이 기능이 탑재되어 있습니다. 이번 과에서는 무선 통신이 무엇이며 유형과 장/단점, 그리고 무선 통신을 적용할 수 있는 분야에 대해서 알아보도록 하겠습니다.

If you were to check for Wi-Fi signals in your current location, how many signals would you find? How many of your belongings have Wi-Fi functionality? Everyday objects such as smartphones, tablets, earphones, speakers, keyboards, mice, and watches are equipped with Wi-Fi capabilities. Additionally, electronic devices like cars, refrigerators, washing machines, and dryers also come with Wi-Fi functionality.

In this chapter, we will explore what wireless communication is, its types, advantages and disadvantages, and various fields where wireless communication can be applied.

1) Introduction[1] 개요

Communication systems can be wired or wireless and the medium used for communication can be guided or unguided. In wired communication, the medium is a physical path like co-axial cables, twisted pair cables and optical fiber links etc. which guides the signal to propagate from one point to other.

Such type of medium is called guided medium. On the other hand, wireless communication doesn't require any physical medium but propagates the signal through space. Since, space only allows for signal transmission without any guidance, the medium used in wireless communication is called unguided medium.

If there is no physical medium, then how does wireless communication transmit signals? Even though there are no cables used in wireless communication, the transmission and reception of signals is accomplished with antennas.

Antennas are electrical devices that transform the electrical signals to radio signals in the form of electromagnetic (EM) waves and vice versa. These electromagnetic waves propagates through space. Hence, both transmitter and receiver consists of an antenna.

1 https://www.electronicshub.org/wireless-communication-introduction-types-applications/

통신 시스템은 유선이나 무선일 수 있고, 통신에 사용되는 매체는 안내되거나 그렇지 않을 수 있다. 유선 통신에서 매체는 동축 케이블, 이중 나선 케이블 및 광섬유 링크 등과 같은 물리적 경로로 신호가 한 지점에서 다른 지점으로 전파되도록 안내한다.

이러한 유형의 매체를 안내 매체라고 한다. 반면, 무선 통신은 물리적 매체를 필요로 하지 않지만 공간을 통해 신호를 전파한다. 공간이 안내 없이 신호 전송만 허용하기 때문에 무선 통신에서 사용되는 매체를 안내되지 않은 매체라고 일컫는다.

물리적 매체가 없다면 무선 통신은 어떻게 신호를 전송할까? 무선 통신에 사용되는 케이블이 없어도 안테나를 통해 신호의 송수신 작업을 수행할 수 있다.

안테나는 전자기파(EM)의 형태로 전기 신호를 무선 신호로 변환하는 혹은 그 반대로 하는 전기 장치이다. 이 전자파는 우주를 통해 전파된다. 따라서 송신기와 수신기 모두 안테나로 구성된다.

Vocabulary

wired : 유선의
wireless : 무선의
medium : 매체
guided : 안내되는
unguided : 안내 없는
co-axial cable : 동축 케이블
twisted pair cable : 트위스트 페어 케이블
optical fiber links : 광섬유 링크
signal : 신호
propagate : 전파하다

on the other hand : 반면에
require : 요구하다
transmission : 전송
transmission and reception : 송수신
accomplish : 성취하다
transform : 변형시키다
electromagnetic (EM) waves : 전자파
vice versa : 반대로
consist of : ~로 구성된다

2) Wireless Communication[2] 무선 통신

Wireless communication (or just wireless, when the context allows) is the transfer of information between two or more points that do not use an electrical conductor as a medium by which to perform the transfer. The most common wireless technologies use radio waves. With radio waves, intended distances can be short, such as a few meters for Bluetooth or as far as millions of kilometers for deep-space radio communications. It encompasses various types of fixed, mobile, and portable applications, including two-way radios, cellular telephones, personal digital assistants (PDAs), and wireless networking.

Other examples of applications of radio wireless technology include GPS units, garage door openers, wireless computer mouse, keyboards and headsets, headphones, radio receivers, satellite television, broadcast television and cordless telephones. Somewhat less common methods of achieving wireless

---

2 https://en.wikipedia.org/wiki/Wireless

communications include the use of other electromagnetic wireless technologies, such as light, magnetic, or electric fields or the use of sound.

무선 통신(혹은 맥락상 무선)은 전송을 수행하는 매개로 전기 도체를 사용하지 않는 둘 이상의 지점 정보간의 정보이다. 가장 일반적인 무선 기술은 전파를 사용하는 경우이다. 전파를 사용하면 의도된 거리는 블루투스 같은 경우는 몇 미터로 짧게, 심우주 무선 통신일 때는 수백만 킬로미터와 같이 멀어질 수도 있다. 이는 양방향 라디오, 휴대 전화, 개인휴대단말기(PDA), 무선 네트워킹을 포함한 다양한 유형의 고정, 모바일 및 휴대용 애플리케이션을 포함한다.

무선 기술의 다른 예는 GPS 장치, 차고 문 개폐기, 무선 컴퓨터 마우스, 키보드와 헤드셋, 헤드폰, 라디오 수신기, 위성 텔레비전, 방송 텔레비전, 무선 전화 등이 있다. 무선 통신을 실현하는 다소 덜 일반적인 방법에는 빛, 자기장 혹은 전기장과 같은 다른 전자기 무선 기술이나 소리의 사용이 포함된다.

The term wireless has been used twice in communications history, with slightly different meaning. It was initially used from about 1890 for the first radio transmitting and receiving technology, as in wireless telegraphy, until the new word radio replaced it around 1920. Radios in the UK that were not portable continued to be referred to as wireless sets into the 1960s.

The term was revived in the 1980s and 1990s mainly to distinguish digital devices that communicate without wires, such as the examples listed in the previous paragraph, from those that require wires or cables. This became its primary usage in the 2000s, due to the advent of technologies such as mobile broadband, Wi-Fi and Bluetooth.

Wireless operations permit services, such as mobile and interplanetary communications, that are impossible or impractical to implement with the use of wires. The term is commonly used in the telecommunications industry to refer to telecommunications systems (e.g. radio transmitters and receivers, remote controls, etc.) which use some form of energy (e.g. radio waves, acoustic energy,) to transfer information without the use of wires. Information is transferred in this manner over both short and long distances.

무선이라는 용어는 통신 역사에서 약간 다른 의미로 두 번 사용되었다. 이것은 무선 전신에서와 같이, 최초의 무선 송수신 기술에 1890년경부터 1920년경에는 라디오라는 신조어가 그 것을 대체하기 전까지 사용되었다. 영국의 휴대용이 아닌 라디오는 1960년대까지 무선으로 계속 언급되었다. 이 용어는 1980년대와 1990년대에 주로 앞에 단락에서 열거된 것처럼, 와이어(전선)없이 통신하는 디지털 기기와 전선/케이블이 필요한 기기를 구별하기 위해 부활되었다. 이것은 2000년대에 모바일 광대역, 와이파이, 블루투스와 같은 기술의 등장으로 인해 주된 사용이 되었다.

무선 작업은 이동 통신 및 행성 간 통신과 같은 서비스를 허용하는데, 이는 와이어를 사용하여 구현할 수 없거나 비현실적이다. 이 용어는 일반적으로 전기통신 업계에서 와이어를 사용하지 않고 정보를 전송하기 위해 어떤 형태의 에너지(예: 전파, 음향 에너지)를 사용하는 통신 시스템(예: 무선 송신기 및 수신기, 원격 제어 등)을 지칭하기 위해 사용된다. 정보는 단거리 및 장거리 모두에서 이러한 방식으로 전송된다.

Vocabulary

electrical : 전기의

conductor : 도체

intended distance : 의도된 거리

deep-space : 심우주

encompass : 포함하다

portable : 휴대의

two-way : 양방향의

somewhat : 다소

common method : 일반적인 방법

electromagnetic wireless technology : 전자기 무선 기술

field : 분야

slightly : 약간

wireless telegraphy : 무선전신술

primary: 주된, 주요

usage : 용도

advent : 도래, 출현

broadband : 광대역, 브로드밴드

permit : 허용한다

interplanetary : 행성간의

impractical : 비현실적인

acoustic energy : 음향 에너지

3) Modes of Wireless Communications[3] 무선 통신의 유형

Wireless communications can be via:

Radio

Radio and microwave communication carry information by modulating properties of electromagnetic waves transmitted through space.

3 https://en.wikipedia.org/wiki/Wireless#Modes

Free-space optical

Free-space optical communication (FSO) is an optical communication technology that uses light propagating in free space to transmit wirelessly data for telecommunications or computer networking. "Free space" means the light beams travel through the open air or outer space. This contrasts with other communication technologies that use light beams traveling through transmission lines such as optical fiber or dielectric "light pipes".

The technology is useful where physical connections are impractical due to high costs or other considerations. For example, free space optical links are used in cities between office buildings which are not wired for networking, where the cost of running cable through the building and under the street would be prohibitive. Another widely used example is consumer IR devices such as remote controls and IrDA (Infrared Data Association) networking, which is used as an alternative to Wi-Fi networking to allow laptops, PDAs, printers, and digital cameras to exchange data.

Sonic

Sonic, especially ultrasonic short range communication involves the transmission and reception of sound.

Electromagnetic induction

Electromagnetic induction only allows short-range communication and power transmission. It has been used in biomedical situations such as pacemakers, as well as for short-range RFID tags.

무선 통신은 다음을 통해 이루어질 수 있다.

라디오

라디오와 마이크로파 통신은 우주를 통해 전달되는 전자파의 특성을 변조하여 정보를 전달한다.

자유 공간 광학

자유 공간 광통신(FSO)은 자유공간에서 전파되는 빛을 이용해 통신이나 컴퓨터 네트워킹을 위해 무선으로 데이터를 전송하는 광통신 기술이다.
"자유 공간"은 조명 빔이 열린 공기 또는 외부 공간을 통해 이동하는 것을 의미한다. 광섬유나 유전체 광파이프와 같은 전송선을 통과하는 광선을 사용하는 다른 통신 기술과는 대조적이다.

이 기술은 높은 비용 또는 기타 고려 사항으로 인해 물리적 연결이 불가능한 경우에 유용하다. 가령, 무료 공간 광학 링크는 네트워크를 위해 배선되지 않은 사무실 건물들 사이의 도시에서 사용되는데, 건물과 길 아래를 케이블로 연결하는 비용은 엄청날 것이다. 또 다른 널리 사용되는 예로는 노트북, PDA, 프린터 및 디지털 카메라가 데이터를 교환할 수 있도록 Wi-Fi 네트워킹의 대안으로 사용되는 원격 제어 및 IrDA(적외선 통신 협회) 네트워킹과 같은 소비자 IR 장치가 있다.

음파

음파, 특히 초음파 단거리 통신은 소리의 전달과 수신을 수반한다.

전자기 유도

전자기 유도는 단거리 통신 및 전력 전송만 가능하게 한다. 그것은 심박조율기와 같은 생물의학적인 상황뿐만 아니라 단거리 RFID 태그에도 사용되어 왔다.

Vocabulary

electromagnetic wave : **전자파**

modulate : **조절하다**

properties : **성질, 특징**

Free-space optical communication (FSO) : **자유 공간 광통신**

propagate : 전파하다
beam : 빔, 빛줄기
contrast : 대비되다
optical fiber : 광섬유
dielectric : 유전체의
impractical : 비현실적인
consideration : 고려, 고려사항
remote control : 리모콘, 원격조절
IrDA (Infrared Data Association) : 적외선 데이터 협회
sonic : 음파의
electromagnetic induction : 전자기 유도
biomedical : 생물의학의

4) Advantages of Wireless Communication[4] 무선 통신의 장점

There are numerous advantage of wireless communication technology, wireless networking and wireless systems over wired cmmunication like cost, mobility, ease of installation, and reliability etc.

① Cost

The cost of installing wires, cables and other infrastructure is eliminated in wireless communication and hence lowering the overall cost of the system compared to wired communication system. Installing wired network in building, digging up the Earth to lay the cables and running those wires across the streets is extremely difficult, costly and time consuming job.

---

4 https://www.electronicshub.org/wireless-communication-introduction-types-applications/#Advantages_of_Wireless_Communication

In historical buildings, drilling holes for cables is not a best idea as it destroys the integrity and importance of the building. Also, in older buildings with no dedicated lines for communication, wireless communication like Wi-Fi or Wireless LAN is the only option.

비용, 이동성, 설치 용이성 및 신뢰성 등과 같은 유선 통신에 비해 무선 통신 기술, 무선 네트워킹 및 무선 시스템에는 수많은 이점이 있다.

① 비용

무선 통신에서는 전선, 케이블 및 기타 인프라 설치비용이 제거되어 유선 통신 시스템에 비해 시스템의 전체 비용이 절감된다. 건물에 유선 네트워크를 설치하고 케이블을 설치하기 위해 땅을 파고 거리를 가로질러 전선을 연결하는 것은 매우 어렵고 비용이 많이 들고 시간이 많이 소요되는 작업이다.

역사적인 건물에서 케이블 구멍을 뚫는 것은 건물의 무결성과 중요성을 파괴하기 때문에 좋은 생각이 아니다. 또한 통신 전용선이 없는 노후 건물에서는 Wi-Fi나 무선 LAN과 같은 무선 통신이 유일한 옵션이다.

② Mobility

As mentioned earlier, mobility is the main advantage of wireless communication system. It offers the freedom to move around while still connected to network.

③ Ease of Installation

The setup and installation of wireless communication network's equipment and infrastructure is very easy as we need not worry about the hassle of cables. Also, the time required to setup a wireless system like a Wi-Fi network for example, is very less when compared to setting up a full cabled network.

④ Reliability

Since there are no cables and wires involved in wireless communication, there is no chance of communication failure due to damage of these cables, which may be caused by environmental conditions, cable splice and natural diminution of metallic conductors.

⑤ Disaster Recovery

In case of accidents due to fire, floods or other disasters, the loss of communication infrastructure in wireless communication system can be minimal.

② 이동성

앞서 언급했듯 이동성은 무선 통신 시스템의 주요 장점이다. 네트워크에 연결된 상태에서 자유롭게 이동할 수 있다.

③ 설치 용이성

무선 통신망의 장비 및 인프라의 설정 및 설치는 케이블의 번거로움을 걱정할 필요가 없기 때문에 매우 쉽다. 또한 예를 들어 Wi-Fi 네트워크와 같은 무선 시스템을 설정하는 데 필요한 시간은 전체 케이블 네트워크를 설정하는 것과 비교할 때 매우 짧다.

④ 신뢰성

무선 통신에는 케이블과 전선이 없기 때문에 환경 조건, 케이블 접속 및 금속 도체의 자연적 감소로 인해 이러한 케이블이 손상되어 통신 장애가 발생할 가능성이 없다.

⑤ 재해 복구

화재, 홍수 또는 기타 재해로 인한 사고 시 무선 통신 시스템에서 통신 인프라의 손실을 최소화할 수 있다.

Vocabulary

advantage : 장점

cost : 비용

mobility : 이동성

installation : 설치

reliability : 신뢰성

infrastructure : 인프라

eliminate : 없애다, 제거하다

lower : 내리다, 낮추다

dig up : 파다

lay : 깔다, 설치하다

historical : 역사적

drill : 구멍을 뚫다(드릴로)

integrity : 완전한 상태, 온전함

dedicated : 전용의

damage : 훼손

environmental conditions : 환경적 조건들

splice : (테이프의) 끝을 이은부분

diminution : 감소

metallic : 금속의

conductor : 전도체

disaster : 재난

recovery : 회복

floods : 홍수

5) Disadvantages of Wireless Communication[5] 무선 통신의 단점

Even though wireless communication has a number of advantages over wired communication, there are a few disadvantages as well. The most concerning disadvantages are Interference, Security and Health.

① Interference

Wireless Communication systems use open space as the medium for transmitting signals. As a result, there is a huge chance that radio signals from one wireless communication system or network might interfere with other signals.

The best example is Bluetooth and Wi-Fi (WLAN). Both these technologies use the 2.4GHz frequency for communication and when both of these devices are active at the same time, there is a chance of interference.

무선 통신은 유선 통신에 비해 많은 장점이 있지만 몇 가지 단점도 있다. 가장 우려되는 단점은 간섭, 보안 및 건강이다.

① 간섭

무선 통신 시스템은 신호를 전송하는 매체로 열린 공간을 사용한다. 결과적으로 한 무선 통신 시스템이나 네트워크의 무선 신호가 다른 신호를 간섭을 일으킬 가능성이 크다.

가장 좋은 예는 Bluetooth와 Wi-Fi(WLAN)다. 이 두 기술은 통신에 2.4GHz 주파수를 사용하며 두 장치가 동시에 활성화되면 간섭 가능성이 있다.

5 https://www.electronicshub.org/wireless-communication-introduction-types-applications/#Disadvantages_of_Wireless_Communication

② Security

One of the main concerns of wireless communication is Security of the data. Since the signals are transmitted in open space, it is possible that an intruder can intercept the signals and copy sensitive information.

③ Health Concerns

Continuous exposure to any type of radiation can be hazardous. Even though the levels of RF energy that can cause the damage are not accurately established, it is advised to avoid RF radiation to the maximum.

② 보안

무선 통신의 주요 관심사 중 하나는 데이터 보안이다. 신호가 열린 공간에서 전송되기 때문에 침입자가 신호를 가로채 민감한 정보를 복사할 수 있다.

③ 건강 문제

모든 유형의 방사선에 지속적으로 노출되면 위험할 수 있다. 손상을 일으킬 수 있는 RF 에너지 수준이 정확하게 설정되지 않았더라도 RF 방사를 최대한 피하는 것이 좋다.

Vocabulary

disadvantage : 단점
concerning : 우려되는
interference : 간섭
security : 보안
interfere : 간섭하다, 방해하다
frequency : 주파수
active : 활성화된
intruder : 침입자

intercept : 가로채다
sensitive : 민감한, 신중을 기하는
continuous exposure : 지속적인 노출
radiation : 방사능
hazardous : 위험한
cause : 야기하다
accurately 정확하게, 정밀하게
establish : 설정하다, 수립하다
avoid : 피하다

6) Applications[6] 적용

Wireless technology can be applied in various fields. The followings are descriptions of the applicable areas.

① Mobile telephones

One of the best-known examples of wireless technology is mobile phones. These wireless phones use radio waves from signal-transmission towers to enable their users to make phone calls from many locations worldwide.

무선 기술은 다양한 분야에 적용될 수 있다. 다음은 해당 영역에 대한 설명이다.

① 휴대전화

무선 기술의 가장 잘 알려진 예 중 하나는 휴대폰이다. 이러한 무선 전화는 신호 전송 타워의 전파를 사용하여 사용자가 전 세계 여러 위치에서 전화를 걸 수 있도록 한다.

6 https://en.wikipedia.org/wiki/Wireless#Applications

② Data communication

Wireless data communications allow wireless networking between desktop computers, laptops, tablet computers, cell phones and other related devices. The various available technologies differ in local availability, coverage range and performance, and in some circumstances, users employ multiple connection types and switch between them using connection manager software or a mobile VPN to handle the multiple connections as a secure, single virtual network. Supporting technologies include:
Wi-Fi is a wireless local area network that enables portable computing devices to connect easily with other devices, peripheries, and the Internet. Cellular data service offers coverage within a range of 10-15 miles from the nearest cell site.

Low-power wide-area networks (LPWAN) bridge the gap between Wi-Fi and Cellular for low bitrate Internet of things (IoT) applications.

Mobile-satellite communications may be used where other wireless connections are unavailable, such as in largely rural areas or remote locations. Satellite communications are especially important for transportation, aviation, maritime and military use.

Wireless sensor networks are responsible for sensing noise, interference, and activity in data collection networks.

Wireless data communications are used to provide a backup communications link in case of normal network failure, to link portable or temporary workstations, to overcome situations where normal cabling is difficult or financially impractical, or to remotely connect mobile users or networks.

– Peripherals

Peripheral devices in computing can also be connected wirelessly, as part of a Wi–Fi network or directly via an optical or radio–frequency (RF) peripheral interface(e.g. wireless keyboards, blooth speakers)

② 데이터 통신

무선 데이터 통신은 데스크톱 컴퓨터, 노트북, 태블릿, 휴대 전화 및 기타 관련 장치 간의 무선 네트워킹을 허용한다. 사용 가능한 다양한 기술은 로컬 가용성, 적용 범위 및 성능이 다르며, 경우에 따라 사용자는 여러 연결 유형을 사용하고 연결 관리자 소프트웨어 또는 모바일 VPN을 사용하여 여러 연결 유형을 전환하여 다중 연결을 안전한 단일 가상 네트워크로 처리한다. 지원 기술은 다음과 같다.

Wi–Fi는 휴대용 컴퓨팅 장치가 다른 장치, 주변 장치 및 인터넷에 쉽게 연결할 수 있도록 하는 무선 근거리 통신망이다. 셀룰러 데이터 서비스는 가장 가까운 셀 사이트에서 10–15마일 범위 내에서 서비스를 제공한다.

저전력 광역 네트워크(LPWAN)는 낮은 비트 전송률의 사물 인터넷(IoT) 애플리케이션을 위해 Wi–Fi와 셀룰러 간의 격차를 해소한다.

모바일 위성 통신은 시골 지역이나 원격 위치와 같이 다른 무선 연결을 사용할 수 없는 곳에서 사용할 수 있다. 위성 통신은 운송, 항공, 해상 및 군사용으로 특히 중요하다.

무선 센서 네트워크는 데이터 수집 네트워크에서 노이즈, 간섭 및 활동을 감지하는 역할을 한다.

무선 데이터 통신은 정상적인 네트워크 장애 시 백업 통신 링크를 제공하고 휴대용 또는 임시 워크스테이션을 연결하여 정상적인 케이블 연결이 어렵거나 재정적으로 비현실적인 상황을 극복하거나 모바일 사용자 또는 네트워크를 원격으로 연결하는 데 사용된다.

– 주변기기

컴퓨팅의 주변 장치는 Wi-Fi 네트워크의 일부로 무선으로 연결하거나 광학 또는 무선 주파수(RF) 주변 장치 인터페이스(예: 무선 키보드, 스피커)를 통해 직접 연결할 수도 있다.

③ Energy transfer

Wireless energy transfer is a process whereby electrical energy is transmitted from a power source to an electrical load that does not have a built-in power source, without the use of interconnecting wires.

④ Medical technologies

New wireless technologies, such as mobile body area networks (MBAN), have the capability to monitor blood pressure, heart rate, oxygen level and body temperature. This technology helps with the intentional and unintentional risk of infection.

③ 에너지 전달

무선 에너지 전송은 상호 연결된 전선을 사용하지 않고 전원에서 내장 전원이 없는 전기 부하로 전기 에너지를 전송하는 프로세스이다.

④ 의료 기술

모바일 신체 영역 네트워크(MBAN)와 같은 새로운 무선 기술에는 혈압, 심박수, 산소 수준 및 체온을 모니터링할 수 있는 기능이 있다. 이 기술은 의도적이거나 의도하지 않은 감염 위험을 줄이는 데 도움이 된다.

Vocabulary

applicable : 적용할 수 있는
differ : 다르다
availability : 유효성, 가능성
circumstance : 상황
employ : 사용하다
handle : 다루다
virtual : 가상의
peripheral : 주변 장치
satellite : 위성
transportation : 교통
aviation : 항공
maritime : 해양
military use : 군사용도
temporary : 임시의
blood pressure : 혈압
heart rate : 심박 수
oxygen level : 산소 수치
body temperature : 체온
intentional : 의도적인
unintentional : 의도하지 않은

☞ 잠깐 쉬어가기 ....

스타벅스 사이렌 오더 어플리케이션 활용
(출처: 대한경제 갈무리, https://www.dnews.co.kr/uhtml/view.jsp?idxno=202308240958125080370)

와이파이 통신 중에는 비콘이 있습니다. 비콘은 가까이에 있는 스마트 기기를 자동으로 인식하는데, 다른 유형에 비하여 범위가 50m까지 넓습니다. 비콘이 적용되는 사례는 우리 생활에 종종 눈에 띄는데요. 특정 식당이나 쇼핑몰에 입장하면 방문자에게 메시지나 쿠폰을 보내는 것이 비콘이 적용된 경우입니다. 스타벅스의 '사이렌 오더'도 대표적인 비콘의 활용 사례라고 할 수 있습니다. 스타벅스 코리아가 2014년에 세계 최초로 만든 '사이렌오더'는 우리나라에서 성공적으로 활약하며 비콘 기반의 시스템을 통하여 보다 고객들로 하여금 스타벅스의 플랫폼 안으로 들어오도록 만들었습니다.

사이렌오더는 매장 방문 전에 주문과 결제를 할 수 있어 혼잡한 시간대에 주문 대기 시간을 줄일 수 있기 때문에 스타벅스의 충성 고객을 더욱 확보할 수 있었습니다. 이용자들이 스타벅스 앱을 설치하여 사이렌오더와 연동된 스타벅스의 선불식 충전 카드인 '마이 스타벅스 리워드'로 구매하게 되는데, 이 회원 수만 2023년 1월 1000만명을 넘어섰다고 합니다. 대용량 용기에 담아 파는 '투고백(To go bag)' 판매량이 주문 방식이 바뀌면서 급증한 것으로 나타났다고 합니다. 투고백을 사이렌 오더로 구매할 수 있도록 주문 시스템을 개선한 이후 약 한 달(2023년 7월4일~7월31일) 만에 누적판매량이 2만 5000개를 돌파했다고 하는데요. 사이렌 오더가 적용되지 않았던 2022년 같은 기간 대비 4배 많은 양으로, 65.8%나 오른 수치라고 합니다. 이처럼 스타벅스 코리아는 비콘을 활용한 사이렌 오더를 사용하면서 고객의 편리성을 증가시키게 되었고 구매력을 높이게 되었습니다.

교육기관에서도 출결을 체크할 때 비콘 방식을 활용하곤 합니다. 물론 꼼수를 부리는 학생들로 인하여 부정 출석체크에 대한 부작용도 만만치 않긴 하지만, 50m 범위에 들어오면 자동 출석 체크되는 기능은 분명 학생이나 교수자에게 편리한 기능입니다.

연습문제

exercises

1~5. 다음 빈 칸에 들어가는 단어로 적절한 것을 넣으세요.

1. The most common ( ) technologies use radio waves.

정답 : ______________________________

2. Communication systems can be ( ) or wireless and the medium used for communication can be guided or unguided.

정답 : ______________________________

3. Radio and microwave communication carry ( ) by modulating properties of electromagnetic waves transmitted through space.

정답 : ______________________________

4. The cost of ( ) wires, cables and other infrastructure is eliminated in wireless communication and hence lowering the overall cost of the system compared to wired communication system.

정답 : ______________________________

5. Continuous exposure to any type of radiation can be ( ).

정답 : ______________________________

6~10. 다음 It이 지칭하는 것을 영어로 쓰세요.

6. It means the light beams travel through the open air or outer space.

정답 : ______________________________

7. It only allows short-range communication and power transmission.
정답 : ______________________________

8. It offers the freedom to move around while still connected to network.
정답 : ______________________________

9. It is a wireless local area network that enables portable computing devices to connect easily with other devices, peripheries, and the Internet.
정답 : ______________________________

10. It is the transfer of information between two or more points that do not use an electrical conductor as a medium by which to perform the transfer.
정답 : ______________________________

연습문제 해답

1. wireless
2. wired
3. information
4. installing
5. hazardous
6. Free space
7. Electromagnetic induction
8. Mobility
9. Wi-Fi
10. Wireless communication

Chapter

11 Computer Security

컴퓨터 보안

학습순서

【 INTRO 】

여러분들은 혹시 여러분들의 계정과 비밀번호가 노출되었다는 메일을 받아본 적이 있습니까? 종종 TV 뉴스나 웹사이트에서 금융권 사이트들이 해커들에게 공격을 받아 고객 정보가 대량 유출되었다는 뉴스를 들어본 적이 있습니다. 또한 랜섬웨어 때문에 피해를 입었다는 회사의 이야기도 종종 들었을 것입니다. 그렇다고 우리가 인터넷 없이 살아갈 수도 없는 노릇입니다. 보안 기술의 발달은 이 보안기술을 위협하는 다른 기술 또한 발달하였음을 의미합니다. 이번 과에서는 어떠한 것들이 컴퓨터 보안을 위협하고, 이를 예방하기 위한 방법은 무엇인지 알아보도록 합시다.

Have you ever received an e-mail stating that your account and password have been exposed? You may have often heard from TV news or websites that financial sites have been attacked by hackers and that customer information has been leaked in large quantities. Also, you may have heard of the company's damage caused by ransomware. But we can't live without the internet. The development of security technology means that other technologies that threaten this security technology have also developed. In this chapter, let's find out what threatens computer security and how to prevent it.

1) Introduction[1] 개요

Computing magazines often define information assurance as "the technical and managerial measures designed to ensure the confidentiality, possession or control, integrity, authenticity, availability, and utility of information and information systems." This information may be in storage, processing, or transit, and the threats to it can be accidental or intentional.

Protecting information resources is not easy. Network technology advances so quickly that IT experts are constantly challenged to keep up. The plethora of valuable information stored on computers and sent through the web provides great potential for hackers and scammers to infiltrate computer security.

There are two main types of hackers. Some hackers use their computers to break into companies' or other people's computers to steal information, such as credit card numbers. This type of computer criminal uses increasingly sophisticated methods to obtain personal information. Other types of hackers are more interested in damaging the receivers' computers and do this by sending viruses through Web sites or e-mail.

컴퓨팅 잡지는 종종 정보 보장을 "정보 및 정보 시스템의 기밀성, 소유 또는 제어,

1 https://www.encyclopedia.com/science-and-technology/computers-and-electrical-engineering/computers-and-computing/computer-security

무결성, 신뢰성, 가용성 및 활용성을 보장하기 위해 설계된 기술적 및 관리적 조치"로 정의한다. 이 정보는 저장, 처리 또는 전송 중일 수 있고 이 정보에 대한 위협은 우발적이거나 의도적일 수 있다.

정보 자원을 보호하는 것은 쉽지 않다. 네트워크 기술은 매우 빠르게 발전하기 때문에 IT 전문가들은 이에 대응하기 위해 끊임없이 도전을 받는다. 컴퓨터에 저장되고 웹을 통해 전송되는 수많은 귀중한 정보는 해커와 사기꾼들이 컴퓨터 보안에 침투할 수 있는 큰 가능성을 제공한다.

해커에는 크게 두 가지 유형이 있다. 어떤 해커들은 자기들의 컴퓨터를 사용해서 회사나 다른 사람들의 컴퓨터에 침입하여 신용카드 번호와 같은 정보를 훔친다. 이런 종류의 컴퓨터 범죄자는 개인 정보를 얻기 위해 점점 더 정교한 방법을 사용한다. 다른 유형의 해커들은 수신자의 컴퓨터를 해를 입히는 것에 더 관심이 있고 웹 사이트나 이메일을 통해 바이러스를 보내서 이것을 한다.

Computer security, cyber security or information technology security (IT security) is the protection of computer systems and networks from information disclosure, theft of or damage to their hardware, software, or electronic data, as well as from the disruption or misdirection of the services they provide.[2]

The field is becoming increasingly significant due to the increased reliance on computer systems, the internet and wireless network standards such as Bluetooth and Wi-Fi, and due to the growth of "smart" devices, including smartphones, televisions, and the various devices that constitute the "Internet of things". Owing to its complexity, both in terms of politics and technology, cyber security is also one of the major challenges in the

2 https://en.wikipedia.org/wiki/Computer_security

contemporary world.

컴퓨터 보안, 사이버 보안 또는 정보 기술 보안(IT Security)은 정보 노출, 하드웨어, 소프트웨어 또는 전자 데이터의 도난 또는 손상으로부터 컴퓨터 시스템 및 네트워크를 보호하는 것은 물론 제공하는 서비스의 중단 또는 잘못된 방향으로부터 보호하는 것이다.

이 분야는 컴퓨터 시스템, 블루투스, 와이파이 등 인터넷 · 무선 네트워크 표준의 의존도가 증가하고 있고 스마트폰, 텔레비전 등 스마트 기기, 사물인터넷을 구성하는 다양한 기기의 성장으로 그 중요성이 커지고 있다. 사이버 보안은 정치와 기술 면에서 모두 복잡하기 때문에 현대 세계의 주요 과제 중 하나이다.

Vocabulary

confidentiality : 기밀성
possession or control : 소유 또는 제어
integrity : 무결성
authenticity : 진짜임, 신뢰성
availability : 가용성
utility : 효용성
transit : 운송
accidental : 우연, 우발의
intentional : 의도적인
advance : 발전하다
expert : 전문가
constantly : 쭉, 끊임없이
challenged : 도전 받는
keep up : 내려가지 않게 하다, 계속 대응하다

plethora : 과다, 과잉
great potential : 큰 잠재력
hackers and scammers : 해커들과 사기꾼들
infiltrate : 침투하다
criminal : 범죄의
sophisticated : 정교한
reliance : 의존
constitute : 구성하다
complexity : 복잡성

2) What is Computer Security Threats?[3] 컴퓨터 보안 위협

Computer security threats are potential threats to your computer's efficient operation and performance. These could be harmless adware or dangerous trojan infection. As the world becomes more digital, computer security concerns are always developing. A threat in a computer system is a potential danger that could jeopardize your data security. At times, the damage is irreversible.

Types of Threats

A security threat is a threat that has the potential to harm computer systems and organizations. The cause could be physical, such as a computer containing sensitive information being stolen. It's also possible that the cause isn't physical, such as a viral attack.

컴퓨터 보안 위협은 컴퓨터의 효율적인 작동 및 성능에 잠재적인 위협이다. 무해한 애드

3 https://www.geeksforgeeks.org/computer-security-threats/

웨어 또는 위험한 트로이 목마 감염일 수 있다. 세계가 디지털화됨에 따라 컴퓨터 보안에 대한 우려는 항상 발전하고 있다. 컴퓨터 시스템의 위협은 데이터 보안을 위태롭게 할 수 있는 잠재적 위험이다. 때때로 피해는 되돌릴 수 없다.

위협 유형

보안 위협은 컴퓨터 시스템과 조직을 해칠 가능성이 있는 위협이다. 중요한 정보가 들어 있는 컴퓨터가 도난당하는 등 물리적 원인이 있을 수 있다. 또한 바이러스성 공격과 같은 물리적인 원인이 아닐 수도 있다.

Physical Threats: A physical danger to computer systems is a potential cause of an occurrence/event that could result in data loss or physical damage. It can be classified as:

Internal: Short circuit, fire, non-stable supply of power, hardware failure due to excess humidity, etc. cause it.
External: Disasters such as floods, earthquakes, landscapes, etc. cause it.
Human: Destroying of infrastructure and/or hardware, thefts, disruption, and unintentional/intentional errors are among the threats.

물리적 위협: 컴퓨터 시스템에 대한 물리적 위험은 데이터 손실 또는 물리적 손상을 초래할 수 있는 발생/사건의 잠재적 원인이다. 다음과 같이 분류할 수 있다.

내부: 단락, 화재, 전력의 불안정한 공급, 과도한 습도로 인한 하드웨어 고장 등이 원인이 된다.
외부: 홍수, 지진, 풍경과 같은 재난이 원인이 된다.
인간: 인프라 및/또는 하드웨어의 파괴, 도난, 운영 중단, 의도하지 않은 오류/의도적인 오류가 위협 요소 중 하나이다.

Non-physical Threats: A non-physical threat is a potential source of an incident that could result in:

Hampering of the business operations that depend on computer systems.

Sensitive - data or information loss

Keeping track of other's computer system activities illegally.

Hacking id & passwords of the users, etc.

비물리적 위협: 비물리적 위협은 다음과 같은 결과를 초래할 수 있는 사고의 잠재적 원인이다.

컴퓨터 시스템에 의존하는 비즈니스 운영을 방해하는 것

민감한 데이터나 정보 손실

타인의 컴퓨터 시스템 활동을 불법적으로 추적하는 행위

이용자의 아이디 및 비밀번호 등을 해킹하는 행위

The non-physical threads can be commonly caused by:

① **Malware**: Malware ("malicious software") is a type of computer program that infiltrates and damages systems without the users' knowledge. Malware tries to go unnoticed by either hiding or not letting the user know about its presence on the system. You may notice that your system is processing at a slower rate than usual.

② **Virus**: It is a program that replicates itself and infects your computer's files and programs, rendering them inoperable. It is a type of malware that spreads by inserting a copy of itself into and becoming part of another program. It spreads with the help of software or documents. They are embedded with software and documents and then transferred from one computer to another using the network, a disk, file sharing, or infected e-mail. They usually appear as an executable file.

비물리적 스레드는 일반적으로 다음으로 인해 발생할 수 있다.

① **악성 프로그램**: 악성 소프트웨어(Malware, 악성 소프트웨어)는 사용자 모르게 시스템에 침투하여 시스템을 손상시키는 컴퓨터 프로그램의 한 유형이다. 악성 소프트웨어는 사용자에게 시스템에 대한 존재를 알리거나 알리지 않음으로써 눈에 띄지 않도록 시도한다. 시스템이 평소보다 느린 속도로 처리되고 있음을 알 수 있다.

② **바이러스**: 스스로 복제하여 컴퓨터의 파일과 프로그램을 감염시켜 작동 불능 상태로 만드는 프로그램이다. 자신의 복사본을 삽입하여 다른 프로그램에 포함시킴으로써 확산되는 악성 프로그램의 일종이다. 그것은 소프트웨어나 문서의 도움으로 퍼진다. 소프트웨어 및 문서에 포함된 다음 네트워크, 디스크, 파일 공유 또는 감염된 전자 메일을 사용하여 한 컴퓨터에서 다른 컴퓨터로 전송된다. 일반적으로 실행 파일로 나타난다.

③ **Spyware**: Spyware is a type of computer program that tracks, records, and reports a user's activity (offline and online) without their permission for the purpose of profit or data theft. Spyware can be acquired from a variety of sources, including websites, instant chats, and emails. A user may also unwittingly obtain spyware by adopting a software program's End User License Agreement. Adware is a sort of spyware that is primarily utilized by advertising. When you go online, it keeps track of your web browsing patterns in order to compile data on the types of websites you visit.

④ **Worms**: Computer worms are similar to viruses in that they replicate themselves and can inflict similar damage. Unlike viruses, which spread by infecting a host file, worms are freestanding programs that do not require a host program or human assistance to proliferate. Worms don't change programs; instead, they replicate themselves over and over. They just eat resources to make the system down.

③ **스파이웨어**: 스파이웨어는 수익 또는 데이터 절도를 목적으로 사용자의 허가 없이 사용자의 활동을 추적, 기록 및 보고하는 컴퓨터 프로그램의 한 유형이다. 스파이웨어는 웹 사이트, 인스턴트 채팅 및 전자 메일을 포함한 다양한 소스에서 가져올 수 있다. 사용자는 소프트웨어 프로그램의 최종 사용자 사용권 계약을 채택하여 자신도 모르게 스파이웨어를 얻을 수도 있다. 애드웨어는 광고에 주로 사용되는 스파이웨어의 일종이다. 온라인에 접속하면 방문한 웹 사이트 유형에 대한 데이터를 컴파일하기 위해 웹 검색 패턴을 추적한다.

④ **웜**: 컴퓨터 웜은 스스로 복제한다는 점에서 바이러스와 유사하며 비슷한 피해를 줄 수 있다. 호스트 파일을 감염시켜 전파되는 바이러스와 달리 웜은 호스트 프로그램이나 사람의 도움이 필요하지 않은 독립형 프로그램이다. 웜은 프로그램을 바꾸지 않고 계속해서 자신을 복제한다. 그들은 단지 시스템을 다운시키기 위해 자원을 먹을 뿐이다.

⑤ **Trojan**: A Trojan horse is malicious software that is disguised as a useful host program. When the host program is run, the Trojan performs a harmful/unwanted action. A Trojan horse, often known as a Trojan, is malicious malware or software that appears to be legal yet has the ability to take control of your computer. A Trojan is a computer program that is designed to disrupt, steal, or otherwise harm your data or network.

⑥ **Denial Of Service Attacks**: A Denial of Service attack is one in which an attacker tries to prohibit legitimate users from obtaining information or services. An attacker tries to make a system or network resource unavailable to its intended users in this attack. The web servers of large organizations such as banking, commerce, trading organizations, etc. are the victims.

⑤ **트로이 목마**: 트로이 목마는 유용한 호스트 프로그램으로 위장한 악성 소프트웨어다. 호스트 프로그램이 실행되면 트로이 목마는 유해하거나 원치 않는 동작을 수행한다. 종종 트로이로 알려진 트로이 목마는 합법적인 것처럼 보이지만 컴퓨터를 제어할 수 있는

악성 프로그램이거나 소프트웨어다. 트로이 목마는 데이터 또는 네트워크를 방해, 도용 또는 손상시키도록 설계된 컴퓨터 프로그램이다.

⑥ **서비스 거부 공격**: 서비스 거부 공격은 공격자가 합법적인 사용자가 정보나 서비스를 얻는 것을 금지하려고 하는 공격이다. 공격자는 이 공격에서 원하는 사용자가 시스템 또는 네트워크 리소스를 사용할 수 없도록 한다. 은행, 커머스(상거래), 무역 조직 등과 같은 대규모 조직의 웹 서버가 피해자들이다.

⑦ **Phishing**: Phishing is a type of attack that is frequently used to obtain sensitive information from users, such as login credentials and credit card details. They deceive users into giving critical information, such as bank and credit card information, or access to personal accounts, by sending spam, malicious Web sites, email messages, and instant chats.

⑧ **Key-Loggers**: Keyloggers can monitor a user's computer activity in real-time. Keylogger is a program that runs in the background and records every keystroke made by a user, then sends the data to a hacker with the intent of stealing passwords and financial information.

⑦ **피싱**: 피싱은 로그인 자격 증명 및 신용 카드 세부 정보와 같은 중요한 정보를 사용자로부터 얻기 위해 자주 사용되는 공격의 한 유형이다. 스팸, 악성 웹 사이트, 이메일 메시지, 인스턴트 채팅 등을 보내 은행 및 신용카드 정보나 개인 계정에 대한 액세스와 같은 중요한 정보를 제공하도록 사용자를 속인다.

⑧ **키로거**: 키로거는 사용자의 컴퓨터 활동을 실시간으로 모니터링할 수 있다. 키로거는 백그라운드에서 실행돼 사용자가 입력한 모든 키 입력을 기록한 뒤 암호와 금융 정보를 빼돌릴 목적으로 해커에게 데이터를 전송하는 프로그램이다.

Vocabulary

efficient : 효율적인

harmless : 무해한

trojan infection : 트로이 목마 감염

concern : 우려

potential danger : 잠재적 위험

jeopardize : 위험에 빠뜨리다

irreversible : 되돌릴 수 없는

viral attack : 바이러스성 공격

occurrence : 발생

short circuit : 합선

non-stable : 불안정한

humidity : 습도

thefts : 도난

disruption : 중단

illegally : 불법적으로

malware : 악성 소프트웨어

inoperable : 실시 불가능한

replicate : 스스로 복제하다

infect : 감염시키다

render : 어떠한 상태가 되게 만들다

embedded : 탑재된, 끼워 넣은

executable file : 실행파일

adopt : 채택하다, 쓰다

primarily : 주로

advertising : 광고

inflict : 괴로움 등을 가하다

proliferate : 급증하다, 빠르게 확산하다

disguise : 변장/가장하다
steal : 훔치다
prohibit : 금지하다
legitimate : 합법적인
victim : 피해자
credentials : 자격 증명
deceive : 속이다
keystroke : 한번 누르기, 치기(키보드를)

3) How to make your system secure 시스템 보안을 하는 방법[4]

From passwords to file encryption, computer security plays an important role. So what do computer users do to keep their computers secure?

Users are to be wary of threats and should start implementing the use of strong passwords as weak passwords would allow hackers to guess them easily and gain access to private user credentials and use them to get monetary benefits. The followings are a reminder when protecting passwords:

Never document passwords in text files or spreadsheets
Avoid saving passwords in the browser
Avoid using personal information like spouse name, date of birth, child's name
Use of complex passwords with a combination of letters (lower-case and upper-case)

4 https://www.geeksforgeeks.org/computer-security-threats/#How to make your system secure:

Use unique-passwords and do not use the same password for different accounts
Deploy Two-factor authentication

암호에서 파일 암호화에 이르기까지 컴퓨터 보안은 중요한 역할을 한다. 그렇다면 컴퓨터 사용자는 컴퓨터의 보안을 유지하기 위해 무엇을 할까?

사용자들은 위협을 경계해야 하며 취약한 암호는 해커들이 쉽게 추측하고 개인 사용자 자격 증명에 접근하여 금전적 이익을 얻기 위해 사용할 수 있기 때문에 강력한 암호 사용을 시작해야 한다. 다음은 암호를 보호할 때 미리 알려 주는 사항이다.

텍스트 파일 또는 스프레드시트에 암호를 문서화하지 않음
브라우저에 암호 저장 안 함
배우자 이름, 생년월일, 자녀 이름과 같은 개인 정보를 사용하지 않기
문자의 조합과 함께 복잡한 암호 사용(대소문자 및 대문자)
고유 암호 사용 및 다른 계정에 대해 동일한 암호 사용 안 함
2단계 인증 사용하기

The second most important key to cyber-security is backing up of data. This is done by saving a copy of your existing data on an external hard-disk so that if your device is stolen or compromised, your backup data would be a savior.

Also, all the wireless network associated with businesses and individuals should be protected with a strong password. This prevents hackers from accessing or hijacking the wireless business network. Make sure that the wireless network is encrypted.

사이버 보안에서 두 번째로 중요한 핵심은 데이터 백업이다. 이것은 외부 하드 디스

크에 기존 데이터의 복사본을 저장하여 수행되므로 장치가 도난당하거나 손상된 경우 백업 데이터가 구원자가 된다.

또한 기업 및 개인과 관련된 모든 무선 네트워크는 강력한 암호로 보호되어야 한다. 이렇게 하면 해커가 무선 비즈니스 네트워크에 액세스하거나 가로채는 것을 방지할 수 있다. 무선 네트워크가 암호화되어 있는지 확인한다.

Based on the above, the following measures should be taken to ensure that your system data is safe and secure:

① Always keep a backup of your data.
② Install firewall software and keep it updated every time.
③ Make use of strong and difficult to crack passwords (having capital & small alphabets, numbers, and special characters).
④ Install antivirus/ anti-spyware and keep it updated every time.
⑤ Timely scan your complete system.
⑥ Before installing any program, check whether it is safe to install it (using Antivirus Software).
⑦ Take extra caution when reading emails that contain attachments.

위에 따라 시스템 데이터가 안전하고 안전하게 보호되도록 다음 조치를 취해야 한다.
① 항상 데이터를 백업해 두기
② 방화벽 소프트웨어를 설치하고 항상 업데이트하기
③ 강력하고 해독하기 어려운 비밀번호(대문자 및 소문자, 숫자, 특수문자 포함)를 사용하기
④ 안티바이러스/안티스파이웨어를 설치하고 항상 업데이트하기
⑤ 전체 시스템을 적시에 스캔하기
⑥ 프로그램을 설치하기 전에 (안티바이러스 소프트웨어를 사용하여) 설치해도 안전

한지 확인하기

⑦ 첨부파일이 포함된 이메일을 읽을 때는 각별한 주의를 기울이기

Vocabulary

wary : 조심하는

monetary benefits : 금전적 이득

document : 문서

two-factor authentication : 2단계 인증

deploy : 효율적으로 사용하다

compromised : 면역 반응 따위가 제대로 발휘되지 못하는, 손상된

savior : 구세주, 구원자

hijacking : 공중납치, 강탈

capital & small alphabets : 알파벳 대소문자

special characters : 특수문자

contain : 가지고 있다, 포함하다

attachment : 첨부 파일

☞ 잠깐 쉬어가기 ....

보안 기술이 발달하는 만큼 그에 따른 보안 위협 사례도 증가하고 있습니다. 예전과 달리 더욱 지능화되었는데요. 일반인에게 카카오톡이나 문제 메시지, 이메일 등으로 가장해서 보내면 수신인이 확인하는 순간 개인정보가 유출되는 피싱이 대표적인 예입니다. 피싱뿐만 아니라 랜섬웨어도 피해가 심각합니다. 랜섬웨어는 한 번 피해를 받으면 회복이 어렵습니다. 과거의 일회성이었던 공격과 달리 요즘 랜섬웨어는 오랜 기간 준비하여 여러 가지 공격을 동시에 혹은 추가로 실행하는 트렌드가 점차 심각해지고 있습니다. 그렇다면 우리는 어떻게 하면 좋을까요?

안랩연구소에 따르면[5] 랜섬웨어의 대처법은 다음과 같습니다.

첫 번째, 'PC 종료하지 않기'

---

5 https://www.ahnlab.com/kr/site/securityinfo/secunews/secuNewsView.do?seq=31063

랜섬웨어에 감염된 것을 인지하면 너무 당황한 나머지 급하게 PC 전원을 끌 수 있는데 이는 잘못된 대처법입니다. 랜섬웨어 감염을 확인한 후, PC 전원을 끄지 않도록 주의해야 합니다. 일부 랜섬웨어는 감염 알림 메시지창이 나타난 상태에서 사용자가 PC를 종료할 경우 PC의 파일들을 삭제해버리기도 합니다. 감염 알림창에 나타난 메시지를 주의 깊게 살펴보고 감염된 랜섬웨어가 무엇인지 파악한 후, 차분하게 피해를 최소화할 수 있는 방안을 찾아보는 것이 바람직합니다.

둘째, '외부 저장장치와의 연결 해제하기'
랜섬웨어 감염이 의심될 경우, 즉시 공유 폴더, USB나 외장하드 등 외부 저장장치와의 연결을 해제하는 것이 좋습니다. 아직 랜섬웨어가 암호화를 진행 중이라면 감염된 PC에 연결된 저장장치 및 공유폴더의 파일들도 암호화될 수 있기 때문입니다.

셋째, '무료 복구 프로그램 검색하기'
신뢰할 수 있는 보안 회사의 홈페이지 등을 통해 감염된 랜섬웨어에 대한 복구툴이 있는지 확인해본 후 빨리 조치해야 합니다. 주요 보안 업체들은 악성코드 분석 및 암호화 기법 분석을 통해 일부 랜섬웨어의 암호를 풀 수 있는 열쇠를 찾아내 암호화된 파일을 복구할 수 있는 툴(프로그램)을 제작해 무료로 제공하고 있습니다.

하지만 최고의 대처밥은 예방입니다. 랜섬웨어는 대부분 불법적인 경로, 확인되지 않은 사이트, 취약한 사이트에서 유입됩니다. 무분별한 다운로드와 접속을 피하는 것이 가장 좋습니다. 또한 PC의 운영체제 및 응용 프로그램, 백신 등을 최신 버전으로 업데이트해 최상의 상태를 유지하는 것이 좋습니다. 마지막으로 중요한 것은 정기적인 백업입니다. 사용자가 스스로 가치있는 자료를 여러 개 백업본을 통하여 저장해 두고 필요시에만 연결하고 사용이 끝나면 분리해 주는 것이 좋습니다.

연습문제

exercises

1~5. 다음 빈 칸에 들어가는 단어로 적절한 것을 넣으세요.

1. Some (   ) use their computers to break into companies' or other people's computers to steal information, such as credit card numbers.

정답 : ______________________________

2. The plethora of valuable information stored on computers and sent through the web provides great potential for (   ) to infiltrate computer security.

정답 : ______________________________

3. A threat in a computer system is a potential danger that could (   ) your data security.

정답 : ______________________________

4. Computer worms are similar to viruses in that they (   ) themselves and can inflict similar damage.

정답 : ______________________________

5. All the wireless network associated with businesses and individuals should be protected with (   ).

정답 : ______________________________

6~10. 다음 It이 지칭하는 것을 영어로 쓰세요.

6. It is a threat that has the potential to harm computer systems and organizations.

정답 : ______________________________

7. It is malicious software that is disguised as a useful host program.
정답 : ______________________________

8. It is a type of malware that spreads by inserting a copy of itself into and becoming part of another program.
정답 : ______________________________

9. It advances so quickly that IT experts are constantly challenged to keep up.
정답 : ______________________________

10. It is a type of computer program that tracks, records, and reports a user's activity (offline and online) without their permission for the purpose of profit or data theft.
정답 : ______________________________

연습문제 해답

1. hackers
2. hackers and scammers
3. jeopardize
4. replicate
5. a strong password
6. A security threat
7. A Trojan horse
8. Virus
9. Network technology
10. Spyware

Reference

Chapter 1

https://en.wikipedia.org/wiki/Fourth_Industrial_Revolution
https://www.rmit.edu.au/news/c4de/industry-4-0-design-principles
https://en.wikipedia.org/wiki/Artificial_intelligence
https://sensiml.com/entity/ai/
https://en.wikipedia.org/wiki/History_of_artificial_intelligence
https://www.javatpoint.com/history-of-artificial-intelligence
https://insights.sap.com/what-is-machine-learning
https://www.latimes.com/world/asia/la-fg-la-fg-0312-south-korea-go-player-20160311-story.html

Chapter 2

https://en.wikipedia.org/wiki/Generative_artificial_intelligence
https://www.gartner.com/en/topics/generative-ai
https://lore.com/generative-ai-history
https://www.mlq.ai/what-is-generative-ai/
https://openai.com/research/dall-e
https://www.zdnet.com/article/best-ai-art-generator/
https://towardsdatascience.com/generative-adversarial-networks-explained-34472718707a
https://arxiv.org/abs/1812.04948
https://openai.com/research/jukebox
https://mubert.com/
https://www.synthesia.io/post/generative-ai-examples
https://www.coursera.org/articles/what-is-generative-ai
https://www.harvardonline.harvard.edu/blog/benefits-limitations-generative-ai
https://fact.technology/learn/generative-ai-advantages-limitations-and-challenges/
https://www.oneai.com/learn/generative-ai-limitations
https://lingarogroup.com/blog/the-limitations-of-generative-ai-according-to-generative-ai
https://www.forbes.com/sites/bernardmarr/2023/05/31/the-future-of-generative-ai-beyond-chatgpt/
https://www.harvardonline.harvard.edu/blog/future-generative-ai
https://www.forbes.com/sites/bernardmarr/2023/07/25/the-future-of-manufacturing-generative-ai-and-beyond
https://www.technologyreview.com/2023/04/27/1072102/the-future-of-generative-ai-is-niche-not-generalized/

Chapter 3

https://en.wikipedia.org/wiki/Computer
https://www.g2.com/articles/history-of-computers
https://ko.wikipedia.org/wiki/이미테이션_게임
https://ko.wikipedia.org/wiki/앨런_튜링

Chapter 4

https://en.wikipedia.org/wiki/Computer_hardware
https://www.techopedia.com/definition/32480/von-neumann-architecture
https://en.wikipedia.org/wiki/Von_Neumann_architecture
https://ko.wikipedia.org/wiki/에니악

Chapter 5

https://www.webopedia.com/definitions/software
https://searchapparchitecture.techtarget.com/definition/software
https://en.wikipedia.org/wiki/Operating_system
https://gs.statcounter.com/os-market-share/desktop/worldwide/
https://gs.statcounter.com/os-market-share/mobile/worldwide/
https://www.wgu.edu/blog/5-most-popular-operating-systems1910.html

Chapter 6

https://en.wikipedia.org/wiki/Bitwise_operation
https://en.wikipedia.org/wiki/Units_of_information
https://www.computerhope.com/jargon/b/bit.htm
https://www.computerhope.com/jargon/b/byte.htm
https://en.wikipedia.org/wiki/Nibble

Chapter 7

https://en.wikipedia.org/wiki/Multimedia#Multimedia
https://en.wikipedia.org/wiki/Multimedia#Major_characteristics
https://en.wikipedia.org/wiki/Multimedia#Characteristics
https://en.wikipedia.org/wiki/Multimedia#Usage/application

Chapter 8

https://en.wikipedia.org/wiki/Database
https://en.wikipedia.org/wiki/Database#Terminology_and_overview
https://en.wikipedia.org/wiki/Database#Database_management_system
https://www.oracle.com/database/what-is-database/#Types_of_databases
https://phoenixnap.com/kb/oltp-database
https://www.oracle.com/database/what-is-database/#relational

https://www.oracle.com/database/what-is-database/#Evolution_of_the_database
https://news.coupang.com/wp-content/uploads/2021/01/image-10.jpeg

Chapter 9

https://en.wikipedia.org/wiki/Computer_network
https://en.wikipedia.org/wiki/Computer_network#Use
https://www.educba.com/what-is-network-topology/
https://www.lifewire.com/lans-wans-and-other-area-networks-817376
https://en.wikipedia.org/wiki/Computer_network#Communication_protocols
https://www.imperva.com/learn/application-security/osi-model
https://www.nia.or.kr/site/nia_kor/ex/bbs/View.do?cbIdx=99870&bcIdx=25604&parentSeq=25604

Chapter 10

https://www.electronicshub.org/wireless-communication-introduction-types-applications/
https://en.wikipedia.org/wiki/Wireless
https://en.wikipedia.org/wiki/Wireless#Modes
https://www.electronicshub.org/wireless-communication-introduction-types-applications/#Advantages_of_Wireless_Communication
https://www.electronicshub.org/wireless-communication-introduction-types-applications/#Disadvantages_of_Wireless_Communication
https://en.wikipedia.org/wiki/Wireless#Applications
https://www.dnews.co.kr/uhtml/view.jsp?idxno=202308240958125080370

Chapter 11

https://www.encyclopedia.com/science-and-technology/computers-and-electrical-engineering/computers-and-computing/computer-security
https://en.wikipedia.org/wiki/Computer_security
https://www.geeksforgeeks.org/computer-security-threats/
https://www.geeksforgeeks.org/computer-security-threats/#How to make your system secure:
https://www.boannews.com/media/view.asp?idx=100260&kind=
https://www.ahnlab.com/kr/site/securityinfo/secunews/secuNewsView.do?seq=31063